The Seattle Public Library

A Gift from the Estate of Margaret Dutton

Received On

MAY -- 2018

Magnolia Library

NO LONGER PROPERTY OF SEATTLE PUBLIC LIBRARY

D1013299

MARE

Tartari Zi
uolhenses

Scythia intra Imaum

Scythia extra
Imaum

Re

Imaus
mons

Regnum C
maniæ

Mare Caspiu

ASIA

R

Mœtla

Aria

Emodij mōtes

chaldæa.

Persia

Dragiana

Indus
flu.

Gan
ges
flu.

Sin⁰ Persic

Gedrosia

India ex

Felix

Cale
chut

INDIA INTRA
Gangem

Sinus
Gangen

a

Achiloa
Zaphala
90

Sin⁰ Barbaric⁰

AEQVATOR

150

160
Cherson

TRAVEL

TRAVEL

A Literary History

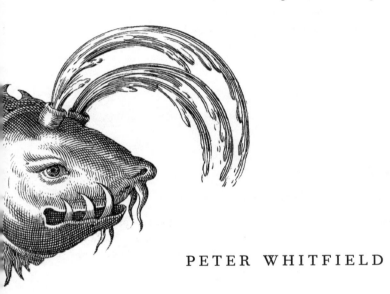

PETER WHITFIELD

Bodleian Library
UNIVERSITY OF OXFORD

NOTE ON QUOTATIONS Some spellings and capitalisation have been modernised. The translations from Diderot's *Supplément au Voyage de Bougainville* on pp. 139–40 and from Chateaubriand's *America* on p. 186 are by the author.

First published in 2011 by
The Bodleian Library
Broad Street
Oxford OX1 3BG

www.bodleianbookshop.co.uk

ISBN 978 1 85124 338 9

Text © Peter Whitfield, 2011

All images, unless specified, © Bodleian Library, University of Oxford, 2011.

Cover: 'Roman Capriccio' by Giovanni Panini. These *capriccio* pictures of Rome combined real architectural features in fanciful settings; they were often bought as souvenirs by eighteenth-century tourists, sometimes with their own figures placed in the foreground. WA 1946.265 © Ashmolean Museum, University of Oxford.

All rights reserved

No part of this book may be reproduced, stored in a retrieval system, or transmitted in any form or by any means, electronic, mechanical, photocopying, recording, or otherwise, without the written permission of the Bodleian Library, except for the purpose of research or private study, or criticism or review.

Cover design by Dot Little
Text designed and typeset in 12 on 16 Monotype Fournier by illuminati, Grosmont
Printed in Great Britain by the MPG Books Group, Bodmin and King's Lynn
on 80 gsm Bookwove Cream

British Library Catalogue in Publishing Data
A CIP record of this publication is available from the British Library

Contents

Preface

PASCAL once wrote that all mankind's misfortunes spring from just one cause: 'he does not know how to sit still in a room.' I like that: it makes me less ashamed to admit that I am a poor traveller. Places interest me, but more and more often the mechanics of getting to them defeats me, especially that nightmare of the modern world, the international airport. For this reason, the inner journeys that people make in their lives have absorbed me more than the outer ones. Therefore I follow Voltaire's advice: when I want to travel, I turn to my library.

But of course if we all took this stance, human history would be fairly uneventful, if it existed at all, for history without travel is unthinkable. First, humanity overspread the earth through the process of migration, forming communities and cultures that flourished for long periods in isolation from each other. Then later, through exploration and resettlement, this isolation was broken down, and the movement began towards the one world which we now inhabit. In this book, the tail end of the migration phase can be traced in a few early texts such as the Book of Exodus and the *Aeneid*. But by far the greater part of my book is concerned with the second phase, in which travel literature becomes a witness, and indeed an agent, in the gradual reintegration of mankind; it becomes a form of discourse through which one civilisation thinks about another, and about itself.

The book's perspective is Eurocentric, because the literature of international travel is predominantly European. Beginning in the ancient and classical world of the Eastern Mediterranean, the book moves west and north, until it becomes a survey of English travel writing. If this appears to be a convenient sleight of hand, it does at least reflect the historical reality that it was the western European nations who travelled to and observed the lands and peoples of America, Africa and Asia, and not the reverse. In this historical process, my book tries to identify successive paradigms of travel and travel literature: we have the literature of exploration, conquest, pilgrimage, science, commerce, romanticism, adventure, imperialism, and so on. Driven on by motives such as these, the English became good at setting up parallel worlds abroad, where they could study other ways of life, perhaps meddle with them, exploit them or laugh at them, but certainly write about them. An attitude of superiority was once endemic in a very great deal of travel writing, and travel literature has become implicated among the forces of colonialism. It is, however, the contention of this book that this has been gradually replaced over the last century by a new humility in the face of the foreign, encouraged by a growing discontent with western civilisation. And even before the modern age, travel writing was the ideal vehicle for the humorist, the eccentric, the loner or the crackpot, who fitted into no easy political or intellectual scheme, whose passion was to escape from his homeland and jaunt through the world as he pleased, with no fixed abode and no fixed identity.

Travel literature is a vast field, impossible to do justice to in a brief survey. Part of its difficulty is that its canon is not well defined. With the exception of a few monuments like Herodotus, Marco Polo, Columbus, Captain Cook, Darwin and so on, any selection will always be slightly arbitrary. How many significant diaries are there

Amerigo Vespucci meets a representative of the people of South America
in a classic image of the encounter between so-called civilisation and savagery,
the naked and the clothed.

of journeys to Italy or voyages across the Pacific in the eighteenth
century, and how many significant journeys in the Near East or India
in the nineteenth? Important but neglected texts are always being
rediscovered and old ones reassessed. In the modern period the flow
of books becomes a cascade; we duck to avoid the torrent, and miss
some treasures. Just after completing this book, I picked up Peter
Levi's *The Hill of Kronos* (1980), which I should have read before. Levi
was a poet, an original and exciting one, and he also played at being
a scholar – I don't mean that patronisingly: he was a scholar, but a
scholar of the imagination, not of the slow, patient, analytical intellect.
These two passions came together in his subtle, sharp-edged memories
of Greece. But what gives his book its real interest is his account of
life under the military junta: here sadness, shame and tragedy darken
his book, and darken the wonder of the Greek idyll he has built up:

how could this horror break in on a world of poetry and scholarship? There must be hundreds of such travel memoirs, each with its own unexpected uniqueness, which happen not to become specially famous, but which are potentially part of the canon of major works.

This is not a social history of travel, and I have not been drawn into discussing mass tourism and its destructive effects. But it's hard to avoid seeing most modern travel as yet another aspect of consumerism, collecting destinations and experiences as we collect electronic gadgets, or cars or properties, while the more attractive parts of the earth disappear rapidly beneath airports, hotels, restaurants, theme-parks, holiday villages, ski stations and the like. But I don't agree with the common view that so-called real travel writing has necessarily died with so-called real travel. In this environment, the worthwhile travel writer has to keep alive the idea of the inner journey, the transforming experience: he or she has to be our eyes and our conscience, reminding us of what is genuine amid so much that is worthless.

Literary critics have been greatly exercised to explain in theoretical terms what travel literature is, as if there must be a single transcendent principle valid for all travel texts. But why should there be? Do we know, in any final, universal sense, what poetry is, or drama, or the novel? Like all these genres, travel writing has taken different forms in different ages, forms which we can describe, but whose essential identity eludes final definition. A travel text is obviously some species of memoir, tied to specific geographical locations, whose aim is to reflect or capture the character of that location and its people. It is tied to reality, but it will inevitably be reshaped in the memory and in the imagination – anyone who writes a postcard home from abroad knows this. When the travel experience is set down on paper, the memoir becomes a theatre in which the writer plays a double part, as both spectator and actor: what is seen is seen through his eyes, but he is also a protagonist of the action. So the writer is not merely recording an experience, he is creating it.

If Pascal were sitting quietly in his room thinking, it would probably be about God and the universe. If he thought of travel at all, it would probably be to wonder if he would understand God and the universe any better if he were to travel abroad a little – which he never did. But that would be a tall order, wouldn't it? That would be asking a great deal of travel literature, just as it would be asking a great deal of poetry, science, philosophy or any other genre. The history of travel literature is complicated: it touches intimately on the way that we in Europe have understood and dealt with the rest of the world. But I think its essence is its record of the ways in which we have tried to escape from our own world, and perhaps from ourselves, to set out on journeys of exploration, whether they result in adventure, poetry, comedy, transgression, wisdom, sadness, suffering or desolation. This sense of escape, surprise, discovery and transformation is the great strength of travel writing, and this is why it deserves a higher place in the pantheon of literature, even though we still cannot exactly say what it is. My hope is that some of this richness can be felt in this brief book.

ONE

The Prehistory
of Travel Writing

Sirmio, bright eye of peninsulas and islands ... Ah what is more
blessed than to put cares away, when the mind lays by its burden, and,
tired with the labour of far travel, we have come to our own home,
and rest on the couch we have longed for? This it is which alone is
worth all these toils.

Catullus (*Carmen* XXXI)

The Ancient World: Ordeal and Conquest

ACCORDING TO one of our great primal myths, human history
began with a journey – the journey out of Eden. How often since
that moment have the experiences of transition and transformation
been associated with travelling – with exile, migration, invasion,
discovery, colonisation, enslavement or escape. Physical space is one
of the two dimensions in which we have our existence, and movement
in space has always been fundamental to human development, both
for the individual and for the group. However, not all movement is
necessarily travel, for the travel writer attempts to crystallise his or
her experience into something novel, something worth recording,
something significant and purposeful.

I

When we think of travel in the remote past, a number of powerful and resonant words come into our minds, words bequeathed to us from the ancient world meaning 'journey', but something much more than a mere journey: Exodus and Odyssey, Epic and Saga, Quest and Pilgrimage. Each of these words has its own distinct meaning, but all convey one of the primal senses of travel – that it was an ordeal, a challenge, an experience to be endured. Travel was associated with suffering, but a suffering which had the power to transform the lives of those who survived it. The physical journey, its beauties and its terrors, somehow lifted the traveller into a higher plane of being, sometimes temporarily, sometimes permanently.

The Book of Exodus is the story of a journey which was nothing less than a revelation of divine power, a journey so important that it forged the consciousness of a people. The delivery from Egypt, the miraculous passage through the Red Sea, the revelation of law on Sinai, and the forty-year journey through the desert – all these comprised the Exodus experience. It was an experience of physical hardship, mental despair and personal conflict among the wandering Israelites, counterbalanced by signs, wonders and miraculous help from God. The end of the ordeal comes in the Book of Joshua, with the crossing of the River Jordan and the entry into the promised land. In the course of that prolonged ordeal, God had revealed his law, his plan for the destiny of mankind. This biblical narrative differs in many ways of course from a conventional travel narrative. Some place names are given – Sinai, Moab, Canaan, Jericho, and so on – but the physical environment remains vague, and we are repeatedly told only of mountain and wilderness. Yet the Exodus narrative expresses powerfully one of the leading paradigms of travel – the image of the journey as a process of transformation in which suffering is strongly implicated, in effect the death of the old life and the awakening of the new. The ancient history of Europe and Asia was shaped by a series of great migrations, as whole peoples sought new territories to conquer or in which to escape hunger or aggression. These peoples were almost always preliterate, so that we rarely have an inner witness to this experience, but the Book of Exodus may provide a unique record of one such migration, a record that is filled with a profound sense of religious and tribal identity.

The second great travel word that echoes to us down from the ancient world tells of us a far more personal and individual journey, indeed it is named for its protagonist: Odyssey. The *Odyssey* too involves suffering, deliverance, transformation and final triumph, but in between comes an action-filled narrative of adventure: shipwreck, combat, love, treachery, encounters with monsters and magic, and the unseen presence of gods and goddesses. The physical setting is now presented far more vividly, indeed the waters and islands of the Aegean are one of the shaping forces of the narrative, and for its original audience the action took place on the borderland between the known and the unknown. The central theme of this adventure is not the consciousness of a people, but the identity of an individual. Formerly a king and a warrior, Odysseus becomes a victim of the gods, man and nature, a castaway, a captive, naked and alone. He is even driven to descend into the underworld, among the spirits of the dead, to beg the prophet Tiresias to reveal his final destiny. Through ten years of ordeal, his life and personality are stripped bare, while his task is to endure, to regain his homeland, and recover his original identity. This he achieves through tenacity and cunning, and his ability to play whatever part is required in any crisis – all qualities which make Odysseus the archetypal traveller-hero. The second fundamental theme prefigured in the *Odyssey* is the encounter with the alien, with forces of nature or forms of humanity beyond normal experience, which test the courage and the understanding of the protagonist.

Another epic journey is recorded in a still more ancient text from Mesopotamia, the *Gilgamesh Epic*, which was already a thousand years old when the *Odyssey* was taking shape. Gilgamesh was half-human and half-divine, the king of the city of Uruk on the Euphrates, and his story is perhaps the first quest narrative in world history. He sets out to find the secret of eternal life, travelling over plains and mountains where no man had ever gone before, seeking the garden of the gods. Both the journey and the garden are evoked in powerful, poetic images of suffering and beauty. Gilgamesh then crosses the ocean to find the seer Utnapishtim, who instructs him how to obtain a magical plant growing on the ocean bed, which alone can confer the immortality he seeks. Gilgamesh dives for the plant and does indeed find it, but during his homeward journey, while he is resting, a snake appears and devours the precious plant. Gilgamesh weeps as he acknowledges that eternal life is unattainable in this world, and he prepares for the death which he now knows is inevitable.

The narrative of the *Gilgamesh Epic* is stark and strongly drawn, and the world that it inhabits is more savage and elemental than that of the *Odyssey*. But its theme of intellectual or spiritual quest is striking and impressive, and once again we see the physical journey used as a metaphor for personal struggle or transformation. This metaphor was not dependent on the literal, historical truth of the narrative. The original readers or audiences of these ancient stories may or may not have believed that these journeys were real. In the case of the Exodus they certainly did, while the other two could have been accepted as poetic constructs. But either way, the message, the symbolic meaning of the journey, is still clear and still valid.

Travel in Classical Literature

The reflective, truth-claiming first-person travel narrative as we know it did not emerge in Greek or Roman literature, but travel did come to play a considerable part in the writing of history, especially military history. The absence of personal involvement, the failure to evoke the experience of travel, physically or imaginatively, means that Greek and Roman authors can scarcely ever be called travel writers in the recognised sense, but their works do undoubtedly form a prehistory of the genre. The seminal figure here was Herodotus, celebrated as the father of history, but who also has some claims to being the father of geography too, at least of human geography. Herodotus, writing between 450 and 430 BC, chose as his great theme the wars between Greece and Persia, but he regarded it as part of his brief to describe the lands and peoples who were involved in this historic conflict – the Persians themselves, of course, but also the Babylonians, Scythians, Egyptians and Indians. Rather than merely narrating events in the course of the war, he chose to portray the conflict as a clash of cultures, to contrast the beliefs, practices and character of foreign nations with those of the Greeks. Central to this contrast was the Greek ideal of freedom, set against the tyranny of Persian society: in the war, the Persians had to be compelled to fight under the threat of the whip, while the Greeks fought willingly for their freedom.

To build up his picture of the barbarian peoples, Herodotus travelled widely throughout the Eastern Mediterranean and Near East, gathering first-hand information. He believed strongly that the prime sources of any historical and cultural analysis should be oral, therefore wherever he went he would question scholars, priests or other spokesmen about their nations' histories, and he often prefaces his descriptions with the phrase 'the Egyptians say', 'the Persians say', and so on. Herodotus clearly had a taste for the marvellous, and he acquired a reputation as a teller of tall stories. This was certainly justified, although he will often enliven his narrative by describing some colourful or bizarre custom, then say that he himself does not believe it. But many of his stories have the authentic ring of first-hand observation, for example his account of the Armenian merchants who ship their wares down the River Euphrates to Babylon: they built specially designed boats made of hides stretched over skins, and once their business was finished they dismantled their craft, which would be impossible to propel upstream, and carried them home on mules. His most extended description is of the Egyptians, a nation which was then part of the Persian empire, and whose antiquity fascinated the Greeks. By his own report he travelled as far south as the first cataract of the Nile, and he speculates on the age-old problem of the river's spring inundation. He found the Egyptians to be the most religiously obsessed people on earth, and he gives minutely detailed accounts of their religious rites and practices, although it has to be said that the inner, underlying beliefs behind them often seemed to escape him. He dwells at great length on the uniquely Egyptian custom of mummification, describing it in somewhat macabre detail, but without shedding any light on why it was done.

Herodotus is a mine of information about these ancient peoples, but there is a certain distance between him and his material, a rather colourless detachment, even a faint hint of contempt. The foreign manner of dressing, eating, writing, mourning, marrying, worshipping, legislating, fighting – all these he declares to be the reverse of the common practice in civilised countries. He writes at times as if he were stirring an anthill with the toe of his boot, and were surprised at the confusion of life that he finds there; all this, he seems to imply, is very un-Greek.

Not long after Herodotus, Xenophon's *Anabasis* was a more immediate, realistic piece of reporting on a foreign land and its people, although its context was a highly unusual one – that of an army in retreat after a disastrous campaign. In Persia in 401 BC, Prince Cyrus set out to seize the throne from his brother, Artaxerxes II, and among those he enlisted in his rebel army were 10,000 Spartan mercenaries. Cyrus's ambitions and his life ended at the Battle of Cunaxa, near Babylon, leaving the Greeks with the choice of surrender or somehow forcing their way out to freedom. They chose the latter course, but the direct route to the Syrian coast was blocked by a large Persian army, so, led by Xenophon, they took the decision to march some 700 miles northward through the mountains of Armenia to the Black Sea. The most famous moment of the march came when Xenophon, at the rear of the column, heard those in the vanguard crying *Thalassa! Thalassa!* – 'The Sea! The Sea!' They had arrived within sight of the shores of the Black Sea near Trapezus: their epic journey was half-over, and soon they would find ships to take them to the Bosphorus. The *Anabasis* (the word means 'the journey up') is permeated by a sense of foreignness – of this band of Greek comrades, defeated, isolated, struggling through an alien landscape, surrounded by an alien people. There is some interesting local colour, for example when Xenophon describes the curious underground dwellings in which the Armenians escaped the rigours of the bitter winter in the mountains. But it is really an adventure story, designed to display the superior character of the Greeks when faced with unpredictable barbarians. It became an immensely popular book, fixing in the Greek mind the geography of northern Mesopotamia and the Black Sea, and bringing a more personal note into historical narrative, a greater sense of the physical reality of the journey.

The heir to both Herodotus and Xenophon as a chronicler of foreign culture and of war was Polybius, the Greek who, in the second century BC, wrote the history of the wars between Rome and Carthage. Polybius was tutor to the younger Scipio, and travelled with him to North Africa to witness the final destruction of Carthage. It is from the pen of Polybius that we have much of our knowledge of Carthage and its people, and more especially the famous description of Hannibal's master plan to invade Italy by crossing the Alps with his army in a surprise attack. This section of Polybius is possibly the first text in which the reality of travel in a high mountain landscape is a central feature – the snow, the passes, the crumbling paths and the ravines. It was not a personal, eyewitness account, of course, but Polybius must have had good sources, written or oral, for his detailed evocation of this celebrated feat. It has proved impossible to establish through which passes Hannibal led his huge invasion force, but since he is said to have followed the Rhone north before striking east, he must have crossed a watershed of 2,000 metres or more, somewhere in the mountains east of Gap. Until recently, every schoolchild knew the story of Hannibal, and was familiar with the image of his war elephants plunging through the Alpine snows.

Polybius is one of a number of classical authors who preserved the memory of another unique journey, that of the Greek navigator Pytheas, who left Marseilles around 310 BC to explore Europe's northern regions. Pytheas is regarded as the discoverer of Britain, or rather as the first to bring Britain into the sphere of the world known to the classical civilisations. Pytheas wrote an account of his voyage, which has not survived, but Polybius summarised its main points, while expressing disbelief about some of it. Pytheas apparently landed in the south-west of Britain and spoke with the tin miners who enjoyed regular contact with traders from the Mediterranean. He then claimed to have sailed around the entire coastline, and to have landed and observed the primitive life of its people. The most frequently discussed part of his narrative concerns his journey to a place which he called Thule, six days' voyage north of Britain, where he reported that the sea congealed so that one could neither sail over it nor walk on it. This was presumably ice, but where was Thule? The Shetlands, the Faroes or Iceland? He also mentions the phenomenon of the midnight sun in midsummer, suggesting that Thule must have been on, or very close to, the Arctic Circle.

The fullest and most dramatic narrative of travel, exploration and warfare in classical literature is the story of Alexander the Great. The original eyewitness accounts of these historic events, composed by official historians who accompanied the expedition, have been lost except for fragments, so that we are now largely dependent on the version composed by Arrian in the second century AD, some four centuries after the events described. The outlines of this epic journey are well known: the marches which took Alexander's army from Macedonia through Persia to the foothills of the Himalayas and back again, covering, with innumerable detours, perhaps 20,000 miles in ten years; the sieges and battles which appeared to prove Alexander invincible; Alexander's desire to penetrate to the far eastern rim of Asia, and his conviction that they would then strike the same ocean which encircles Europe and Africa; his ambition to build an empire to which 'there would be no boundaries but those which God himself has made for the whole world'; the final refusal of his exhausted army to push any further east; their terrible homeward journey across the arid plains of southern Persia, during which the men died in their thousands; and the end of the great adventure with Alexander's death in Babylon at the age of just 32, and the swift fragmentation of his dream empire. This is not a personal narrative, but an epic, dominated by the presence of Alexander: it is almost a non-fictional equivalent of the Homeric portraits of Achilles and Odysseus, throughout which Alexander, with his energy, invincibility and thirst for conquest, remains an enigma. The stage on which this epic is played out is geographical, but the whole focus of the narrative is military. The stance of Greek superiority which we noticed in Herodotus here takes an extreme, imperialist form: the lands and peoples Alexander encounters have little interest in their own right; they exist merely to be conquered, they are incidental features in his vast egocentric world. This is a feature which will recur in varying degrees in travel literature over the centuries. 'I came, I saw, I conquered' is hardly an ideal credo for the travel writer, but it surfaces again and again, sometimes overtly, sometimes in more subtle disguises; for many writers, foreign environments and peoples are there to be tamed.

Caesar himself contributed to the military-historical tradition, of course, writing in his carefully chiselled prose about his campaigns in France, Germany and Britain between 60 and 50 BC. He wrote in some detail about these barbarian peoples, their social customs, their religion and their economies, and his work is of value as one of the very few considered pictures we have of Celtic or Germanic culture. Like Herodotus, he must presumably have used interpreters and spokesmen to get his facts, and misinformation or misunderstanding must often have intervened. Caesar describes the Gallic tribes as living in some form of feudalism, ruled by two elite classes, Druids and Knights, the former being the custodians of religion, culture and law; the latter providing the fighting strength. They believed in reincarnation, and this was apparently a great spur to their courage in battle. But where did Caesar get the idea that the Druids could write, and that they used the Greek characters? Could he have seen runic writing and misunderstood it? The Germanic people he describes as entirely absorbed in hunting and fighting, and worshipping only the gods of sun, moon and fire. He leaves us in no doubt that the peoples of Britain, Gaul and Germany are mere barbarians, fragmented tribes, almost permanently at war among themselves; they live according to irrational custom; they are not a nation like Rome, with a unified law and culture. The paradigm of travel as conquest presented figures like Caesar with a challenge, a role they must play. That role demanded the severest mastery of themselves and their forces, and of the people and environments they encountered. Their texts reflect this hard, impersonal ethic of travel.

Something of this ethic is also to be found in Rome's answer to Homer's *Odyssey*: Virgil's *Aeneid,* which reverts to the more ancient paradigm of travel as quest or ordeal. Virgil planned his epic poem as a kind of retrospective myth, explaining the origin of Rome and its people. Like the *Odyssey*, it includes a long period of wandering and trial for its hero, and it culminates in a violent battle to gain his destined homeland. For Aeneas as for Odysseus, the Mediterranean was a place of conflict and suffering, where his character is tested and his identity is formed. But the whole thrust of this epic is to show the birth of Rome and her rise to power as divinely ordained, and Aeneas as the first chosen instrument of this great plan. Personal ambition and glory have no part in this scheme, indeed throughout his wanderings Aeneas is portrayed as a suffering hero, constantly sacrificing his own interests and impulses in order to fulfil the duty which the gods have imposed upon him. He must undergo the trials of his great journey over sea and land to reach a place which is both his destination and his destiny – the two words are intertwined. This was clearly a pagan equivalent of the Exodus story, a myth of the founding of a nation through a great and terrible journey.

If the direct personal travel narrative as we know it failed to emerge in classical literature, an outstanding example of another genre – the travel guide – did appear. Pausanias' *Guide to Greece* occupied its author for some twenty years, from around 160 to 180 AD, and this timing was fortunate, for the writer was able to observe and describe the rich remains of a classical culture in decline but still living. This sense of decline is easily felt in his text, for again and again Pausanias speaks of cities that are shrinking, villages deserted, temples roofless and shrines half-ruined. He nowhere gives a clear statement of his aims in writing this book, but his interest is overwhelmingly in the historical and religious sites, many of which are described in minute detail. He is far less interested in landscape or people, and his prose is cool and detached, with his own personality kept very much in the background; the idea of the 'traveller's tale' was quite foreign to Pausanias. But the *Guide to Greece* is a long book, and inevitably something of the life of contemporary Greece does emerge. We learn that even at this date, places such as Corinth and Delphi were already haunted by professional guides, who preyed mercilessly on visitors, showing them the sites and telling them their history. Pausanias of course listened to what they had to say, but he conducted extensive literary researches of his own, and gave full accounts of the significance of the sites, including the legends and the religious practices associated with them. The survival of his book was a remarkable piece of luck for later scholars, for it provides an unrivalled catalogue of the physical fabric of Greek culture towards the end of the classical era, and of the beliefs which lay behind it. Many modern excavations have confirmed the accuracy of Pausanias' reports. It was the great anthropologist Sir James Frazer who said that without Pausanias 'The ruins of Greece would for the most be part a labyrinth without a clue, a riddle without an answer. His book furnishes the clue to the labyrinth, the answer to many riddles.'

One further strand emerged in classical literature, tangential perhaps to travel, but destined to become an important component of it: the lure of marvels and natural wonders, sometimes mere caprices, but sometimes more threatening, even nightmarish. There is something of this in Herodotus, but the first mature expression of it comes in Pliny's *Natural History*, completed around 75 AD, an encyclopedia of Roman science but liberally sprinkled with dragons and monsters, and with monstrous races of humans – people with no head but faces in their chests, with the heads of dogs, with one leg on which they hopped, with feet that were webbed or cloven, and so on. These stories were multiplied by the later writer Solinus, known unflatteringly as 'Pliny's ape', and they reappeared in medieval legends, in works like the anonymous *Wonders of the East*, which was a more fantastic version of the familiar bestiary, illustrated with vivid pictures of grotesque creatures, animal and human.

The Christian Era: Pilgrims and Crusaders

It would probably be an exaggeration to call Pausanias' cool, detached work a pilgrimage among the religious sites of dissolving paganism, yet very soon a strange, new and powerful element did enter travel writing, and it clearly came with the advent of Christianity. It seemed that in the era of the new faith, from the third century onwards, a new sense was born of the sanctity of the world. The results in literary terms were narratives of pilgrimage and narratives of miraculous adventure, and both these genres seemed to demand a new structural device, a new standpoint for travel writing, namely the eyewitness. It is in these Christian narratives that the first-person narrator, the traveller himself, becomes an essential presence, journeying to the exotic places of the world, responding to them in his intellect and his imagination. The great primary destination was of course the Holy Land, for by a series of historical chances the centre of gravity of the Christian World had shifted westwards from its birthplace to Rome. By the fourth or fifth century there were hundreds of thousands of devout Christians throughout the Mediterranean and Roman Europe who knew of the setting of Christ's life only through the biblical stories, and who longed for more, for a sense of the reality of the sanctified land. Perhaps this longing was strengthened by the reported discovery of the true cross in Jerusalem in 327 AD by St Helena. Moreover, because the journey from western Europe to Palestine was long, difficult and dangerous, the idea was born that it was an act of sacrifice or endurance for a noble end, and one which would earn spiritual rewards. Few people could undertake this journey personally, but the desire to experience it vicariously was a natural one. Thus travel writing acquired a new and distinct audience with a deep and committed interest in narrative, topographical description and the personal witness of the author. To make a pilgrimage was, in the words of Saint Jerome, 'To enter the grotto of our Saviour, to weep with our sister and with our mother in the sepulchre of the Lord ... to see Lazarus come forth bound with grave clothes, and to see the waters of the Jordan, made more pure by the baptism of the Lord.' To evoke such experiences was a new kind of challenge for the travel writer.

Perhaps the earliest, prototype pilgrimage narrative is that entitled *Peregrinatio ad terram sanctam* ('Pilgrimage to the Holy Land'), which appeared over the name Egeria, although nothing is known of the author except that she was member of a religious order, and her text takes the form of a letter to her sisters in that order. She may have lived at any time from the fourth to the sixth century, and even her nationality is uncertain. Her story is brief, unadorned and consistently focused on the sacred places: this is the sole reason for her going. She gives few incidental details of the journey itself, but is concerned only to record that she has been there, 'in that place', as she repeatedly proclaims, where the sacred or the miraculous has been revealed momentarily in our world. Her route was from Egypt, duplicating the path of the Exodus into Sinai, and these sacred events therefore were those of the Old Testament as well as the New:

> As we moved along, we came to a certain place where the mountains through which we were travelling opened out to form an immense valley, vast, quite flat, and extremely beautiful; and across the valley there appeared Mount Sinai, God's holy mountain. ... This is the vast and very flat valley where the children of Israel tarried during those days when the holy man Moses climbed the mountain of God; and he was there for forty days and forty nights. This is also the valley where the calf was made, and to this day its location is shown, for a large stone set there stands on the very spot.
>
> (*Diary of a Pilgrimage*, pp. 49–50)

The style is simple and repetitive, but there are interesting questions in the background: surely Egeria travelled in a party, not alone? How did she plan her journey in the total absence of maps? Was there already a tourist network to smooth her path? Perhaps so, and surely she had guides, for the place of the calf was shown to her. What of the people who lived their lives in these holy places – were they Christians, Jews or neither? On all these matters she is silent; she is merely witnessing that these places exist, and that the traditions are true, for they have left their mark on the landscape and in the common memory. This is true above all in Jerusalem, where the churches marking the holy sites are catalogued, but even here Egeria's own voice and personality are muted, for the importance of the journey lies in the holy site itself, not in the individual who sees it. The pilgrimage narrative was established with Egeria's letter, but it would be hugely developed and enriched by future travellers.

The path of that development becomes clear when we move forward some three centuries to the narrative of Arculf, recorded in the late seventh century in *De Locis Sanctis* ('On the Holy Places') a somewhat richer and more imaginative text, and one that shows a transition to new themes. The slight oddity about this account is that it was not written by Arculf himself: he was a French bishop who happened to be shipwrecked off the west coast of Scotland, and he related his adventures to Adamnan, abbot of the Iona monastery, who committed them to paper, thus curiously prefiguring the case of the most famous travel narrative of all – that of Marco Polo, which was also written down by an intermediary. Is it possible that the livelier, more colourful account of the Holy Land given by Arculf is a result of questioning by his collaborator? Was Arculf compelled to satisfy Adamnan's curiosity, to feed his imagination, in a way that Egeria had not attempted? Perhaps we get a hint of this in the very structure of the text: it is not a chronological account of Arculf's journey, but goes straight to the heart of the matter with a description of Jerusalem, then fans out to encompass other sites of less importance. The hallmark of Arculf/Adamnan's style is the new sense of wonder which they bring to the story, for in this portrait of Palestine the miraculous is never far away. In Jerusalem there stands a column marking the spot where a dead man returned to life when touched by the holy cross. The bowl from which Christ drank at the Last Supper is preserved in one church, the spear that pierced his side in another, while the stone that sealed the sepulchre is also to be seen, now shattered. Another stone marks the spot on which Abraham prepared to sacrifice Isaac. On Mount Olivet, every year on the day of the Ascension of Christ, a mighty wind blows through the church that was built there, and Arculf was among those who felt its force; at the same place the last footprints Christ made on earth are still visible, and no human power is able to erase them. In Bethlehem, Arculf saw the stream in which the infant Jesus was first washed after his birth, a stream of marvellous purity.

The second novelty of this text is its interest in the present-day reality of the region of Palestine: Arculf describes the colour of the River Jordan, the vineyards on Mount Olivet, and – ominously – the presence of a 'Saracen prayer-house' on the site of the Temple. The Holy Land is no longer a museum, but a real, living place, although its inhabitants are still entirely invisible. This interest extends further, to certain non-biblical places seen en route: the city of Constantinople and its churches are fully described, and there is an entirely secular description of the port of Alexandria and of the crocodile-infested River Nile. Even the volcanoes on the islands of the Tyrrhenian Sea, seen on the homeward voyage, are colourfully evoked. The rules of the pilgrimage narrative are being greatly expanded, and are being linked to a sense of wonder at exotic places. To the original motive of the pilgrim – religious piety – the new motive of curiosity about the world has been added, although this too has still a religious basis, for the wonders of this world display the infinite power of God, showing that the miraculous is all around us now, as it was in the days of the Bible. The experience of travel and the writing it engenders are both changing and maturing, opening windows in the imagination.

In Christian travel narratives, the element of the marvellous was heightened to become the utterly miraculous in *The Voyage of St Brendan*, composed at some unknown date after the year 600. This fantastic story of faith and adventure had a real enough setting in the journeys of Christian missionaries around the western coasts of Britain, including the voyages of St Patrick and St Columba, who brought Christianity to Ireland and Scotland, and those who took

St Brendan celebrating mass on the back of a whale. The St Brendan legends were presumably based on the sea voyages of Christian missionaries in the Early Middle Ages, heightened with miracles and wonders.

the cross to the Faroes and Iceland. But St Brendan's voyage supposedly took him far out into the Atlantic, where he touched on island after marvellous island, each offering its own miraculous revelation of God's creative power – and perhaps too his inclination to humour. On one island – which he calls the Paradise of Birds – he encounters flocks of birds who speak and sing in Latin, and who are Lucifer's fallen angels, placed there by God as a form of mild punishment. Far less pleasant was the fate of Judas Iscariot, found alone on a barren rock, released periodically from hell to be tormented by the demons which inhabited the island. Brendan encounters sea monsters and icebergs and creatures which hurl burning volcanic lava at his ship. He lands on a whale's back, mistaking it for an island, and incurs the creature's wrath when he kindles a fire there. The culmination of seven years' adventuring comes when he finds the Isle of the Blest, a kind of second Eden where saints and martyrs await the end of time. To modern ears, St Brendan's voyage sounds closer to that of Edward

Lear's 'Jumblies' or 'The Owl and the Pussycat' than to any historical narrative. Yet it was taken seriously for centuries, and chart-makers even of the Renaissance and the Age of Discovery still felt compelled to place Brendan's islands in the empty spaces of the North Atlantic. The Brendan stories have a sense of seafaring authenticity, but an even greater sense of imagination, the vision of a world alive with miracles and divine power.

One element, missing since the *Odyssey* and the *Aeneid*, but which the Brendan narrative brings back into travel writing, is the sea, and the idea of the sea as the unknown, out of which terror, wonder or discovery may emerge. This sense is present in much of the literature of northern Europe in the post-classical age, in the poetry, the history and legends of the Norse peoples. The Old English poem 'The Sea-farer' may have been composed in the eighth century, and it evokes the harsh reality of the northern seas in a way that contrasts strongly with the warm, wine-dark waters of Homer's Mediterranean:

> … I, wretched and sad, dwelt a winter
> on the ice-cold sea on the paths of the exile,
> deprived of dear kinsmen,
> hung round with icicles; hail flew in storms.
> There I heard nothing but the roar of the sea,
> the ice-cold wave.
>
> ('The Seafarer', ll. 14–19)

The sea is present in the background of much of the Norse saga literature, prose or poetry, fact or fiction, which embodies the history and beliefs of the people who raided and migrated from Scandinavia through eastern Europe, the Mediterranean and the north Atlantic. Occasionally it moves from the background into the foreground, as in the *Saga of Eric the Red*, which tells of events beginning at the very end of the tenth century. Banished from Iceland for manslaughter, Eric sailed west and established a new settlement on Greenland. This story, especially the deeds of Eric's son, Leif Ericsson, are full of interest since Leif and his companions became the first Europeans to set foot in America. The story is told in the third person by a narrator, but with direct speech, perhaps authentically reported, perhaps invented.

The Greenland colony was desperately handicapped by its lack of timber for building and for fuel, and this provided the motive for Leif's new venture to the west in the year 1001. In due course he struck a coastline, 'level and wooded, with broad white beaches wherever they went, and a gently sloping shoreline', somewhere presumably on the coast of Labrador. Coasting further south they entered a wide strait and made a landfall upon a large, pleasant, well-watered island, with green grass, salmon rivers and little frost. Experts are unanimous that this was Newfoundland, where the Norsemen built houses and spent the winter. 'Nature was generous here', wrote the chronicler, 'and the days and nights were more nearly equal than in Greenland.' The celebrated problem with the Newfoundland identification is the Norsemen's discovery of 'wild grapes' growing in abundance, from which Leif christened the new territory Vinland. The enigma of grapes growing so far north has never been resolved, but the unmistakable remains of a Norse settlement have been discovered on the northern coast of the island. After Leif's return to Greenland, three attempts were made over the next dozen years to colonise Vinland. In the course of one of them, a child named Snorri Thorfinnson was born, the first European child to be born in the Americas, some 575 years before the more famous Virginia Dare in the ill-fated Roanoke colony in Virginia.

For all the promise of Vinland, however, there was a shadow over this paradise: *skraelings* was the picturesque name given by the chronicler to the aggressive people who either inhabited the place or who visited it in strength in their canoes. There were the predictable battles and casualties, enough to destroy the confidence of the hardy Norse sailors, and drive them away for ever. It is impossible to say to which aboriginal people the *skraelings* belonged. The impact that these people had on the colonists was enough to ensure that the Americas were left free from the attentions of Europeans for a further five centuries. The story of Vinland was always known among the Scandinavian people, but not elsewhere. Columbus made clear references to the geographical books that influenced him, and there is no Norse literature on that list. It was the mid-nineteenth century before Scandinavian scholars published this saga, and revolutionised the history of North American discovery. Full of incident, readable and based on eyewitness reports, the central narrative of Eric the Red's saga has the added historical importance of being confirmed by modern archaeology.

We might expect that the theme of religious travel that was so clearly forged in the pilgrimage literature would be strengthened and greatly enlarged in the age of the Crusades; but this conspicuously failed happen. Between 1095 and 1300 several hundred thousand western Europeans went to fight in the Holy Land, and, despite the horrifying death toll, the majority returned to tell the tale. Scores of narratives, long and short, scholarly and popular, emerged from this momentous experience, but in all of them geography and travel form merely the background setting, and remain always secondary to the fervour of the great religious cause, and to the military adventure. In this sense we are back with the stories of Alexander, Caesar and Xenophon. Some of them are eyewitness accounts, including some of the most famous such as those by Villehardouin and Joinville, but their concern is to set down and explain a sequence of vivid and stirring events, not to paint a first-hand picture of Palestine and its people. Battles, heroic deeds, treachery, storms, famine, disease, miraculous deliveries, political conflicts – these fill the Crusader narratives. Some general impressions of the region do inevitably emerge: the heat and the hostility of the arid landscape and of the people, or the magnificence of certain cities like Antioch. Suffering and striving, physical and mental, are constant themes, so that the Crusades re-enact the ancient paradigm of travel as ordeal. The narratives are imbued with religious fervour, of course, but we are conscious too of political and racial hatreds, directed not only against the occupying Muslims, but seething among the supposedly Christian allies.

If we look for any understanding of the spirit of the Near East, of the land itself and the meaning of this great clash of cultures, we look mostly in vain. Only rarely do we get something as novel and thought-provoking as the reflections of Fulcher of Chartres, written around 1127 as he looks back on the success of the First Crusade:

> I pray you, consider and reflect on how God has in our times changed West into East. For we, who were occidentals, have now become orientals. The man who was a Roman or a Frank has, in this land, been turned into a Galilean or a Palestinian. He who was once a citizen of Reims or of Chartres has now become a citizen of Tyre or of Antioch. We have already forgotten the places where we were born; many of us either do not know them or have never even heard of them. One among us now has his own houses and retainers, just as if he possessed them through hereditary or family right. Another takes as his wife, not a woman of his own stock, but rather a Syrian or Armenian, or even, occasionally, a Saracen who has obtained the grace of baptism. ... One may possess vineyards while another has farms. ... Those who were needy have here been enriched by God. Those who had a few pennies, here possess countless bezants. He who had not a village, here possesses a God-given city. Why should one who has found the East to be like this return to the West? Nor does God wish to burden with poverty those who have vowed to follow (or, rather, pursue) him with their crosses. You see, therefore, that this is a great miracle, most astonishing to the whole world. Who has ever heard of such a thing? For God wishes to make us all rich and to draw us to himself as the dearest of friends.
>
> (*The Crusades: A Documentary Survey*, pp. 74–5)

This astonishing passage seems to portray the Crusade – perhaps inadvertently – as a form of colonisation; it suggests that one of its hidden motives may have been to export turbulent fighting men from western Europe, to give them a theatre for their warlike energies, and suitable rewards at the end of it. The Crusades were movements of naked conquest, and, as with the pilgrimage narratives, the people of Palestine are still invisible, and the land is still not an object of curiosity in its own right; it is the battle for possession of it and the glory of that possession that dominate these narratives. We have retreated a pace or two here, even from the degree of personal experience contained in Arculf's text, back into the impersonal prehistory of travel. Only a few make a point of enriching their narrative with geographical descriptions, sometimes giving snapshots of their journey from France or Germany through the wilds of Hungary, Romania and Bulgaria. Odo of Deuil made his way via the Rhine and the Danube, and was an unusually acute observer of life in foreign places: some of his notes have the sting of personal experience. He acknowledges Constantinople as possessing a magnificence that makes it the glory of the Greeks, but his own feeling about the place is far less flattering:

> The city is rather squalid and smelly and many places are afflicted
> with perpetual darkness. The rich build their houses so as to overhang
> the streets and leave these dark and dirty places for travellers and for
> the poor. There murder and robberies occur, as well as other sordid
> crimes which love the dark. Life in this city is lawless, since it has
> as many lords as it has rich men and almost as many thieves as poor
> men. Here the criminal feels neither fear nor shame, since crime is not
> punished by law nor does it ever fully come to light. Constantinople
> exceeds the average in everything – it surpasses other cities in wealth
> and also in vice. (p. 110)

With the exception of isolated passage like these, the literature of the Crusades cannot be termed travel literature, for the whole focus of the narratives is elsewhere – not on the place itself, but on the religious passion which had taken the Crusaders there, and on the military glory or the suffering which awaited them.

As a kind of footnote to the pilgrimage and the Crusade, there is unique narrative of a journey through the lands of the Jewish Diaspora, with Jerusalem as its melancholy goal. In the early 1170s,

Benjamin of Tudela set out from Spain, and travelled via France, Italy, Greece and Asia Minor to the Near East. In each city he records how many Jewish inhabitants there are, making much of those who are learned scholars or of ancient families, mentioning many of them by name. The writing is terse and factual, and from it we learn nothing of Benjamin himself or of his intentions in making his journey, but we cannot doubt that it was a personal form of pilgrimage. His story is full of curious details, for example that Rome is home to 200 Jews, some of them highly respected officers of the Pope. In Corfu he finds but one Jew, a dyer, while in Baghdad he claims 40,000, living in peace and prosperity under the rule of an enlightened caliph. Jerusalem is a place of unspoken sadness, inhabited by numerous people of all races and tongues, but where just two hundred Jews 'dwell in one corner of the city, under the tower of David'. Fifteen years earlier, Benjamin writes, the tombs of David and Solomon had been discovered, a discovery attended by such threatening omens that the authorities swiftly resealed the tombs for ever. From Hebron, however, Benjamin brings back a classic Jewish story: here the tombs of Abraham, Isaac and Jacob are to be found; but the gentiles are fleeced by the guides and shown false tombs, while the Jews can see the real ones – for only a little extra! Not far away, he reports, the remains of the Tower of Babel still stand, split by the 'heavenly fire' which drove its builders mad. Benjamin's story is refreshing for its quality of difference, its unexpected angles, its unstated but all-consuming motivation, and its restrained sadness for what has happened to his scattered people.

The Lure of the East

Religion as a source of travel literature was not exhausted by pilgrimage and Crusade, for rather unexpectedly a third important motive appeared, namely embassies and missions to the distant and formidable civilisations of eastern Asia. Between 1200 and 1240 Genghis Khan united the Mongol tribes into an invincible fighting force which conquered China, while his son, Ogadei, later overran Russia and parts of Europe as far as eastern Germany. The devastation they wrought filled Europe with a terror of this 'scourge of God', and the Latin west may have been spared destruction only by the timely death of Ogadei and the withdrawal of the Mongol forces. In this interlude, Pope Innocent IV seized the opportunity to open diplomatic relations with the Mongols, or Tartars as they were commonly known, by sending several brave men to penetrate into their heartland, to discover what their religion was, and if possible to persuade them to 'Give over their bloody slaughter of mankind and to receive the Christian faith'. Between 1245 and 1255, two well-documented papal embassies travelled to find the Great Khan in his capital at Karakoram. The first party was led by a Franciscan, Friar Carpini, who, astonishingly, was over 60 years old when he set out on his terrible overland journey, while the other was led by another friar, Willem of Rubruck. These were both momentous journeys of cultural discovery, into regions never before described by Europeans. Willem travelled as an emissary of Christianity, but was actually sent by King Louis of France.

Carpini's courage must have been severely tested when travelling through southern Russia, as he witnessed the effects of the Tartar invasion. In and around Kiev, for example, 'We found an innumerable multitude of dead men's skulls and bones lying upon the earth. It was once a very large and populous city, but it is now ... brought to nothing, for there do scarce remain 200 houses, and the inhabitants of these are kept in extreme bondage.' The travellers' safety was apparently assured only by the Pope's written commission – which they had succeeded in translating into Russian, Arabic and Mongol – that they were engaged on important business to the Great Khan. In his narrative and in Rubruck's, the desert or steppe of central Asia enters the European imagination for the first time: its undreamed-of scale, the bitter cold, the emptiness, and the hallucinatory nature of the journey. After fifteen months' travelling Carpini reached Karakoram in time for the enthronement of Kuyuk, Ogadei's son, an event which became an orgy of eating and drinking. Kuyuk appeared to Carpini, 'Of mean stature, very wise and polite, and passing serious and grave in all his demeanour.' Apparently some knowledge of Christianity existed among the Mongols, in spite of which the Khan's reply to the Pope was a threat to wipe him out if he did not come in person to make his submission to the Khan, and with this discouraging reply Carpini had to make the arduous journey back to Italy.

Rubruck's work was slightly more precise in its geography and more personal and anecdotal in tone. He states firmly that the Caspian Sea has no outlet into the ocean; he describes the yurts, the great felt tents in which the nomadic Mongols lived; he describes the Chinese written script; the scattered communities of Nestorian Christians in Asia, known by rumour in Europe; he gives an early account of Buddhism, which he encountered in Tibet; he identifies the Chinese as the people known in Europe as 'Seres' – the bringers of silk. Rubruck was not greatly impressed by Karakoram, which he thought no bigger than a village. There was now a new Khan, Mangu, who, enthroned in a tent of cloth of gold, he found to be a little man, and decidedly the worse for drink at their audience; in fact endless drinking parties appeared to be the chief means of relieving the monotony of life at the Mongol capital. Bearing an obscure but high-sounding message to the Pope, Rubruck returned, as Carpini had done, to write his memoirs, which became well known, and were cited by Roger Bacon for example in his geographical works, while a version of them was printed by Hakluyt in 1598.

There were no further papal missions to the Mongols for some thirty years, for they turned their attention to devastating the Caliphate of Baghdad, after which they moderated their thirst for conquest. Mangu was succeeded as Great Khan by his brother Kublai, who established his capital at Shang-tu – the Xanadu of Coleridge's 'Kubla

Khan'. Kublai was apparently a far more enlightened ruler than his predecessors, interested in the calm, rational administration of his empire. A period known as 'the Mongol peace' opened, when travel and communication between Asia and Europe became easier, and this formed the setting for the most celebrated piece of travel writing yet produced in the west – the book of Marco Polo. Marco's father and uncle, Nicolo and Maffeo, both jewel merchants, had made the journey to China in 1265–70, and had been well received by the Khan. In 1271 they set out for the second time, this time taking the 17-year-old Marco with them.

Why was this journey and the record which Marco made of it so different from any previous journey, and why did it become so important in the history of travel writing and exploration? The answer is that, perhaps without attempting to do so, it introduced a new genre of literature, and that this innovation was instantly recognised and welcomed by its readers. In Marco's narrative we have no motive of religion or of conquest; it was not part of any official embassy to the great Khan, and there seems to be no political dimension; the text is not a learned dissertation on history or culture; although it relates many marvellous things, these are not of a fantastic or miraculous kind. In other words Marco appears to have no ideology, no extra-literary motive: for the first time the journey, the destination, the experience itself, are centre stage. Nor is the presence of the traveller himself diminished: the record is – within certain limits – personal; it is what the writer saw and lived through. It is not presented as a didactic text, but as a work of creative memory, born out of the consciousness of the writer. It presupposes a curiosity about the world for its own sake, and it fed and stimulated that curiosity.

Having said this, Marco Polo's text is certainly not a plain un-varnished record of his experiences; it bristles with problems which have exercised the commentators for centuries, problems that are both literary and historical, and a few of them must be mentioned. The narrative was composed by Marco with the help of another writer, Rusticello, while both men were held in prison in Genoa some few years after Marco's return to Italy in 1295. Rusticello was a writer of fictitious romances, and it is therefore reasonable to wonder how far Marco's original narrative may have been altered by him or embroidered for effect. Although generally giving the appearance of geographical precision, it is often difficult, or even impossible, to follow the route of Marco's journey across Asia, while some parts of his narrative appear to be asides or digressions based on hearsay and not on personal experience; his descriptions of India and Japan come into this category. Marco and his family apparently remained in China for some seventeen years, and he claims that they were in the service of the emperor; yet precisely what they did during that time is never revealed. He omits to mention some very basic facts about China: the nature of the Chinese language and its system of writing, the habit of drinking tea, and the existence of the Great Wall are a few such omissions. This puzzle has even led scholars to suggest that Marco never visited China at all, but picked up second-hand accounts of the country in the ports of the Levant, and fabricated his journey. Other scholars have argued that each of these omissions is capable of explanation. The process of composition with Rusticello took place around 1298, more than twenty-five years after Marco first set out for China, and the critical reader will wonder how all the experiences which he narrates can have remained so sharp and clear in his memory, unless he kept a journal at the time.

Marco and his book became known as *Il Milione* – which might mean either 'the million man' or 'the million story' – because of his breathtaking descriptions of the magnificence of China: the Khan's great dining hall where 60,000 men could be served at once; the Khan's wardrobe of 12,000 robes of cloth of gold; his possession of 100,000 white horses; his fleet of 15,000 ships; of the city of Hangchow, with its lakes and islands where more than 100 sumptuous banquets were held simultaneously, and so on. This superabundance is central to Marco's message about the world of the east, that everything is marvellous, the human world shining with wealth and magnificence, the natural world full of exotic and beautiful animals, and the earth bursting with crops, fruits, precious metals and gems. Everything is on a far grander scale than in Europe, for this is another world. The Khan himself is like a demigod, ruling over this dream landscape:

> You must know that a large lion is brought before the Great Lord. And as soon as the lion sees the Great Khan, it crouches down before him, making signs of great obeisance; and you would think it knew him for its lord and master.
>
> (*The Travels of Marco Polo*, p. 138)

We are continually reminded of Marco's authority as an eyewitness, that, marvellous as all this may appear, it must all be true because Marco saw it. This is Rusticello's introduction:

> And all who read this book or hear it read, must believe it, as all the things contained in it are true. For I tell you that ever since the Lord our God did with his own hands mould our first Father Adam, there never was up to the present day any man, Christian or Pagan, Tartar or Indian or of any other race whatsoever, who knew and explored so great a part of the various regions of the world and of its great marvels, as this Messer Marco knew and explored.   (p. 1)

Yet, despite all his detailed descriptions, Marco's own personality does not really emerge, and he remains only a voice, a witness. Nowhere is there a vital anecdote, some incident that is trivial, colourful or funny, something that gives a sense of the living experience. We wish that Marco himself could have fallen in love with a beautiful Chinese princess, perhaps even sailed with her back to Venice; that he could have taught the Khan Italian and instructed him about European culture; that he could have fought in a battle, or become lost in the interior and been rescued; that he could have studied with Taoist monks, or fallen sick and been cured by acupuncture. But nothing like this ever happens and there is no direct speech anywhere: the voice proceeds smoothly and evenly, but always on the surface of things, while, as in the narratives of the pilgrimages or the Crusades, the indigenous people as people are unheard or invisible. Marco appears to have no ideology, but he unquestionably shaped his text into an imaginative construct, he had a vision of the east which he wished to share, so that for all his claims to truth, it cannot be taken at face value as a report. William of Rubruck's text is plainer, more personal, more humorous and realistic: it conveys more sharply what it felt like to be in China, and yet it was Marco's book – grander in its claims but more confused and contradictory and less immediate in feel – which became a classic.

So the genre of travel writing was launched with this text, which came to be seen as a true description of the East, a world that lay waiting beyond Europe: mapmakers of the fourteenth century adopted Marco's Asian place names, and in eastern China they placed little vignettes of the Great Khan on his throne. Uncertainty about the religion of the Khan – he did not appear to be Muslim or Buddhist or anything else that western observers could put a name to – prompted the dispatch of Franciscan missionaries such as Odoric of Pordenone, who established a small Christian presence in China, and whose reports generally confirmed those of Marco Polo.

Historically, the importance of Marco's book is hard to exaggerate, for its portrait of the wealth and magnificence of Chinese civilisation excited the envy of Europe, and thus created the essential conditions for the Age of Discovery. The East became a dream-vision, and Marco's text, read and studied by princes, merchants and navigators, was one of the principal sources of European Renaissance geography. Columbus believed it absolutely, and when the European explorers set out to find a sea route to the East they were not seeking new lands, but new routes to lands already known – known above all from Marco

Polo's book. For this reason it was arguably one of the most influential books ever written. Yet few travellers followed in the footsteps of the Polos: for one thing the Mongol peace did not last very long, for in 1370 the Chinese rose against their Mongol masters and drove them from their country back to the steppes. For another, the power of the Ottoman Turks had already closed the Near Eastern ports to European traders, and the door to the East, temporarily opened by the Rubruck, the Polos and Friar Odoric, was shut once again.

Perhaps this renewed inaccessibility of Cathay was the context that inspired the second great medieval travel narrative, *The Travels of Sir John Mandeville*, composed in the 1350s, which became if anything still more popular than Marco Polo, and still more of an intellectual tease, its reputation rising and falling and rising again over the centuries. Originally read as a colourful and thought-provoking account of a journey to the Holy Land, and beyond, to Cathay, it was, following the great Age of Discovery, dismissed as a pack of lies. It has now been rehabilitated as a richly imaginative work, a tapestry into which many strands of knowledge, belief, humour and cultural criticism have been consciously woven. The complex relationship between the manuscripts, which exist in several different languages, the problem as to whether a writer named Sir John Mandeville ever existed, the question of whether he ever set foot in the countries he describes – all this has created a scholarly puzzle that will probably never be resolved. What is not in doubt, however, is the charm of Mandeville's narration, or the extent of his influence; his book became the accepted account of the lands beyond Europe, studied and trusted for some two centuries and more after its first appearance around 1360. It was admired by Leonardo da Vinci, and it was read and reread by Columbus while preparing for his great voyage.

The first part of Mandeville's text is an account of a pilgrimage to the Holy Land, not wildly unlike other such narratives, but with some very individual touches, such as Mandeville's private conversation with the Sultan of Egypt, in which the Muslim ruler aroused the shame of the Christian pilgrim with his scathing attack on the moral degradation of western society. But it is in the second part of the book that we are led into an exotic and miraculous world, as Mandeville takes us through parts of central Asia, India, the Indian Ocean islands, Cathay, and the fabled countries even more distant. Here we are back in the world of Pliny, Solinus and *Wonders of the East*, among cannibals, giants, hermaphrodites, men who walk on all fours, men with one huge foot, men who hiss instead of speaking, men with no eyes or noses, men who live on scents instead of food, men who worship animals, women whose eyes can kill with one glance, and so on; there are trees which, when tapped, yield honey, wine or venom, and other trees whose fruit contains living creatures; there is the fountain of eternal youth; the valley of devils or 'Vale Perilous'; the mountains where the legendary creatures Gog and Magog are imprisoned; the bizarre kingdom of the assassins – a false paradise maintained by an evil ruler with the help of drugs; and the mysterious empire in Asia of the fabled Christian king Prester John. The geographical framework of this eastern world is extremely vague, and no map could possibly be drawn of it.

What are we to make of all this? Is this a romance in the medieval tradition, grafted on to a pilgrimage narrative which may possibly be genuine? The literary sources of the second part have been clearly identified, some from the legend and fable tradition, others from genuine travel narratives, including those of the merchant travellers to Cathay. Is Mandeville, then, simply a plagiarist? Was the longest journey he ever made the one to his nearest library, as one critic alleged? Was he in fact creating a parody or satire on the travellers' tale genre? Occasionally he will tell a tall story, then add, 'If it is true or not I cannot say, God alone knows.' He is cautious about the belief that Noah's Ark is still to be seen on Mount Ararat. When told about the fruit which contains living animals, he responded by telling his hosts in Cathay that this was not so very wonderful, for in his own land there were trees which bore living birds as fruits. Near the end of his story these tongue-in-cheek remarks reach their culmination when he admits that, 'Of Paradise I cannot speak properly, for I have not been there, and that I regret.'

Some critics have seen Mandeville as composing a description of the world, a medieval compendium, but with a first-person narrative voice. Others have preferred to see in him the first English novelist, using travel as Malory, Cervantes, Defoe or Fielding would use it much later – as a dimension through which a narrative may develop. Both readings underline the undoubted fact that travel writing can inhabit a borderland between truth and fiction. Whether the writer can move freely, deliberately, in a single text, from one to the other, is another matter. To most readers, the credibility of the whole work depends on the credibility of all its parts – this is the common-sense position. The travel genre is so difficult to define because it is so inclusive – anything can get into it. The last word on Mandeville will probably never be given, but, even more strongly than Marco Polo, he embodies one of the dominant themes of travel literature – the search for novelty, for what is alien, for what stretches our imagination and awes our mind – this is what the traveller travels for, and what his readers look for in his report.

One of the most persistent and alluring of the legends recounted by Mandeville is that of Prester John, the supposed ruler of a mysterious Christian kingdom far to the east. Presumably based on tenuous knowledge of the heretical Nestorian Christians, who had migrated east in the fifth century, and who survived in parts of Western Asia and India, the legend acquired a topical urgency at the time of the Crusades. The idea of joining strength with a Christian army coming from the rear of the Muslim forces was an attractive and powerful one. In the thirteenth century a document purporting to be a letter from Prester John to the rulers of the West was circulating, and it offered precisely the alliance that the West was seeking. It was of course a literary forgery, and by the fourteenth century the failure of any Christian king to reveal himself in Asia led to the ingenious relocation of Prester John to Abyssinia, to the ancient Christian community long established there. As late as 1487, King João II of Portugal dispatched Pêro da Covilhã as a secret emissary to seek Prester John in the mountains of East Africa. En route, the disguised Covilhã became the first known European to enter Mecca. He succeeded in reaching the court of the Emperor of Abyssinia, Eskender, but, whether by choice or by compulsion, he did not return to Europe, marrying and settling there for some thirty years. In 1520 another Portuguese, a Franciscan missionary named Francisco Alvares, found Covilhã, rather like a proto-Stanley finding a proto-Livingstone. Alvares returned to Europe, and in 1533 he delivered a report to the Pope on the state of Christianity in Abyssinia, which included descriptions of its remarkable rock-cut temples, carved according to legend by angels. A fuller account of his travels was published as *The Prester John of the Indies* in 1540. By then, of course, following the era of maritime discovery, the entire framework of geography and world politics had changed, and Alvares's text became a kind of epitaph to the legend of Prester John.

Mandeville had an exact contemporary whose approach to travel writing could not have been more different. While Mandeville in fourteenth-century England was composing his enigmatic fantasy – if that is what it is – in distant Morocco Ibn Battuta was setting down his record of forty years' ceaseless wandering through the length and breadth of the Islamic world. Battuta probably travelled further than any other human being before the Age of Discovery, and his journeys were the more remarkable because he had resolved never to cover the same ground twice. But his narrative approach is as far removed from Mandeville's as it could possibly be: direct, anecdotal, inquisitive, humane, Ibn Battuta's personality is the thread that holds his long, episodic text together. We cannot be sure that everything he wrote is true, but by his own account he visited Muslim Africa, East and West, Constantinople, all of Arabia, Persia, Turkestan, India, Ceylon, the Indian Ocean islands, and China itself. He was a wealthy man who travelled in some style, with companions and servants, and took new wives in several cities. He was a scholar, motivated by a deep piety and a curiosity to see Muslim civilisation and Muslim law in action, yet he was by no means uncritical of what he saw: his evocation of the rule of the Sultan of Delhi, Mohammed Tuglaq, is unforgettable. This diabolical tyrant, in whose city Battuta lived for eight years, was also a patron of scholars and a great dispenser of charity, and Battuta affirms that his gates were thronged daily with those awaiting his charity, but also with those awaiting a hideous death at his hands. In order to purge Delhi of his enemies, the Sultan once expelled every single inhabitant, driving them from their homes out into the countryside; then, standing upon his palace roof survey-ing the silent, deserted city, he felt intoxicated by the luxury of power and utter peace. Battuta was baffled, horrified and fascinated by his bloodthirsty career. Battuta's text was unknown in Europe before the nineteenth century, when his direct, idiomatic style came as a revelation to readers who knew medieval travellers only as pilgrims or retailers of marvels and miracles.

The Holy Land had been for centuries the great focus of interest of European travellers, and apparently this situation did not change after the Islamic reconquest of Jerusalem in 1187. The journey was certainly not without dangers, but Chaucer's Wife of Bath had been three times to Jerusalem, and the number of narratives and guides for pilgrims continued to grow. Each had something to add to the col-lective experience, but none was more individual than that written by William Wey, a fellow of Eton College, around 1465. Wey made two journeys to Jerusalem, in 1458 and 1462, having previously travelled to Compostella, and he chose to divide his work into four distinct parts.

He gives some helpful practical advice to the traveller on what he will
need on the journey, and suggests that Venice makes a good point of
departure and place to stock up on clothing and equipment. To this
practical advice he adds a careful list of journey times between all the
principal towns en route, from Dover to Jerusalem; indeed he presents
his work as an itinerary in businesslike fashion, almost a medieval
Baedeker. He then offers a fascinating description of Venice itself at
the height of its power and magnificence, for he was there during the
Feast of St Mark, and he also witnessed the election of a new Doge,
with its attendant ceremonials. But the real oddity of Wey's text lies in
his account of the onward journey from Venice, written in charmingly
naive metrical rhymed verse:

> Fro Venyse to Port Jaff by the see
> Hyt ys ij^m [one thousand] myle and hundrys thre;
> And yn that see ther ys a place
> Wher the whale swalowyd Jonas.
> Ther ys in the same, besyde that,
> A ston that seynt Petyr fyschyd at.
>
> (*The Itineraries of William Wey*, p. 8)

and so on. We can only speculate that perhaps Wey intended these
jingling couplets to be memorised by pilgrims, and recited to while
away their time at sea. Wey confirms that Christian pilgrims are
indeed permitted to enter Jerusalem for certain fees, but that travel in
other parts of Palestine could be dangerous, and that some sites may
be effectively out of bounds. The final component of Wey's work was
the most unusual – a list of the major places of interest on a map of
the Holy Land.

Two decades after Wey, another pilgrimage narrative included a
map of the Holy Land, and was to be far more influential for the
simple reason that it was printed, while Wey's text had come just a few
years too early to catch the printing revolution, at least in England.

Bernhard von Breydenbach was a canon from Mainz, and his text is a practical itinerary, like Wey's – there are no marvels or miracles here. He made his pilgrimage in 1483–84, accompanied by an artist named Erhard Reuwich, who drew a series of fine views of Mediterranean ports including Venice, which appeared as woodblock illustrations in this, the first illustrated travel book to be printed. It was a natural transfer to the print medium of the tradition of manuscript illustration, already found in certain travel texts such as Marco Polo and Mandeville. In Breydenbach's book, Reuwich's masterpiece was a magnificent map-view of the Holy Land, showing towns and geographical features in elevation. The city of Jerusalem is given on a scale much enlarged above the rest of the map, and the whole effect is quite spectacular. Illustration would add a new dimension to travel publication: the travel writer represented the intellectual curiosity of the reader back at home, but the illustrator would increasingly feed the visual imagination.

There is one travel narrative from the Middle Ages which stands out as a personal and charming memoir, unconnected to any other text. In 1336 Petrarch, the great poet and humanist scholar, a long-time resident of the Vaucluse, set out to climb the nearby Mont Ventoux, the extinct volcano which rears up out of the plains north-east of Avignon. He had no special reason for doing so, except to discover what could be seen from the summit. Unable at first to find anyone to accompany him, he pressed his younger brother into service. En route, the pair met an old man on the lower slopes who tried to dissuade them from going on, but then agreed to act as their guide. The climb was physically difficult, over arid, rocky ground, and the way was confusing. Several times Petrarch became tired, and lagged behind, claiming he was seeking a better path, but found that he was merely losing height, and he had to bear the laughter of his brother when he rejoined. Arriving at the summit, he was deeply struck by the view of the Alps which pointed the way to Italy, and of the sea sparkling below Marseilles. The most extraordinary episode in this text is that

Petrarch took with him on the ascent a copy of *The Confessions* of Saint Augustine, and how many mountaineers have ever done that? Petrarch's brother suggested that they perform an act of sortilege, opening the book at random to see what commentary or guidance the saint could offer them. Petrarch did so, and read the words:

> And men go about to wonder at the heights of the mountains, and the mighty waves of the sea, and the wide sweep of rivers, and the circuit of the ocean, and the revolutions of the stars, but themselves they consider not.
>
> (*The Ascent of Mount Ventoux*, p. 9)

Petrarch was thunderstruck at this unnerving coincidence, and they made their way down from the mountain by moonlight in a very chastened frame of mind. They halted for the night at an inn, where Petrarch tells us that he immediately set down what had happened, while the impression of it was fresh in his mind. The result was a unique document, which perhaps may stand as the earliest text in the vast literature of mountaineering.

The most profound and resonant journey narrative to come out of the Middle Ages, however, had nothing to do with real geography, with mountains, foreign lands and their kings, with merchants or seaman, with pilgrimages, marvels or monsters or divine miracles. It may seem odd to discuss Dante's *Divine Comedy*, completed around 1320, in terms of travel literature, yet quite plainly it tells of a journey, and the poem cannot proceed without the dramatic metaphor of movement in space. Dante's journey takes him beyond the confines of this world, into levels of the created universe which are inaccessible to living creatures. As he is guided through hell, purgatory and heaven, Dante is permitted to observe, and in part to experience, the suffering and the bliss which wait behind the veil of this life, and he is in no doubt of their intense, physical reality. His journey begins on a specific day in a real forest, and ends with his leaving the earth and

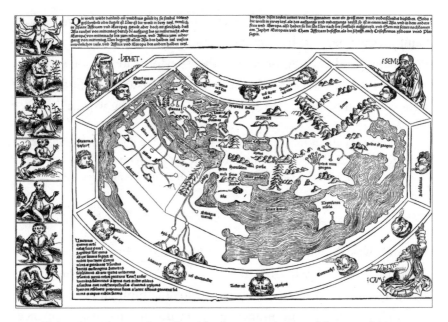

World Map from the *Nürnberg Chronicle* of 1493, on the eve of the Age of Discovery,
showing the subhuman creatures of medieval legend who were believed to dwell
at the edges of the known world.

ascending through the successive spheres of heaven towards God.
Yet throughout he remains a living man, the only living creature
in the story, for the rest are shades. The journey is the framework
upon which the poet builds a vision of the entire universe, but the
development of that vision is presented as a real, personal experience,
a real journey involving purification through suffering and awakening.
It clearly takes us back to the archetypal paradigm of travel with
which we began – the conviction that travel is deeply purposeful: as
we move through space, we are changed, we discover, and we are
transformed.

TWO

The Age of Discovery

As I know that you will be pleased at the great victory with which
Our Lord has crowned my voyage, I write this to you, from which
you will learn how in thirty-three days, I passed from the Canary
Islands to the Indies with the fleet which the most illustrious king
and queen, our sovereigns, gave to me. And there I found very many
islands filled with people innumerable, and of them all I have taken
possession for their highnesses, by proclamation made and with
the royal standard unfurled, and no opposition was offered to me.
To the first island which I found, I gave the name *San Salvador*, in
remembrance of the Divine Majesty, Who has marvellously bestowed
all this; the Indians call it 'Guanahani'. To the second I gave the name
Isla de Santa Maria de Concepción; to the third, *Fernandina*; to the
fourth, *Isabella*; to the fifth, *Isla Juana*; and so to each one I gave a
new name.

Christopher Columbus (*The Four Voyages of Columbus*, vol. I, p. 2)

THESE WERE the first words which Christopher Columbus sent
back to Europe, announcing his dazzling achievement of crossing
the Atlantic, of discovering unknown lands, and of taking possession of them for his royal patrons. He did not add, but he perhaps
believed, that his voyage had opened a new era in world history, and,

incidentally, in travel literature. He presents his adventure naturally enough as a 'victory', and the new lands as abounding in all manner of wealth and beauty, but, as we shall see, this rhetoric was used to conceal fundamental uncertainties about this new world.

Marco Polo's book had acted like a stone cast into the pool of European consciousness, and its ripples, instead of diminishing, continued to spread and agitate the waters in the two centuries following the writer's death. To reach the East, to trade with the Indies and Cathay, to see and touch the magnificent kingdom which Marco had described, became an overwhelming desire on the part of European monarchs, soldiers, merchants and navigators. All European nations possessed a class of elite, unemployed young men, bred to an ideology mingled of warfare, adventure, royal service and national pride. The Crusades, a natural outlet for their fierce energies, were over, and they looked around for new theatres in which to display their prowess. The possibility of overseas adventure, exploration and conquest brought these ambitions into focus, and the seafaring nations of the western Mediterranean began to ponder how they might outflank the Muslim powers who barred their passage to the fabulous lands of the East. By 1450 the Portuguese were involved in a deliberate process of exploration, pushing further and further down the western coast of Africa, searching for a sea route to the East. Meanwhile by 1480, at least one geographical theorist – Columbus – had studied every available map and geographical book he could lay his hands on, and had become convinced that a simple, radical but logical alternative existed: to sail west across the Atlantic in search of Cathay.

By 1493 Columbus arrived back in Seville with news of his discovery; six years later Vasco da Gama was in Lisbon reporting on the first voyage around the coast of Africa to India; two decades after that, Ferdinand Magellan's exhausted crew, without their dead captain, dragged themselves back to Seville to claim the first circumnavigation of the world. Over several thousand years, humanity had been developing in isolated civilisations – in Europe, India, China and Central America. But these momentous events signalled the beginning of the end of that isolation. The first steps had been taken towards creating the one world which we now inhabit.

For travel literature, the impact of these events would be seismic. Almost overnight the known world doubled in size, and became immensely more complex. The newly discovered territories were unknown worlds, inhabited by unknown creatures, resembling ourselves but in some ways disturbingly unlike us. The Holy Land, the remains of the Tower of Babel, the Kingdom of Prester John, even the Great Khan in Cathay – these would soon be forgotten, for they belonged to the intellectual past. To these new-found lands, the classical and biblical writers, the scholars and poets of the old world, seemed to offer no guidance. Even the explorers who had found them were not sure where they were, or what they were. Were these new lands islands off the coasts of Cathay? This was Columbus's often-repeated belief, yet nothing that he found resembled anything that Marco Polo had described. The act of taking possession of these lands in the name of the kings of Europe suggested quite clearly that they were seen as virgin territory. To some extent, these claims were clearly made to satisfy the explorers' masters, to ensure their continued patronage, to offer them what all monarchs desired – the enlargement of their kingdoms. But the act of claiming possession also presented an enormous challenge that was both physical and intellectual. They must return to reconnoitre and map these territories, and they must somehow try to understand their character, and that of the people who inhabited them. Where did these people come from? How did they – and their 'new world' – relate to the family of mankind who lived in the 'old world', the world whose creation was described in the Book of Genesis? Did they possess a form of civilisation, or were they mere savages, scarcely distinct from animals? The first news reports and the later, fuller descriptions of the navigators had somehow to

A sixteenth-century ship threatened by nightmarish sea monsters,
a picture symbolising the barriers of fear confronted by the navigators of
the Age of Discovery.

find new imagery and a new intellectual framework in which to place
these newly discovered realms. It is symbolically significant that one
of the last world maps to be published on the very eve of the Age of
Discovery – that in the great *Nürnberg Chronicle* in 1493 – still showed
the edges of the known world to be filled with the subhuman creatures
from the Pliny–Mandeville tradition; after 1500 no world map showed
them any more, for they had been replaced by images of the real
'savages' found in the new world.

It must be said that the first generation of explorers were neither
great intellects nor great writers. Columbus and Vespucci, and the
companions of da Gama, Cortés and Magellan, saw themselves prima-
rily – and quite justifiably – as men of action, participants in a great
adventure. Their writing naturally emphasised the drama and the
hardship they had faced, and the resourcefulness with which they had
pressed on to triumph. Therefore the twin themes which they seized

upon were the hostility of the sea which they must conquer in order to reach these new lands, and the alien nature, or the outright savagery, of the people whom they encountered. This was an unknown, threatening world into which they had ventured, one which demanded strength, courage and ruthlessness from those who hoped to master it. Yet it was a world of primitive beauty, a virgin world teeming with potential riches, and it evoked in equal measure the wonder and the greed of the Europeans.

The Voyages of Christopher Columbus

Of all the great early explorers, it is fitting that Columbus should be the most intriguing. What was his true objective? What did he really believe he had found? And what relationship did he envisage between the new world and old? A generation after Columbus's death, a Spanish historian called his discoveries 'the greatest event since the creation of the world, excluding only the incarnation and death of him who created it'. This grandiose claim matches the tone of Columbus's letters and journals, for it is clear that he was seeking something more than a new sea route to the east: he was seeking a new heaven and a new earth. He was setting out to inaugurate a new era in world history, to claim the world for Christianity. He emphasised that when he had first approached the Spanish monarchs he was no mere adventurer, seeking a business partner, but that 'the Holy Trinity moved me to come with this message into your royal presence'. Encountering the indigenous people of the Caribbean, we hear from Columbus for the first time the idea that they imagined the European visitor to be a god descended out of heaven. During the return from his first voyage, he was beset by great storms, and was so tormented by the thought that his ship might be lost, and with it the knowledge of his great discovery, his great service to God and Spain, that he wrote out a brief account of his voyage, sealed it in a waterproof cask and committed it to the sea. His own name seemed to blaze with significance for him: he was Christopher, 'the Christ-bearer'; yet at the same time this was the man who rushed to assure his Spanish masters of the wealth in gold and crops and natural resources that awaited them in the 'Indies', and who immediately began planning their future exploitation as Spanish colonies, plans which included enslaving the indigenous populations.

In his reports Columbus had somehow to combine the idea of finding a new world with the idea of finding what he had expected – that is, finding the Indies. The impossibility of reconciling these conflicting ideas set up tensions within his mind that go far to explain the contradictions, obscurity and incoherence that we find in his letters. It also explains why he could never produce a map of his discoveries. On the first voyage he carried letters from the Spanish Crown to the Great Khan of China, which of course he was unable to deliver, but he did not hesitate to claim possession for Spain of the lands of Cuba and Hispaniola, while still affirming that they were islands off the coast of China. To grasp the absurdity of this, we have only to imagine the situation reversed: imagine a Chinese fleet landing on the Balearic Islands and claiming possession of them for the Great Khan. Columbus's disastrous failure as a colonial administrator seems to have deepened his religious mania, forcing him to claim a more exalted role as an explorer and missionary. His letters concerning the third and fourth voyages are reports from a mind on the edge of some vision or revelation, but one which remains tantalisingly out of reach. Coasting off Venezuela on the third voyage in 1498, he hints at a psychological breakthrough, noting, 'I have come to believe that this is a mighty continent which was hitherto unknown.' But this hint is not followed up, and we hear no more of the idea of a new continent. The crucial factor seems to have been his observations at the mouth of the Orinoco river: how, he mused, could such a huge volume of fresh water pour down from a mere island? He even wondered if this lushly forested tropical coastline might hide the Garden of Eden, the earthly paradise, which medieval geographers and mapmakers had located at the eastern limit of the world. Tradition taught that from that garden there flowed the four great rivers, the Tigris, the Euphrates, the Nile and the Don; was the Orinoco really one of these, or a fifth outpouring from paradise? 'These lands', he wrote, 'are those in which I am assured in my heart that the earthly paradise lies.'

The fourth voyage of 1503 was his final attempt to break through the land barrier of Central America into the sea that would finally lead to the true Indies. He was beset by storms that were apocalyptic in their violence:

> For nine days I was lost, without hope of life; eyes never saw the
> sea so high, so rough ... There was I, held in a sea turned to blood,
> boiling as a cauldron on a mighty fire. Never did the heavens appear
> more terrible. For a day and a night they blazed like a furnace, and
> the lightning darted forth in such flashes that I wondered every
> moment whether it had destroyed my masts and sails; ... we all
> believed that the ships must be consumed.... The crews were already
> so broken in spirit that they longed for death as a release from such
> martyrdom.
>
> (*The Four Voyages of Columbus*, vol. II, p. 86)

In this extremity he was granted a vision in a dream, and heard a voice reaffirming his divine mission, saying:

> He caused thy name to sound marvellously in the land. The Indies,
> which are so rich a part of the world, He gave thee for thine own; thou
> hast divided them as it pleased thee, and He enabled thee to do this.
> Of the barriers of the Ocean sea, which were closed with such mighty
> chains, He gave thee the keys; and thou wast obeyed in many lands and
> among Christians thou hast gained an honourable fame. (vol. II, p. 92)

And yet within a few sentences he has turned from this almost messianic self-portrait to yet another catalogue of the gold, pearls and spices with which this land – he is now speaking of the Central

American mainland – abounds, and which lie open to their conquerors. The simplicity of their defenceless people is held up as a great advantage:

> All this makes for the security of the Christians and the assurance of their dominion, and gives great hope for the honour and increase of the Christian religion. And the voyage thither will be as short as to Española, since it will be with the wind. Your Highnesses are as much sovereigns of this land as at Jerez or Toledo; your ships may go there as if they were going home. Thence they will obtain gold: ... Gold is most excellent. Gold constitutes treasure, and he who possesses it may do what he will in the world, and may so attain as to bring souls to Paradise. (vol. II, pp. 102–4)

This extraordinary link between gold and Christianity, earthly power and spiritual glory was to be absolutely central to Spanish exploration and conquest in the Americas. It is to be found also among the chroniclers of the Portuguese maritime empire, and scarcely less forcefully among the explorers of the Protestant nations, the English and the Dutch. It amounted to a theory of cultural destiny – that the European maritime nations were destined to bring Christianity and civilisation to a pagan and savage world, and their reward was to be the wealth and riches which the indigenous populations themselves were incapable of appreciating or valuing. It is impossible to understand the psychology of the conquistadors and their successors without grasping this scale of values, first articulated here by Columbus. It would be easy to dismiss all this as hypocrisy and cynicism on a grand scale, an elaborate mask for naked greed and cruelty. Yet it seems clear that it was truly believed by the navigators, by the fighting men, by the merchants and by the princes who sent them. We have to see it as a reaction, a defensive response to the discovery of this new world, and of the inexplicable people they found there, perceived to be somewhere between the animals and humanity. They stood outside all received knowledge: the classical authorities, the biblical authorities, the scientific authorities, knew nothing of them; indeed they seemed almost to stand outside God's creation. This encounter with Europeans, so the navigators believed, must be as much their destiny as ours, their moment of awakening from the pagan darkness in which they had lived. These beliefs would dominate and guide the structures of European colonialism and imperialism which would prevail for four centuries. The mystery and confusion within Columbus's mind was a presage of so much that was to follow.

The implications for travel writing were immense. Throughout the sixteenth century, those who travelled beyond Europe would be explorers, bringing back reports from places which did not yet exist on the map or in the understanding or the imagination. They were first footfalls, first glimpses, first encounters, the explorer feeling his way as he went, but always with this sense of rapacious superiority, that it was his destiny to tame these savage Edens. Their writings are of deep historical interest, but there is a constant feeling that they rarely reach a level of imagination or insight worthy of their subject. They came from the pens of soldiers and adventurers, men of action, not philosophers or poets, and their minds and motives were not what we should expect of those who were exploring new worlds; they cannot interpret what they see.

Columbus's pride would no doubt have been deeply wounded had he known that the new world which he was the first to see would be named for a rival explorer, a fellow Italian in the service of Spain. Amerigo Vespucci claimed to have made four voyages across the Atlantic between 1497 and 1504, and like Columbus he penned several letters to his patrons describing them, but in very different style. Vespucci is noticeably calmer, far less religious, and more analytical than Columbus. The most significant of these letters relates to his third voyage, when he claims to have followed the coast of South America down to a latitude of 50 degrees south – far further than any previous navigator. He differentiates between the various groups

The other great threat discovered in the New World was the reported cannibalism
of its inhabitants, depicted here on the margins of the Sebastian Münster world map
of 1532.

of indigenous people, he dismisses the old geographical theory of
climates as untenable, he refers to flora and fauna with more precision,
and he describes the stars and constellations of the southern heavens.
All this gives a slightly more reflective air and a quasi-scientific precision to his writing. Like Columbus he makes some use of the rhetoric
of paradise – the fragrance, verdure and abundance of the land, and
the nakedness of the inhabitants – but unlike Columbus he displays
no religious fervour, and does not dwell on promises of gold. He does,
however, introduce certain themes that would become standard in this
kind of text: the cannibalism of the people – or at least some of them
– and their lawless social and sexual mores. They have, he says, no
private property, no law, no authority and no religion; they couple
with whom they like, and take wives and husbands as they wish; in a
word, 'they live according to nature'. His description of salted joints
of human flesh hanging from house beams would influence European
images of America for generations.

But Vespucci's greatest fame came from his explicit statement that this vast land was a continent, 'which may be called a new world', of which the men of previous ages had no knowledge. This was the truth which Columbus must have glimpsed, but which he always resisted, and the text in which it occurs was published under the title *Mundus Novus*. This text was widely reprinted and read throughout Europe: it was picked up by the German geographer Martin Waldseemüller, who proposed that this new world should be named after Vespucci, slightly altering his Christian name, Amerigo, by analogy with the other 'A' continents. Thus on Waldseemüller's great world map of 1507, the name 'America' appears for the first time, but placed in South America. Through the agency of Waldseemüller, Vespucci also scored over Columbus in giving to the world a strikingly clear and authoritative map, embodying this revolution in geographical knowledge. At the head of this map, Vespucci is portrayed as the discover of the new world, counterbalanced by Ptolemy, the geographer of the old world.

The Conquest of America

The Spanish approached the new world with an aggressive conviction of their superiority, their destiny as Christians and conquerors, and within that ethos lay the seeds of inevitable tragedy for the indigenous populations, nowhere more so than in the campaigns of conquest over the kingdoms of Mexico and Peru. Those who led those campaigns were no more travel writers than the Roman generals or the Crusaders were, but the accounts they gave of those doomed civilisations are in places unforgettable. Hernán Cortés was astute, cunning and ruthlessly focused on his own objective, which was conquest pure and simple, but nevertheless he sent a series of clear and perceptive reports back to the King of Spain, which succeeded in evoking some of the complexities of Mexican politics, the richness of its physical culture, and above all perhaps the magnificence of the lake city of Mexico, resembling a more savage Venice. It comes as a considerable surprise to hear Cortés say at one point that 'the manner of living among these people is very similar to that in Spain, and considering that this is barbarous nation, shut off from a knowledge of the true God or communication with enlightened nations, one may well marvel at the orderliness and good government which is everywhere maintained.' Even the ageing soldier Bernal Díaz del Castillo, recalling the conquest years later, remembered his first sight of the great city, 'rising from the water like an enchanted vision'. But through the heart of this magnificence flowed a dreadful poison – the bloodthirsty religious rites which sustained the social and priestly elite. In Cortés's letters and in Díaz we find a complete reversal and rejection of the Eden imagery used by Columbus; indeed the grotesque idols, the nightmarish temple sacrifices and the depraved priests make this aspect of Mexican life seem more like hell than paradise. The peoples native to Hispaniola had apparently been innocent of any formal beliefs, but this savage parody of a religion seemed to offer the Spanish exactly the justification they needed to attack and destroy the indigenous culture. Cortés relates with pride how he overthrew the idols in the Aztec temples, and years later the ageing and impoverished conquistador would seek help from his king, recalling his deeds in high-minded religious terms:

> I have laboured, going sleepless, eating poorly and at times not at
> all, bearing armour on my back, risking my life in dangers, freely
> spending my means and years, and all in the service of God, bringing
> sheep into His fold in a hemisphere far removed from ours, as yet
> unknown and unwritten of in the scriptures, increasing and spreading
> the fame and dominions of my King, bringing under his yoke and
> royal sceptre many and great realms and kingdoms of barbarous men
> and peoples, conquered by my own person.
>
> (*Five Letters 1519–1526*, pp. xvii–xviii)

The Cortés letters and Díaz's *True History of the Conquest of New Spain* are the twin pillars on which much knowledge of conquest

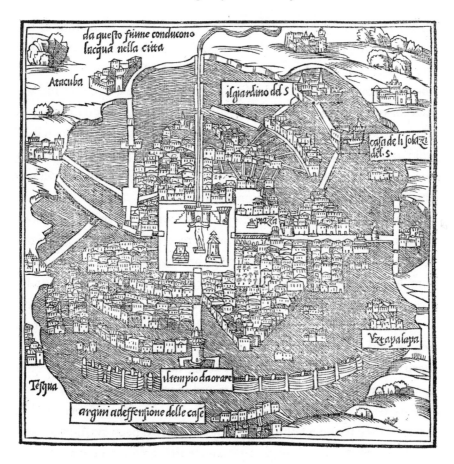

Map view of Mexico City, the Aztec capital built on islands in a great lake and compared by the conquistadors to Venice, from Münster's *Cosmographey*, 1578.

and pre-conquest Mexico rests. Likewise our knowledge of the first encounters with the Inca empire rests on a very few key eyewitness documents. Francisco Pizarro, the chief conqueror of Peru, was a ruthless soldier of fortune who left no account of his experiences for the simple reason that he was illiterate, but he was followed by others more sensitive and alive to the history and culture of South America. Among these, none was more remarkable than the youthful Pedro de Cieza de León, who as a mere child of 12 had watched the arrival of

Pizarro's brother Hernán at Seville in 1534, and the unloading of the first treasure ship laden with Inca gold and silver. Soon afterwards were published the first anonymous reports of the events in Peru, the wondrous kingdom of the Incas, Pizarro's attack upon it, and the murder of the Inca emperor. The young Pedro de Cieza de Léon was among the next wave of Spanish adventurers to set out in search of gold and glory, and within the year he was cutting his way through the jungles of present-day Panama and Colombia, seeking a route to the Pacific and any tribes who possessed gold.

What motivated Cieza de Léon to become a writer we cannot explain, but, without formal education or encouragement, he began almost at once to make notes of what he saw, notes that would grow into his magisterial book *The Chronicle of Peru*. Part history, part geography, part travel memoir, this is a book whose richness is worthy of its subject, which enables us to re-create in our imagination this region and the tragedy which overwhelmed it. Before the entry into Peru, Cieza de Léon tells of the exotic, dangerous camp life in the jungle, the great lizards, the jaguars and the anacondas, one of which, twenty feet long, 'was speared by Pedro Jimon with his lance, and in its belly they found a young deer, whole as it had been swallowed, and we Spaniards were so hungry that we ate the fawn, and even a part of the snake.' He tells of the American Indians' use of arrows poisoned with curare, and their stockaded villages, guarded by watchtowers on top of which were spiked the heads of their enemies. He does not gloss over the savagery of what he saw and heard, admitting that the Spaniards had inspired such fear among the indigenous people that often they would hang themselves from the trees rather than fall into their hands. But the Indians themselves were utterly without mercy, and he reports that 'these Indians are so given to the eating of human flesh, that they are known to seize women on the point of giving birth, and swiftly slit their belly with their knives and extract the child, which they roast and eat.' Once the Spaniards found a big cooking pot in a village, full of boiled meats, and were so hungry that their one thought was to eat; but when they had taken their fill, one of the Spaniards fished from the pot a human hand with fingers on it.

But there was room for gentler passions: 'As my Captain knew', wrote Cieza de Léon, 'that I was curious to know the secrets of the Indians, he gave me Catalina' – this being the name he gave to a beautiful Indian girl who became his mistress. Amid these scenes, he incredibly wrote his journal, using a drumhead for a table and a condor's feather for a quill. Paper was his big problem, scarce and expensive as well as fragile: some of his most important pages he rolled up into lengths of bamboo, sealing the ends with wax. Moving south, Cieza de Léon and his companions entered Peru, and over some four or five years traversed much of the country, following the marvellous Inca highways from cacti-filled valleys to the heights of the Andes at over 16,000 feet, and crossing the dizzying river gorges via the heart-stopping rope bridges. He provides the first account of Lake Titicaca and its region, with the extraordinary houses of the dead, the large stone towers in which the dead were placed with food for the next life, and attendant women to accompany them. His journey ended at the great silver mine of Potosí, which he sketched, this becoming the first picture of it to appear in Europe. He became fascinated by the history of Peru, and in Cuzco and other cities he spoke with the old conquistadors who had settled there in the former palaces and temples, and, more important, with the Inca lords who still survived, and who told him of their pre-conquest life. He never sought to minimise the storm of cruelty and injustice unleashed by his countrymen:

> I should have wished not to relate the cruelties of my countrymen
> ... I would rather escape from a narration of battles, and leave
> them unwritten, [but] people must know about such great evils and
> the brutal deaths inflicted by both sides. ... Were one ordered to
> enumerate the great evils, injuries, robberies, oppression, and ill
> treatment inflicted on the natives during these operations ... there
> would be no end of it ... for they thought no more of killing Indians

than if they were useless beasts ... when I came from Catagena, I saw a Portuguese named Roque Martin, who had the quarters of Indians hanging on a porch to feed his dogs with, as if they were wild beasts.

(The Incas, pp. lvii–lix)

From Cieza de Léon we get a picture of men cut off from their history, custom, law and restraint, merging psychologically with the jungle in which they now lived, and reverting to savagery, in the manner of the castaway children in *Lord of the Flies*. He conceived a great admiration for the Inca civilisation, its achievements in government, art and engineering, untainted by the rivers of blood which had stained the culture of the Aztecs.

Cieza de Léon himself took part in some of the final battles in the conflict between the warring conquistadors, then in 1550 he returned home to Seville, bearing his precious freight of manuscripts, amounting to some 8,000 pages. The first part of his great work was published with royal approval in 1553, but by that time he lay mortally ill of some unknown malady, perhaps a tropical disease brought back from the lands where he had spent sixteen years of his short life. He died in 1554, aged only 32, and the subsequent fate of his writing is both interesting and sad. It was at first widely admired for its wealth of information and its humane attitude, but later, when Catholic Spain came under attack for its savage treatment of the Indians, especially from Protestant England and the Netherlands, it suited the Spanish to play down the 'black legend', and Cieza de Léon's work was now seen as too frank and too polemical. The rest of his work was left in obscurity; no further parts were published, and only in the nineteenth century were his manuscripts rediscovered and re-evaluated. An astonishing achievement for a young, uneducated soldier, we receive from this book as from few of the others of this generation a genuine sense of a living human being, watching, thinking and distilling his own personal vision in these strange lands.

The theme of conquest, with its attendant conflict and cruelties, was given visual form in the European books of the sixteenth century, culminating in the series of travel texts issued by the Frankfurt publisher Theodore de Bry in the 1590s. These would have been the contemporary equivalent of 'The New World – the Movie', with hundreds of engravings of the explorers' ships at sea, their encounters with indigenous peoples, and above all their battles with them. A very few minutes spent with de Bry are enough for most people today before they turn away in disgust from the endless scenes of slaughter on the one hand and cannibalism on the other, yet on the evidence of these books this, rather than any vision of a new Eden, was the dominant image of the encounter with America. One of the most influential of de Bry's stories was that of the German mercenary soldier Hans Stade, who was captured by Brazilian cannibals, but who managed to survive the ordeal and escape, to publish a gruesome and widely read account of their practices.

Fifteen years after Cieza de Léon's book, there appeared the first part of another unique eyewitness account of the wars in South America. Alonso de Ercilla had taken part in the prolonged attempts to pacify the fierce Araucanian Indians, experiences which inspired his epic poem *La Araucana*, the first such poem to emerge from the Americas. Although flowery and repetitive in style, it is chiefly remarkable for the way in which the proud resistance of the American Indians makes them, rather than the Spaniards, the ultimate heroes of the conflict.

Our sense of historical injustice inevitably colours our reading of these early new world narratives: to counterbalance this injustice, we long for the Europeans to suffer too, and some of the most graphic travel accounts derive their strength precisely from this sense of a reversal of fortune – of the fierce conquistadors becoming themselves victims of the lands which they had sought to subdue and pillage. It was through these narratives of ordeal that the conquistadors truly discovered that they were the foreigners, the intruders, and that they must pay for their arrogance. One such journey was the first navigation of the Amazon, by a party commanded by Francisco de Orellana, who crossed the Andes from Quito in 1541 in association with Gonzalo Pizarro, in search of the fabled lands of El Dorado. Near the junction of the Coca and Napo rivers, western tributaries of the still unknown Amazon, they built boats in which Orellana was dispatched to reconnoitre and gather food. Not surprisingly, once embarked upon the river, Orellana and his companions were unable to turn back, and were swept forward into the unknown, while Pizarro and his men dragged themselves half-starved back through the mountains to Quito. Orellana had begun a 3,000-mile journey through the uncharted rainforests, during which they endured attacks from animals and from savage tribes, sickness and starvation. Among the party was a Dominican friar named Gaspar de Carvajal, who wrote a dramatic account of their ordeal.

Some of his descriptions are what we might expect – the Spaniards reduced to eating toads and serpents, the battles with the American Indians with their poisoned arrows, whose death's-heads were nailed to the trees by the riverside – but others are more puzzling. From the boats he claimed to have seen large stone-built highways cutting through the jungle, and on one occasion they went ashore and found a great villa filled with treasures, including glazed pottery as fine as the best porcelain they had ever seen; these reports are strange because their setting should have been far outside the limits of the Inca dominions. The most famous incident of all was the encounter with the fierce female warriors, which caught the imagination of Europe, and led to their identification with the Amazons of classical legend, and hence to the naming of the great river. 'We ourselves saw them fighting in front of all the Indian men,' claimed Carvajal, 'and they fought so courageously that the men did not dare turn their backs. These women are very white and tall, and have their hair very long and braided and wound about the head, and they are very robust and go about naked.' They were said to live apart from all men, but to meet with a neighbouring tribe once a year for the purpose of mating; the girls they kept and raised, but the male children they are said to have killed.

After more than half a year, Orellana's boats finally reached the mouth of the Amazon, and with great difficulty crossed the tidal bore to emerge into the Atlantic, and to make their way north to Cubagua on the Venezuelan coast. It had been an epic of suffering, unsought by its protagonists, during which many of them had lost their lives, and Orellana himself had been blinded in one eye by an Indian arrow. In the great Spanish gold hunt, they were spectacular losers, for they brought back not a single ounce, but they had crossed South America and placed the world's greatest river on the map. Orellana must have felt that this river was his destiny, for he returned only to die in the course of a second battle with the Amazon.

The suffering of the invader was also the theme of one of the first narratives of the North American interior. In 1527 a large expedition left Cuba, intending to explore from Florida northwards, anticipating the discovery of other advanced civilisations like those of Mexico. But a series of accidents and misjudgements brought disaster, and the survivors, having landed, lost contact with their ships, and were compelled to struggle back westward along the coast of Texas, attempting to reach Mexico, some by sea on makeshift rafts and some by land. Some fell into the hands of hostile peoples, but a very few, among them Álvar Núñez Cabeza de Vaca, succeeded in winning the trust of their captors. These few lived among the American Indians for six years, sharing their semi-nomadic existence, hunting and trading, learning their language and their customs. Cabeza de Vaca owed much of his success to his knowledge of healing, and he seems to have been venerated as a kind of medicine man. He moved among several different tribes, but for all of them life was harsh in the extreme, a never-ending search for always inadequate food, with hunger and death never far away. They were in many ways very unlike the plains Indians to the north, with a far narrower material culture and belief system. Their social life centred on rigid family and kinship rituals, and elaborate practices connected with the dead.

Cabeza de Vaca eventually found his way back to civilisation, nine years after his departure from Cuba, but the experience was not a happy one: accompanied by several hundred American Indian followers, he was trekking through northern Mexico when they encountered a party of Spanish slave-hunters, who saw his companions only as potential slaves, against which he protested angrily. He had already seen the effects of Spanish slaving activity in the region: settlements abandoned or burnt, the people hiding for fear of the Christians. Cabeza de Vaca was almost dazed by his return to European life, and found himself unable for some time to wear western clothes or to sleep anywhere but on the ground. His years with the American Indians had changed his life and personality. Cabeza de Vaca's vivid memoir, published in Spain in 1542, is among the earliest and most important records of the European encounter with the land and people of North America. By sharing their harsh life, he came to see and understand the American Indians as people – a simple but profound mental leap which his compatriots were unable to make. His experience, and that of Orellana's party, were accidents of history, personal, unplanned and unsought, sideshows in the great drama of conquest, but this is precisely what gives them their significance.

The Portuguese and the Pacific

By contrast, one of the true epics of the age of discovery, Magellan's first crossing of the Pacific Ocean, is commemorated in a narrative which is self-consciously a record of great historic events, an adventure story built around a heroic leader. The Italian Antonio Pigafetta sailed with Magellan, and was among the few survivors of this terrible three-year ordeal, the first circumnavigation of the earth, and it was he who wrote the essential eyewitness account of it. But Pigafetta has only three themes: first, the character of Magellan – whom he calls the Captain-General or the Great Captain – tenacious, single-minded, skilful, utterly dedicated to his objective; second, the primitive savagery or simplicity of all the native people they encounter; third, the loneliness and implacable hostility of the sea. As a Portuguese leader in command over Spaniards, Magellan was constantly on his guard against threats to his authority, and, as Pigafetta reports, he responded with an iron hand, crushing a suspected mutiny and executing the rebels; Pigafetta saw this as admirable proof of Magellan's all-consuming fidelity of purpose. One of Pigafetta's best-known passages concerns the inhabitants of Patagonia, who he asserts were giants, more than twice the height of the Europeans. The explorers were in close and repeated contact with these giants, taking them aboard their ships, and learning much about their life and beliefs. These reports became famous throughout Europe: every account of Patagonia and every map for the next hundred years and more would be illustrated with images of savage giants. Shakespeare knew of them, and remembered that they venerated a great devil named Setebos, a name he borrowed in *The Tempest* for the god worshipped by Caliban and his mother, the witch Sycorax. But the enigma of the Patagonian giants has never been solved: no evidence of a race of giants would ever be found anywhere in South America.

It was through Magellan's determination that the strait which now bears his name was eventually found, the crucial maritime gateway from the Atlantic into the uncharted Pacific. So tortuous is this channel that the fleet was over a month passing through it. When the ships emerged into the open sea, they fired their guns in triumph, little knowing the ordeal that now awaited them. For more than two months the mariners sailed over trackless water, suffering tortures from heat, thirst and starvation, dying daily, with no conception of where they were or when they would ever sight land. They ate the very rats they caught on board the ships, and so desperate were they that a market in rats sprang up, in which they were auctioned to the highest bidder. 'There had never been', writes Pigafetta, 'such a voyage before.' Finally arriving among what would later be the Philippine Islands, Magellan cruised from one island to another, trading a little and attempting to convert the indigenous people to Christianity. In a senseless skirmish on the island of Mactan, he was killed, to Pigafetta's great grief, losing the honour of completing the first circumnavigation. One of the incidental aims of Pigafetta's memoir was to build up the mystique of the clove, the ultimate motive for this agonising voyage: it grows uniquely, he claims, on one island, Tidore, on the mountain slopes, almost always hidden from human view by mist, like a kind of holy grail. Nevertheless they were able to obtain 25 tons of the dried flower buds, which were worth a small fortune in Europe.

Three years after setting out, one ship from the original fleet, crewed by only eighteen survivors, finally limped home to Seville, under the captaincy of Juan del Cano. Pigafetta would later present to the king not gold or silver, but a manuscript account of the adventure, although probably not the full-length narrative, which was published first in a French translation in Paris in 1525. Ironically, the three years of the voyage itself had rendered the achievement almost worthless: when it began, the aim was to find at last a westward sea route to the Indies, which Columbus and all his successors had failed to do, America itself being then of secondary interest. But while Magellan's ships were at sea, Cortés had discovered the gold kingdom of Mexico, so that Spain acquired overnight a fabulous overseas empire, and no new fleet of any nation would attempt to cross the Pacific for another fifty years. From Pigafetta we receive almost no sense of this vast new world which Magellan was opening for his king and for mankind: to buy spices and bully the native people are his twin concerns. Invaluable as it is to historians, this text lacks any vision commensurate with its subject, and any historic or geographic sweep tends to become lost in detail.

If we demand vision, we must turn to the most surprising travel text to emerge from the Age of Discovery, Luís de Camões's narrative poem *The Lusiads*, which was long regarded as the Portuguese national epic. Published in 1572, it relates the deeds of many illustrious Portuguese, but principally the career of Vasco da Gama, and his first voyage to India via the Cape of Good Hope. Camões was himself a man of action who had fought in North Africa, where he lost his right eye in fighting against the Moors, before sailing to seek his fortune in India, finding instead only hardship, imprisonment and shipwreck. In spite of this, he held fast to his belief in the Portuguese national destiny to carve out and rule its maritime empire, a destiny that he presents in divine or even cosmic terms. In the most extraordinary scene of the poem, the sea nymph Thetys leads da Gama up to a mountaintop, and, spreading out before him a miraculous map of the world, prophesies the future glories of the Portuguese nation as it throws its chain of ports and colonies across Africa, India, the Far East and Brazil. This is possibly the most overt statement anywhere of the belief that it is Europe's destiny to spread Christian civilisation over the earth, and its right to crush all opposing creeds and cultures. There is no more illuminating guide to the psychology of the Age of Discovery than *The Lusiads*.

Camões's epic was one of a small number of imaginative responses to the voyages of discovery. An earlier work was Sir Thomas More's celebrated novel *Utopia*, which gave a new word and a new concept to the European languages. *Utopia* shares none of the triumphalism of *The Lusiads*; indeed it turns the cult of European superiority on its head, by imagining an explorer who lands on a distant island which is in every way more rational, civilised and humane than European society. More then uses this fantasy location to castigate the inequality, violence, greed and injustice which rule all known and familiar kingdoms, including Tudor England. More's own blueprint of an ideal society includes the abolition of absolute monarchy, of money and of enforced religious doctrine, the prime sources of political and social conflict. Unfortunately, the price to be paid is a form of communism, sustained only by a deadening uniformity of thought and social life, worse even than in Plato's *Republic*.

More's *Utopia* was an intellectual flight of fancy, but it picked up a very real and significant thread in the Age of Discovery which most of its protagonists had missed. The navigators and explorers had shown that mankind lived in multiple worlds and multiple cultures. Aggression, destruction, Christian triumphalism, European hegemony – these were not the only possible responses: it was possible that Europeans would encounter cultures superior to their own, which would provoke new insights into western values. The encounter with alien worlds might become a process of discovery in an intellectual or even a spiritual sense. This insight, this possibility, is a theme that develops steadily as travel literature matures; indeed it may have been a precondition for the emergence of what we call travel literature from its origins in narratives of warfare or exploration. One of the few critical philosophical responses to the Age of Discovery came from the pen of Montaigne, who perceived the naked greed behind the great adventure:

> So many Cities levell'd with the Ground, So many Nations exterminated, so many millions of people fallen by the Edge of the Sword and the richest and most beautiful part of the World turn'd upside down, for the Traffick of Pearl and Peper: Mechanick victories!
>
> ('Of Carriages', Book III, p. 174)

In Portugal and Spain the Age of Discovery produced an important and psychologically revealing form of travel-related literature: the historical-geographical chronicle. The prototype was Azurara's *Chronicle of the Discovery and Conquest of Guinea*, which tells the story of the gradual exploration of the West African coast from 1420 to 1450. Chronicles like this deliberately set out to transcend the personal narrative: they represented the official interpretation of history and they were informed by the spirit of national glorification which later reached its culmination in Camões. These chronicles appeared some decades after the events they describe; they were works of historical research and mature reflection. The immediate news of the discoveries was given in letters and pamphlets, which were often printed in considerable numbers, but which were of course ephemeral, so publishers would gather them together in collections. A massive landmark of the new geographical awareness came with the *Cosmographia Universalis* which Sebastian Münster first published in Basle in 1544, a descriptive encyclopedia of the newly enlarged world. Clearly not travel literature, this kind of work, like the historical chronicles, marked the integration of travel into the literary discourse of the Renaissance. Travel was now not merely a realm of action, not an incidental factor in military campaigning, in pilgrimage or in trade, but an intellectual force which had reshaped man's understanding of his world. Travel would increasingly become a realm of thought, an experience which led to re-evaluations of the world and of the traveller's own personality.

The Way of the North

The first overseas empires of the Age of Discovery were carved out by the Spanish and the Portuguese: with papal blessing these two nations were authorised to divide between them the riches of the new world. This dual hegemony lasted for half a century until the rivalries unleashed by the Reformation spurred the Protestant nations, England and the Netherlands, to seek their own place in the sun overseas, and the sea routes to them. Already, in the 1530s, the French had identified northern North America as their own potential *Terre Neuf* and had dispatched Jacques Cartier to reconnoitre it, and if possible to find that elusive passage – which must surely exist – through or around the continent and into the Pacific. Cartier made three voyages, eventually penetrating the St Lawrence as far inland as the site of Montreal, but his attempts to plant colonies there foundered in the bitter Canadian winters, for which the French were quite unprepared. Cartier recorded the names of two American Indian settlements on the St Lawrence – Hochelaga and Stadacona – which would appear on maps for a century, while the name Canada apparently referred to a region or kingdom further to the west. One significant feature of the narratives of the Cartier voyages is the absence of conflict or slaughter, indeed the friendly relations which the French succeeded in establishing with the Huron Indians in their villages, with whom 'they made good cheer', and who provided them with eels, maize, melons and medicinal plants.

At least this was the claim of Cartier's narrative: reading between the lines, there seems to have been considerable tension between the two groups of people. Cartier's act in setting up a large cross and taking possession of the territory angered the American Indians. In his first voyage Cartier took the chief's two sons – by agreement as he claimed – back to France for a year, returning them on the second voyage. But then he took, by force or trickery, the chief himself, Donnacona, and several others, who never saw their homes again. The cold forests of Canada clearly offered no prospects of fabulous gold kingdoms to excite the kind of bloody aggression which the Spaniards showed in central America, but Cartier, desperate for some evidence of his achievement, took the American Indians as exotic living trophies.

These experiences did not encourage any further French voyages for a further sixty years, but they did establish the French claim to Canada. In England, however, armchair geographers conceived their own answer to the problem of tapping into the wealth of the Indies – 'the way of the north'. As early as 1527, Robert Thorne, a merchant in Seville, wrote to Henry VIII, 'Out of Spain they have discovered all the Indies and Seas Occidentall, and out of Portingall all the Indies and Seas Oriental.' Fanciful maps were produced by cartographers as reputable as Mercator and Ortelius showing the North Pole as a land mass clearly distinct from the Asian and American coasts, with open sea lying between them. On this flimsy basis, a succession of English ships set out confidently into the harsh, impenetrable, ice-filled seas north of Norway and north of Labrador in search of the imagined sea passages to the Pacific via the north-east and the north-west. Neither passage would be found for three more centuries, but the quest for them would yield some narratives interesting in their own right, and some follow-up journeys into the interior of Russia.

The 'way of the north' began when Sir Hugh Willoughby and Richard Chancellor set sail from London in 1553 in search of the almost legendary kingdom of Muscovy, ruled over by the all-powerful Ivan the Terrible. Their route lay around the North Cape of Norway, but the two ships became separated, and Willoughby was beset by ice on the Kola Peninsula, where he and all his crew died. Chancellor was more fortunate, passing the Peninsula into the White Sea, where he found 'No night at all, but a continual light and brightness of the Sun shining clearly upon a huge and mighty sea.' He reached the port of Archangel, from where he travelled over to Moscow, and was granted an audience with the fearsome Tsar, who welcomed him with some warmth, however, and offered trading privileges in furs, timber, tallow and cordage to the Muscovy Company that he represented. Chancellor returned safely to England, where his unflattering reports of life in Russia did not seem to deter his friends. Moscow outside the royal palace was, he said, little more than a collection of wooden huts, and in many of the towns which he passed en route the inhabitants relieved their miserable existence by endless drinking, while the dead lay frozen in the streets, to be eaten by dogs. Nevertheless an important trade contact had been made, which was followed up by Chancellor's successors.

The Northeast Passage interested not only the English but the Dutch, and in the 1590s Willem Barentsz led three expeditions around the North Cape into the sea which now bears his name. Each time he explored the coasts of Novaya Zemlya but was halted by ice in the Kara Sea. His final voyage of 1596–97 is the most interesting, for it contains the earliest account of an overwintering above the Arctic Circle. When their ship became locked in ice, the sailors built a hut from its timbers on Novaya Zemlya, where they were forced to remain for seven months before the seas opened and they could escape in the two ship's boats. The monotony of the Arctic night was dreadful, and they suffered psychologically and physically, half-frozen despite the fire of driftwood, and half-suffocated from its fumes. Their stores from the ships were supplemented by birds and foxes – the latter they used both for food and for making fur caps. Bears were both enemies and blessings, their strength being so ferocious as to threaten to tear down the hut, but their fat yielding invaluable oil for lighting, and their fur protective clothing. Their only light relief came when they marked Christmas, especially on Twelfth Night, when they drank and made merry, and crowned one of the crew King of Novaya Zemlya. When the sun finally reappeared they walked, ran and stretched their joints by playing golf on the snow.

When they were at last ready to depart, Barentsz left a letter in the hut describing their experiences. This hut, frozen and weather-beaten but almost intact, was found almost three centuries later in 1871, by Norwegian seamen, filled with the possessions the Dutch had left behind, including Barentsz's manuscript. But Barentsz himself was one of those most weakened by their privations, and he died after only a week at sea. The others found supplies in Russian ports, and struggled home to Amsterdam in November 1597, where 'the people wondered to see us, having esteemed us long before that to have been dead and rotten.' The experience of Barentsz and his crew became a pattern, for no subsequent explorers could pass the ice of the Kara Sea; despite the assurance by no less a figure than Gerard Mercator that 'the voyage to Cathay by the East is doubtless very easy and short', the search for the Northeast Passage languished for two centuries.

Likewise the story of the Northwest Passage began with an initial burst of confidence, as Martin Frobisher, John Davis, Henry Hudson and others set out through the Arctic ice for Cathay. They succeeded in placing their names upon the maps of the region, but in little else. To encourage their backers, each voyage was reported as a noble failure, Davis for example claiming that 'The North-West Passage is a matter nothing doubtful, but at any time almost to be passed, the sea navigable, void of ice, the air tolerable and the waters very deep.' Frobisher, having convinced himself that Baffin Island was Asia, then forgot his geographical aims as his voyages descended into a comic and deluded gold rush. Hundreds of tons of useless rock were quarried from the foreshore and shipped back to England for testing, but they were destined to repair the streets of London, for they contained nothing but iron pyrites, or fool's gold. The most significant occurrence was the first modern encounter with the Innuit people, who, the Europeans noted excitedly, looked distinctly Asian in appearance:

> These people I judge to be a kind of Tartar ... They are of the colour of a ripe olive, which how it may come to pass, being borne in so cold a climate, I refer to ye judgement of others, for they are naturally borne children of the same colour and complexion as all the Americans are, which dwell under the equinoctiall line. ... They go clad in coats made of the skins of beasts, as of seals, deer, bears, foxes, and hares. ... They have boats made of leather, and covered clean over, saving one place in the middle to sit in, planked within with timber.
>
> (*The Three Voyages of Martin Frobisher in search of a passage to Cathia and India by the North-West*, pp. 281–4)

But these people proved often to be hostile and violent, and brutish in their manner of living, and this was decidedly a bleak and inhospitable land, which led nowhere and had in itself few attractions, save those that Hudson Bay would later reveal as giving access to fur-trading routes to the interior of Canada. The abiding image of these early ventures into the north-west must be the melancholy Victorian painting of Hudson with his son, cast away in 1610 by his crew and drifting towards his inevitable death among the ice floes. Hudson's story has been pieced together from a number of sources: the survivors reported that he was a poor leader, and dishonest in his allocation of food; they claimed too that the actual leaders of the mutiny had – rather conveniently – been killed later in a fight with some indigenous people. Back in London the mariners who returned from this voyage were eventually tried for mutiny, but were acquitted.

Later, in 1631–32, two independent expeditions under Captains Luke Foxe and Thomas James concluded that the search for the Passage was hopeless. The accounts of all these northern voyages tend to be repetitive, as harsh and featureless as the region itself: the ice, the wind, the barren land, the primitive inhabitants, the sufferings of the seafarers, all described in a language that begins as the spare semi-official language of the seaman's log, but that occasionally rises, in a movement of release, into something approaching poetry. There is something arresting in these early descriptions of navigation in icy waters, and the writing of Foxe in particular was formerly identified as a source which Coleridge used when composing 'The Ancient Mariner', although this is now thought less likely:

> The ship is anchored, the watch is set, a mark is set on the lead-line, and sleep like a thief doth slily steal upon me. ... This morning *Aurora* blusht, as though she had ushered her Master from some unchaste lodging, and the airs so silent as though all those handmaids had promised secrecy.
>
> (*The Voyages of Captain Luke Foxe and Captain Thomas James in search of a North-West Passage*, pp. 394–5)

Are these narratives of the empty sea really travel literature? Paradoxically, their most memorable incidents often take place on land, and this is certainly true of Thomas James's voyage. Hemmed in by ice and forced to winter on Charlton Island in the south of the bay, he was preparing to leave in June 1632 when he decided to light a beacon fire in celebration. He climbed a high tree to watch for any response from the native people. But the fire spread rapidly in the high summer wind, and in an almost comic scene James scrambled desperately down the tree to find his camp enveloped by the flames which eventually swept for miles through the dry mosses and trees. Both James and Foxe made it safely back to England, and published their separate accounts, without advancing the search for the Northwest Passage, but establishing early landmarks in English maritime literature.

English Seafaring and Colonisation

The quest for the northward passages to the East had begun as the attempt by northern European nations to outflank Spain and Portugal. The truce or gentleman's agreement which left Hispanic power unchallenged in America, the East Indies and the Pacific broke down in the rivalries engendered by the Reformation, and their culmination came in Francis Drake's circumnavigation of the world of 1577–80. Drake was a classic product of England's years of religious persecution under Queen Mary Tudor, and anti-Catholic venom had become one of Drake's ruling passions. His raids on Spanish ports and shipping formed a calculated campaign of defiance and revenge against what he regarded as a malignant power threatening the entire world. In effect he was licensed by Queen Elizabeth to act as her unofficial terrorist, to harass Spain on the other side of the world. His circumnavigation began when be became the first non-Spaniard to pass the Magellan Strait and raid the undefended Spanish settlements of South and

Central America: his crossing of the Pacific and Indian oceans was simply his chosen homeward route.

Drake himself was no writer, but several of his companions were, notably the fleet's chaplain, Francis Fletcher, whose journal of the voyage formed the basis of the account published some years afterwards as *The World Encompassed by Sir Francis Drake*. Lively and readable, this is basically an adventure story with dashes of politics and religion, the whole being dominated by the resolute figure of Drake, steering between danger and triumph like a miniature Odysseus. Fletcher tells us of the personal conflicts within the fleet, which Drake crushed by summarily executing his chief enemy; he tells us of the strange, savage inhabitants of South America, who he is convinced have been made more vicious and intractable by the cruel treatment they received at the hands of the Spaniards; he tells us of the wildness of the seas and of the intense physical suffering of the mariners in those remote waters; he tells with great pride of Drake's daring acts of piracy against the Spanish; he tells of the colony of New Albion founded in California, where Drake was crowned king by the adoring indigenous people; and he tells us of the interminable ordeal that was the homeward voyage across the Pacific and Indian Oceans. At times taking the form of a matter-of-fact journal, Fletcher's work nevertheless possesses a strong sense of the dramatic and epic qualities of this voyage, which he showed in his evocation of its critical moments, such as this storm:

> We were rather to look for present death then hope for any delivery, if God Almighty should not make the way for us. The winds were such as if the bowels of the earth had set all at liberty, or as if all the clouds under heaven had been called together to lay their force upon that one place. The seas were rolled up from the depths, even from the roots of the rocks, as if it had been a scroll of parchment ... and being aloft were carried in most strange manner and abundance, as feathers or drifts of snow, by the violence of the winds, to water the exceeding tops of the high and lofty mountains. Our anchors, as false friends in such a danger, gave over their holdfast, and as if it had been

Drake crowned by American Indians in 1579 in 'Nova Albion', somewhere on the Californian coast. This event was often used to justify England's claim to sovereignty over North America.

with horror of the thing, did shrink down to hide themselves in this miserable storm.... So that the violent storm without intermission; ... the most mad seas; the lee shores; the dangerous rocks; the contrary and most intolerable winds; the impossible passage out; the desperate tarrying there; and inevitable perils on every sides did lay before us so small likelihood [*sic*] escape present destruction, that if the special providence of God himself had not supported us, we could never have endured that woeful state.

(*The World Encompassed by Sir Francis Drake*, pp. 85–6)

To come through such storms alive was part of the nationalistic myth which Fletcher and other writers on Drake were seeking to build up. These voyages, like those of some of the other early navigators, were unique experiences, unrepeatable because they were the first to explore these unknown and dangerous regions on the other side of the world. This uniqueness means perhaps that they are not travel narratives in the ordinary sense of the word, but are epic and heroic. Yet any travel narrative must endeavour to be unique in some way, for if a journey is repeatable at will, by anyone to order, then we have left the realm of travel literature and entered that of the guidebook. These Drake documents exemplify the formula of the early exploration narrative: the achievement is central, and therefore the writing is direct, veering from homely detail to the dramatic, not overintellectual, often fired by national pride, and often portraying a central hero figure.

But the heroic failure may make a more striking narrative than the heroic triumph. Ten years after Drake, Thomas Cavendish became the second Englishman to harass the Spanish in the Pacific and circumnavigate the world. In doing so he missed the Armada, and, perhaps by way of compensation, Cavendish swiftly began to plan yet another blow against Spain, a repeat voyage through the Magellan Strait with a fleet of five ships. But they never reached the Pacific, for the venture disintegrated into chaos and ended with Cavendish's own death. Storm, shipwreck, internal dissension, and fights with both native people and Portuguese in Brazil shattered the fleet, leaving a single ruinous ship to limp home. Cavendish himself kept a record of what happened, a document written in wild, tortuous language, filled with bitterness against those he felt had betrayed him and with the resolve never to return home in failure:

> [T]o England I would never give my consent to go, and that if they would not take such Courses as I intended, that then I was determined that ship and all should sink in the seas together. ... & now by this what with grief for him & the Continual trouble I endured amongst such hell-hounds, my spirit was clean spent wishing myself upon any desert place in the world there to die, rather than thus basely to return home again.

> (*The Last Voyage of Thomas Cavendish*, pp. 122–6)

As Cavendish slept, his men would alter course, seeking to save their own lives by guiding him across the Atlantic back to England by stealth against his will. How he died no one knows: perhaps through sickness, perhaps assassinated by one of his desperate sailors, or possibly by his own hand, in line with his stated determination to 'perform or die'. The motif of suffering, always associated with epic travel, is at its most visible in the sea narrative.

The late Elizabethan age was also capable of producing a very different kind of narrative. The very beginning of England's history as a colonising power was marked by a cool, analytical memoir of the earliest English venture into North America, Thomas Hariot's remarkable little book *A Brief and True Report of the New Found Land of Virginia*, published in 1588. Hariot was an acutely intelligent man, a scholar and a scientist, who travelled with the first party sponsored by Sir Walter Ralegh to found the Roanoke colony. The venture was not a success, but Hariot's work was a genuinely new look at America and its indigenous peoples. It is typical of Hariot's thoroughness that he set himself to learn the Algonquin language before he even sailed, being taught by two American Indians brought back to London the year before. Strikingly absent from Hariot is the explorer's traditional deep addiction to gold or stories of gold: Hariot's aim is to make a serious and careful case for the future of Virginia as a viable colony, and his book was not written to flatter a patron or tease out new sponsorship money.

The most interesting part of Hariot's work is his sympathetic account of the American Indians. One of the guiding principles of the colonists – some of them at least – was that good relations with the American Indians would be useful or even vital to them. Hariot found them naturally intelligent, but obviously they were preliterate, with few tools, arts or crafts, and they had no sense of recorded history, only oral legends and traditions. They regarded European artefacts with amazement – the compass, the gun, the sword, the clock, the book. They worshipped many gods with human form, and believed the soul to be immortal. The interesting point here is that Hariot must have had lengthy conversations with the American Indians to have grasped these beliefs. They were, he says, very impressed with his talk about the one supreme God, and one of the strangest things of all in his book is this: he reports that in any village where the American Indians opposed, or plotted against, the colonists in any way, a large number of deaths among the American Indians followed. The American Indians themselves, he says, became convinced that this was divine punishment inflicted by the Europeans' God. They even asked the colonists to persuade their God to attack and kill their enemies for them. Hariot's approach to these matters forms an early example of ethnography, thoughtful and quasi-scientific; he appears to be the last person to want to invent stories of this kind for any evangelistic purpose. Hariot's book was widely read and highly influential.

The second landmark of Elizabethan travel literature was Ralegh's *Discovery of the Large, Rich and Beautiful Empire of Guiana*, of 1595. It is well known that Ralegh set out for Guiana in a deliberate attempt to rehabilitate himself with the court, to bring glory to himself and his country. This explains the balance in the text between action and reflection: this was an adventure, but an adventure with a far-reaching purpose. From the outset the story is dominated by gold, for Ralegh's aim was to find the legendary kingdom of El Dorado; he failed, but he makes his failure into a romance of near-success. Discussing the history and situation of Guiana, Ralegh was convinced that it was closely allied to the Inca kingdom of Peru, only its wealth was still more fabulous. The great gateway into the country was the Orinoco, and Ralegh is at his best when describing the mighty flow, the tortuous channels, the man-eating snakes, the heat and the torrential rains of this great uncharted river. Ralegh notoriously describes certain monstrous races of man with faces in their chests, exactly like those of the ancient Pliny–Mandeville tradition; yet he is careful to emphasise that he never saw them with his own eyes, but merely heard about them. As with Hariot, one of Ralegh's guiding principles was to deal justly with the indigenous peoples, and he points up very forcibly the contrast here with the behaviour of the Spanish. The women of Guiana, he remarks, are fine and beautiful, but, despite their nakedness, none was ever touched by his men. Ralegh, a famous womaniser, does not blush to confess how struck he was by the wife of one of the chiefs:

> That *Cassique* that was a stranger had his wife staying at the port where we anchored, and in all my life I have seldom seen a better favored woman: She was of good stature, with black eyes, fat of body, of an excellent countenance, her hair almost as long as herself, tied up again in pretty knots, and it seemed she stood not in that awe of her husband, as the rest, for she spoke and discoursed, and drank among the gentlemen and captains, and was very pleasant, knowing her own comeliness, and taking great pride therein. I have seen a Lady in England so like her, as but for the difference of colour I would have sworn might have been the same.
>
> (*The Discovery of the Large, Rich and Beautiful
> Empire of Guiana*, pp. 46–7)

Surely no travel writer of the time but Ralegh would have paused in his account of the 'savages' of the Orinoco basin to sketch a scene of a social beauty holding court as if she were a European princess, and one wonders if the final sentence contained a private clue which a select few would recognise. Another of the peculiarities of Ralegh's text is that he gives hundreds – perhaps even thousands – of names of places, tribes and individuals: he has taken the trouble to learn and transcribe them, as if he is recognising for the first time their individual reality, that they are not meaningless features encountered in his search for gold. Perhaps the most significant cultural breakthrough lies in the extended conversations which Ralegh had with some of the chiefs, whom he names, while his men caroused with the American Indians in strong native liquor. With one chief in particular, Topiawari, Ralegh engages in political discussion, telling him about England and Queen Elizabeth, and offering to make common cause with him and his tribe against the cruel and hated Spaniards. This may possibly be the first record of a native American being treated as a human being, with a name and a culture of his own, not a dumb figure to thrust aside or cut down by the invading Europeans.

Ralegh and his party were inevitably defeated by the hostile jungle, and retreated downriver and back to Trinidad. He writes of Guiana as unspoiled and as yet unclaimed, and promotes it as potentially the linchpin of a grand strategy that shall undermine and eventually defeat Spanish power in the new world. In the hands of Ralegh and Hariot, English travel literature acquires some political and cultural maturity.

The clearest possible expression of England's consciousness of the new ear of travel and exploration came with the publication of Richard Hakluyt's great collection, *The Principal Navigations Voyages Traffiques & Discoveries of the English Nation*, in 1589, revised and enlarged in 1598–1600. Hakluyt devoted his entire life to collecting, editing and printing over one hundred English narratives, supplemented by many foreign ones, and he bequeathed almost as many again for later publication by his friend and disciple Samuel Purchas. Hakluyt used his contacts in the maritime world, the commercial world and the diplomatic world to obtain records of returning travellers, whether they were ships' logs, merchants' journals or diplomats' letters, and these sources provided ample evidence of the way overseas travel from Elizabethan England increased in scope and importance. Partly modelled on earlier collections published in Europe, such as that by the Venetian Ramusio, Hakluyt's book was unquestionably a major landmark in the history of travel literature. Yet in most cases we have to acknowledge that the literary quality of his texts is not high; in fact few of them qualify as literature at all. They are memoirs of historical importance, with episodic interest, but they do not possess either the form or the psychological maturity that we look for in literature. The reasons for this are sometimes obvious, sometimes elusive.

In the first place Hakluyt makes no secret of his nationalist motive: his avowed purpose is to show that England has caught up with, or even surpassed, the deeds of other nations, especially of course Spain:

The Age of Discovery

[I]n this most famous and peerless government of her most excellent
Majesty, her subjects through the special assistance, and blessing
of God, in searching the most opposite corners and quarters of the
world, and to speak plainly, in compassing the vast globe of the earth
more than once, have excelled all the nations and people of the earth
... who ever heard of Englishmen at Goa before now? what English
ships did heretofore ever anchor in the mighty river of Plate? pass
and repass the unpassable Strait of Magellan, range along the coast of
Chili, Peru, and all the backside of Nova Hispania, further than any
Christian ever passed ... & last of all return home most richly laden
with the commodities of China, as the subjects of this now flourishing
monarchy have done?

(*The Principal Navigations Voyages Traffiques &*
Discoveries of the English Nation, vol. 1, p. xx)

The world-view implicit in passages like this, and in the entirety of
Hakluyt's great work, is the essential legacy of the Age of Discovery.
It is as if a veil or curtain had been drawn back, revealing for the first
time regions of the world that were open and accessible, and that it was
the destiny of Europeans to explore, to exploit and perhaps to conquer.
True, this destiny was not to be fulfilled without danger and hardship
to themselves, for the great barrier of the sea lay between these regions
and Europe. But it was these very dangers which gave nobility and
glory to the game of exploration, which pitted one group of mariners
and explorers against another, one nation against another. The storms
at sea, the conflicts with native peoples or with rival nations, the battles
with nature and the battles with man, the sense of arduous adventure
and tenacity of spirit, whether leading to triumph or failure – these
are the themes which fill the narratives of Hakluyt. Hakluyt's work
was continued by Samuel Purchas in his collection of travel narratives,
Hakluytus Posthumus or Purchas his Pilgrimes, 1625.

Not concerned with overt and bloody conquest, as the Spanish
conquistadors were, the Elizabethans nevertheless still made travel
a matter of competition, conflict and achievement, and the ultimate

achievement was the European seizure of the right and freedom to range through the world, exploring, trading, taking, colonising or killing. In this triumphalist world-view, there was no place for subtle psychology, and personality emerges only through action. Those records which fulfilled something approaching an official purpose – for monarchs, patrons or employers – were always more formulaic than the more personal narratives of people like Cieza de León, Cabeza de Vaca, Hariot or Ralegh. Despite all the adventures of Drake, Magellan, da Gama, Cortés, Cartier and the others, it seems that the discovery of the world did not in itself necessarily provide the material of great literature, unless it could also be illuminated by the discovery of man himself, or, in some form, of God. It must be significant that Shakespeare, who named his theatre 'The Globe', and who was well aware of the new worlds beyond Europe, of the ordeals, adventures and glory which they promised, still made only a few passing references to them, and chose never to use them as the setting of a play. All his interest centred on inner drama of humanity, and he found that drama in the intellectual complexities of European life.

The narratives from the Age of Discovery are major historical documents, but paradoxically they lack a historical perspective, and a cultural one. Their purposes were narrow, and consequently there is a naivety or crudity common to much of this writing. The explorers set out to gain wealth and glory, not knowledge or understanding. They left us the first eyewitness accounts of the unknown; but to do justice to the unknown is a profoundly difficult and demanding task, and the very qualities which made the sixteenth-century explorers so ruthlessly successful as fighting men probably unfitted them to interpret the worlds they discovered. The effect of the Age of Discovery on travel literature was to redefine its setting, its scope and its entire world, to redraw the conceptual map upon which any episode of travel takes place. But a deeper and more adequate response to the new worlds would emerge only slowly and fitfully over the following two centuries.

THREE

The Seventeenth Century:
The Non-conquerors

Hakluytus Posthumus, or Purchas His Pilgrimes. Contayning a History of the World, in Sea voyages & lande-Travells, by Englishmen & others. Wherein Gods Wonders in Nature & Providence, The Actes, Arts, Varieties, & Vanities of Men, with a world of the Worldes Rarities, are by a World of Eywitnesse-Authors, Related to the World … Illustrated with Notes, Enlarged with Discourses. Adorned with pictures, and Expressed in Mapps.

Title of book by Samuel Purchas, 1625

WHILE THE Age of Discovery was revolutionising the map of the world, and offering European travellers the prospect of adventure, ordeal and conquest in the new world, a less aggressive form of travel was still very much in evidence in the old world. Merchants, ambassadors, missionaries, scholars – plus a few unclassifiable individuals – were making their way through much of Europe and parts of Asia and Africa, observing and reporting, enjoying or complaining about what they saw, but not conquering it. The unclassifiables might almost be called the first sightseers, travelling for no other reason than curiosity, although a strong dash of eccentricity and egotism entered into the personalities of most of them. Perhaps even at that early date the idea of writing a book lay in the back of their minds, for one of the obvious results of the Age of Discovery was to strengthen the link between travel and writing. Any significant journey could, and perhaps should, be commemorated in a significant text. For the explorers and conquerors of the sixteenth century, the meaning of 'significant' was obvious, but for the non-conquerors and travel writers of the seventeenth century the task was to redefine what was significant.

The Adventurers

Ludovico di Varthema can be seen as an early prototype of the old-world travellers of the seventeenth century. An Italian – about whom almost nothing is known except what emerges from his book – he made an extensive journey between 1502 and 1508 which took him through the Near East, Arabia, Persia, India and the Indian Ocean, yet for no specific motive that he cared to reveal. He tells us he was inspired by 'the desire to behold the various kingdoms of the world' and 'to ascertain the situations of places, the qualities of peoples, the diversities of animals, the varieties of the fruit-bearing and odoriferous trees of Egypt, Syria, Arabia Deserta and Felix, Persia, India and Ethiopia.' But what this grand rhetorical flourish really means never clearly emerges. In Damascus Varthema joined a large group of hajj pilgrims, and became (so far as we know) the first European to enter Mecca and Medina. How he achieved this – how he mastered Arabic so quickly, for example – we never learn, nor how he maintained himself financially during his travels. He was occasionally detained as a suspicious character, but seems always to have secured his freedom, once by feigning madness and then arousing the passion of a Sultan's wife. Considering how little prior knowledge of Muslim culture he can have had, his description of Mecca and the pilgrimage is marvellously evocative and accurate. He then made his way through Aden and

Oman to Hormuz, whence he sailed to Goa, and then around the coast of India. His description of India and its people was the most detailed to have appeared to that date, dwelling largely on the wonder and barbarity of oriental customs; he has, for example, a memorable early account of *sati*, the self-immolation practised by noble widows:

> Do not imagine, however, that she is unwilling to do this; she even imagines that she shall be carried forthwith into heaven. And thus running violently of her own free will, she ... throws herself into the midst of the fire. And immediately her relations ... fall upon her with sticks and with balls of pitch, and this they do only that she may die the sooner. And if the said wife were not to do this, she would be held in like estimation as a public prostitute is among us, and her relations would put her to death.
>
> (*The Travels of Ludovico di Varthema*, p. 207)

In his travels further east, to Burma, Java, Sumatra and the Spice Islands, Varthema's account becomes less precise, and there is some suspicion that these may be fictitious, or may have been left deliberately vague. He claims to have returned by ship via the Cape of Good Hope to Europe, where he published his *Itinerario* in Rome in 1510. Did Varthema's long, garrulous, but personally unrevealing narrative conceal something? Was he spying, or at least gathering information for some merchant or prince, perhaps trying to pin down the true source of the coveted spices which the Portuguese had believed to originate in India itself? His book had a great impact, and it may be significant that the first confirmed voyage to the Spice Islands took place in 1512, thus following quickly upon Varthema's publication, which was read with excitement as the first new European text on the lands east of India since the era of Marco Polo and Mandeville.

Varthema is not deep or philosophical, but racy, adventurous, rather disconnected, at times almost comical, his text reading almost like an early picaresque novel. But if this is true of Varthema, it is true a thousandfold of another traveller to the Orient, the Portuguese Fernão

Mendes Pinto, who created a travel book that ranges from the Red Sea to Japan, and is packed with historical glimpses of these regions that were unique in their time, but that seize our attention above all as a vivid personal adventure story. Pinto sailed for the East in 1537, and spent the next twenty-one years as soldier, sailor, buccaneer, merchant, prisoner, doctor, ambassador and missionary. He was shipwrecked, kidnapped, fought in bloody battles, was imprisoned, sold into slavery, released, feted by noble and distinguished figures in the Orient, and he contrived many times to act the part of a fly on the wall of history. His travels and adventures – if they really happened – are almost impossible to summarise, for he presents us with a personal, hands-on account of the reality of the Portuguese maritime empire, of all the men on the make, scheming, struggling and risking their lives to secure their fortunes. The Portuguese achievement in wresting the Indian Ocean trade from the powerful Muslim fleets was a fabulous one, but Pinto's book reminds us of the underside of this glorious epoch, the greed and cruelty, and the sufferings of the common soldier or trader. Yet throughout it all Pinto maintains a spirit of optimism, of wonder at all the extraordinary things that he saw, and a sense of humanity amid all the cruelty of the Orient. He travelled through much of Tartary and China, and it is in his pages that we first hear of the figure of the Dalai Lama, whom Pinto saw preaching. But not long afterwards Pinto and his companions heard of an island where great Chinese kings had been buried, along with hoards of treasure. They duly plundered the island, but were captured by the angry Chinese, flogged and sent to Peking in chains, giving him the chance to describe the Chinese judicial and prison system. He was sentenced to hard labour on the Great Wall, and after securing his freedom he spent some time observing the Chinese way of life, of which he gives many telling, out-of-the-way details, for example in a Peking eating house, he tells us, the waiters present the diners with a menu listing the dishes on offer, a custom then unknown in Europe.

Perhaps Pinto's greatest claim to fame was as the discoverer of, or at least the first European visitor to, Japan, where he claimed to have been blown off course by a tempest. He was soon on intimate terms with the local ruler and his family, introducing them to the wonders of firearms, demonstrating his musket and gunpowder, which the Japanese eagerly copied. This episode has been examined minutely by historians, and almost all that he says is authentic, with the signal exception that no other source can be found which mentions Pinto's name in this historic first encounter between Japanese and Europeans. This is the crux of Pinto's vibrant and readable text – is it true? His book, entitled *Peregrinations*, was published in Lisbon in 1614, some thirty years after his death, and for obvious reasons it became an international best-seller; but most readers regarded it is a romance, and Pinto soon acquired the nickname Mendax ('Liar') Pinto. More recent scholars have emphasised the core of historical truth in his writings, but there is no doubt that he chose to build his material into a dramatic narrative, a succession of personal adventures and incidents told with apparent naivety, but in fact realised with considerable literary skill. His text resembles nothing so much as a picaresque novel, whether from the pen of Cervantes or of Defoe. The problem of truth versus fiction in Pinto's narrative has thrown up a literary-historical puzzle similar to that of Marco Polo. One definitely authentic feature of Pinto's story, however, supported by external documents, is his contact with St Francis Xavier, the Jesuit missionary to the East. Pinto gives a remarkable portrait of the spiritual power of this enigmatic man indeed he at one point contemplated entering the Jesuit order in order to assist Xavier.

Ambassadors and Merchants

Nearer to home in Europe lay the kingdom of Muscovy, wrapped in such obscurity that its very existence was little more than a rumour.

In 1517 and again in 1526 the Austrian Sigismund von Herberstein was sent on two exploratory missions on behalf of the Emperor Maximilian I to the court of the Tsar in Moscow. Herberstein's reminiscences, published in Vienna in 1549 as *Rerum Moscoviticarum* was the first real description of Russia to appear in Europe. It is the work of a professional diplomat, and as such it pays special attention to court matters, the history of the kingdom, and a geographical description of its towns and provinces. Russia at that time was seen as a land remote from Europe, the northern rim of the known world, its very name synonymous with cold, cruelty, ice and darkness, so that a journey there was a very risky business. Herberstein's account did not exactly dispel this image. The journey from Vienna took him four months, through regions laid waste by the Russian winter and the long-drawn-out war with Poland. Bears maddened with hunger would attack the villages, he said, and when a man spat, his saliva would freeze before it hit the ground. Although well received by the Tsar (incidentally he does not use this word, but refers simply to the Grand Prince, Vasily Ivanovich) he was lodged in a house with a team of official attendants, who watched him strictly to ensure that he went nowhere and saw no one without their knowledge. One of their tactics to keep him in check was the compulsory evening drinking bout, drawn out by a thousand and one loyal toasts which Herberstein dared not refuse. The violence and insecurity of the country meant that his host provided him with an armed escort of 200 soldiers for his return. He reported that Moscow, although large, was almost entirely built of wood, and so dirty that bridges had been raised over the more filthy thoroughfares; the people were cunning and deceitful and drank heavily. Only the 'Fortress' – the Kremlin – boasted buildings of note, designed and constructed by architects brought in from Italy. Herberstein's book was very widely read, and many in western Europe noted his claim that it was possible for ships to pass from northern Europe into the White Sea, around the north of Scandinavia.

In terms of trade and potential wealth, it is rather hard to understand the lure of Russia in the sixteenth century, yet such was the rage for seeking new lands that it attracted a series of European travellers. But without Herberstein's foundation text it is hard to imagine that the London Muscovy Company would have dispatched Anthony Jenkinson on his ambitious and truly amazing journey through Central Asia in 1557–60, the account of which was published by Hakluyt in 1589. The journey had as its ultimate object the opening of an overland trade route to Cathay for the first time since the era of Marco Polo. Jenkinson with two companions emulated Chancellor in sailing via the North Cape to Archangel, and travelled on to Moscow to negotiate trade concessions with the Tsar. In April 1558, he embarked on the Moscow river and proceeded to the Volga, on a four-month voyage southward to Astrakhan and the Caspian Sea. He reports that the city of Astrakhan had been devastated by plague and famine, the streets littered with the dead, and its desperate inhabitants willing to sell their own children for a loaf of bread; here he acquired a young Tartar girl whom he took back to England and presented to Queen Elizabeth. At Astrakhan the Tsar's writ ended, and Jenkinson and his little party had now to live on their own wits and skills in an unknown, unstable and highly dangerous region. Having secured a boat and negotiated the Volga delta, he became the first Englishman to sail into the Caspian Sea. Surviving storms and bloodthirsty pirates, he landed on the Mangishlak Peninsula, and set off into the steppes, the land of predatory tribesmen who lived by violence and robbery, owing no allegiance to any law or sovereign. Even the resourceful Jenkinson found it impossible to deal with them as he made his way through towns like Khiva and Bokhara, threading his way cautiously among the feuding tribes, and the bands of marauding outlaws. They were a harsh and formidable people who used no money, but survived by barter or robbery, and lived on mare's milk and horseflesh.

The Englishmen reached Bokhara in safety, three centuries after
Marco Polo, but the peace of Kublai Khan which had enabled the
Polos to proceed onward to Cathay had been shattered long ago,
and Jenkinson realised clearly that to travel further into this anarchic
region was to invite death. He also saw that no trade of any importance
would be possible here, and he had reluctantly to turn back and retrace
his steps via the Caspian and the River Volga to Moscow, where
he presented the Tsar with a yak's tail, and with very discouraging
reports of the regions on his south-eastern borders, which the Tsar
himself had never seen. Jenkinson would return again to central Asia,
attempting to open a trade with Persia, but with no greater success.
He left a picture of the troubled, ungovernable regions of central Asia
that resonates all too grimly today; but he was a master of the offbeat,
whimsical or gruesome detail too:

> There is a little River running through the midst of the said City
> [Bokhara], but the water thereof is most unwholesome, for it breedeth
> sometimes in men that drink thereof, and especially in them that be not
> there borne, a worm of an ell long, which lieth commonly in the leg
> betwixt the flesh and the skin, and is plucked out about the ankle with
> great art and cunning, the Surgeons being much practised therein, and
> if she break in plucking out, the party dieth, and every day she cometh
> out about an inch, which is rolled up, and so worketh till she be all out.
> And yet it is there forbidden to drink any other thing than water, &
> mares milk, and whosoever is found to break that law is whipped and
> beaten most cruelly through the open markets, and there are officers
> appointed for the same who have authority to go into any mans house,
> to search if he have either Aquavita, wine, or brage, and finding the
> same, doe break the vessels, spoil the drink, and punish the masters of
> the house most cruelly.

(Early voyages and travels to Russia and Persia, p. 83)

By the early seventeenth century English commercial interest had
shifted south to India, and the idea of infiltrating the enfeebled Portuguese empire in south Asia. The Levant Company, established in

1580, was in a sense the successor of the Muscovy Company and the forerunner of the East India Company. In 1583 a party of half a dozen was dispatched to reconnoitre possible routes and markets between Constantinople and Mogul India, and their adventures were recorded by the adventurous Ralph Fitch. From Syria they descended the Euphrates and Tigris via Baghdad to Basra, and took ship for Hormuz, where they were promptly arrested at the instigation of the Venetian merchants already trading there. Handed over to the Portuguese, they were sent for trial in Goa, thus creating the historical oddity that the first party of Englishmen to set foot in India arrived there as prisoners. In Goa they skipped bail and made a dash for the Mogul territories, out of reach of the Portuguese. In the new imperial city of Fatehpur they were received in audience by the great Akbar, presenting letters from Queen Elizabeth to him. Here the party decided to go their separate ways, Fitch pushing east down the Ganges through Benares and Patna to the delta. Here he took ship to Burma, and left the first English description of the royal city and court of Pegu, enlarging on the King's harem, the white elephants, the gilded pagodas and the streets lined with palm trees. He then visited Malacca to investigate the trade with the Spice Islands and China, before turning for home, after eight years of groundbreaking reconnaissance for the English merchants. Fitch definitely reinforced the traditional image of the east as a place of wonders, where almost everything is rich and splendid, but very often alien and irrational, not least the religious system of the Brahmins:

> They will kill nothing not so much as a louse: for they hold it a sin
> to kill anything. They eat no flesh, but live by roots and rice and
> milk. And when the husband dieth his wife is burned with him, if she
> be alive: if she will not, her head is shaven, and there is never any
> account made of her after. They say if they should be buried, it were a
> great sin, for of their bodies there would come many worms and other
> vermin, and when their bodies were consumed, those worms would

lack sustenance, which were a sin, therefore they will be burned. In Cambaia they will kill nothing, nor have anything killed: in the town they have hospitals to keep lame dogs and cats, and for birds. They will give meat to the ants.

(*Ralph Fitch: England's Pioneer to India and Burma*, pp. 60–61)

The white elephants of the King of Burma provide Fitch with a wonderful opportunity to develop the twin themes of splendour and irrationality. Only the king may possess these creatures; if he hears of one whose owner will not yield it to him, he would rather make war upon him than permit him to keep it; they are housed in pavilions and fed from dishes of silver and gold, washed daily in the river by 'a gentleman which doth wash their feet in a silver basin', but there can be no explanation for this extraordinary practice – it is merely a function of the absolutist power of these Eastern kings, in whose courts everything is 'fair' and 'rich' and 'marvellous'. And yet Fitch writes with a merchant's eye of the produce of the East; the peppers, the cloves, the precious stones, the pearls and the silk – where these originate and how the trade in them is conducted.

When Fitch's memoirs were published by Hakluyt in 1589, their opening sentence included the words, 'I did ship myself in a ship of London called the Tiger, wherein we went to Tripoli in Syria, and from thence we took the way to Aleppo.' If this sounds oddly familiar, it is because Shakespeare read it and filed it away somewhere in his memory, and brought it out to use in the weird rhyme of the first witch in *Macbeth* that includes the line: 'Her husband's to Aleppo gone, Master o' th' Tiger…'

Fitch was a private individual, travelling on behalf of his commercial backers. But it was the radically changing world map of the sixteenth century that made formal international diplomacy a necessary and important part of the political landscape. The tensions between Catholics and Protestants in Europe, and the drive towards empire and trade far beyond Europe, made the accredited ambassador a more and more familiar figure in the courts and capitals of the world. The European approach to the virgin lands of America was outright conquest, but in dealing with the mature nations of Asia, diplomacy was essential, and a stream of special ambassadors were dispatched from the rival European capitals to negotiate for alliances and trading privileges in the Near East, Persia, India, Burma, China and the Indian Ocean. These men travelled thousands of miles, often in great danger, and would often spend years attempting to fathom the power structure in these exotic courts, and to gain the ear of the people who mattered; often they achieved absolutely nothing, except to gather the material from which to write amusing narratives on their return.

But what constituted a true ambassador? Some of the best-remembered travellers who claimed that title were really private adventurers with their own agendas, seeking their own fortunes. The two Sherley brothers, for example, Anthony and Robert, put Persia on the map for English readers with their accounts of their travels in that country, but they had no official status and in fact were regarded with some suspicion by the Crown and government in London. Of the two, Anthony, the elder, had the more unsavoury reputation, having been a mercenary soldier on land and a pirate at sea. He was one of those inspired by the example of Drake and Hawkins into believing that plundering overseas was a gallant profession for an Elizabethan gentleman. The idea of the great Persian expedition was to woo the formidable Persian ruler Shah Abbas first into forming an alliance between Persia and Christian Europe against their common enemies, the Turks, and second to establish trading relations between Persia and England; both of these schemes seemed to promise rich possible rewards. Sherley had no royal authority from Queen Elizabeth or her ministers, but vowed to succeed in this plan or die in the attempt; he even spoke fancifully of converting the Shah and all his kingdom to Christianity. Sherley took with him a group of two dozen friends and servants, including Robert Sherley, who at just 19 years of age was too young to have acquired a reputation as wild as his elder brother.

As Sherley and his party travelled overland through Muslim territory, the group were treated with contempt and were spat upon in the streets of cities like Aleppo and Baghdad, victimised and defrauded by the local governors. Nevertheless they had time to notice the habit of the menfolk of sitting cross-legged, 'drinking a certain liquor which they do call coffee, which is made of a seed much like mustard seed, which will soon intoxicate the brain'; it has been suggested that this is possibly the earliest reference to coffee in English literature. They were also astonished and impressed by the use of the carrier pigeons which were trained to bring news of the great caravans during their crossings of the deserts. Joining a caravan of returning Persian pilgrims, they made their way through the Zagros mountains into Persia itself.

The contrast between the hostile and vicious Turks and the civilised, hospitable Persians is a constant theme of Sherley's narrative, but this was clearly part of his political plan. Shah Abbas had a fearsome reputation as a despot, a man who did not hesitate to torture or murder members of his own family if he felt they threatened him, yet he was in some ways an enlightened ruler, who built the beautiful royal city of Isfahan, and who had a certain degree of cultural openness – two of his favourite wives were Christians. A later English witness, Thomas Herbert, would describe him as 'Of low stature, but a giant in policy, his aspect quick, his eyes small and flaming.' The Shah was known in England as 'The Grand Sophy', apparently a corruption of the Arabic title *Safi al-Din* – 'pure in faith'.

The Sherleys arrived at the then capital Kazvin in time to see the Shah return in triumph from one of his campaigns, entering the city with the heads of twelve hundred Uzbeks brandished on pikes, with the thundering of drums and trumpets, and a horde of courtesans, 'riding astride in disorder and shouting and crying in every direction as if they had lost their senses, frequently approaching the person of the king to embrace him'. Sherley took the opportunity to kiss the royal stirrup and introduce himself with a speech emphasising that the Shah's worldwide fame was such that he had come from far off, from a great queen, to pay homage to him. The Shah was extremely affable, claiming that he 'esteemed the sole of a Christian's shoe more than the best Turk in Turkey,' thus greatly encouraging Sherley in his hopes for his mission.

The Shah accepted both of Sherley's principles, the alliance with Europe and the trade treaty, and Sherley himself was named as the Shah's special envoy to the courts of Europe to cement the arrangement. Thus, paradoxically, the mercenary adventurer and self-appointed English ambassador to Persia became the official Persian ambassador to Europe. Evidence of the Shah's serious intent appeared in his demand that Robert Sherley must remain in Persia, as a hostage to Anthony's good faith and behaviour. Anthony prepared to make his homeward journey via the Caspian Sea and Muscovy, the route that Jenkinson had taken forty years before. Yet Sherley's diplomatic efforts at the court of the Tsar were a humiliating failure, an omen of his subsequent reception in the other capitals in Europe. He was forbidden to re-enter England, abandoned his grand Persian plan, and lived latterly in Spain and elsewhere as a kind of political con man, perpetually trying to sell some scheme to someone or other. In 1600 there had appeared an anonymous *True Report* of Sherley's journey overland *to Casbine in Persia, and his entertainment there by the great Sophie.* Sherley later earned a little money for himself by writing his own *Relation* of his travels into Persia, published in 1613. *Twelfth Night* was composed in 1601, and it is significant that in that work Sir Toby praises Cesario's skill as a swordsman with the words, 'They say he hath been fencer to the Sophy' – surely an echo picked up by Shakespeare from the earlier book.

Robert Sherley, left behind in Persia for almost ten years, was also the subject of two books about that country, from which he emerges with more integrity and credit than his brother. He acquired the Persian language, married a Persian princess and fought in the Shah's wars against the Turks. At last, exasperated by the failure of Anthony's mission, the Shah sent Robert as his new official ambassador to pursue the great alliance with Europe. Dressed in Persian costume, Robert and wife repeated Anthony's round of the European courts, where he was well received, but where he found little enthusiasm for a Turkish war. He had an unpleasant interview with his disgraced brother in Rome, was painted with his wife in costume by Van Dyck, received by King James in London, and shuttled to and fro between London and Isfahan for vague hypothetical discussions with the Shah. Returning for the third time in 1627, he found the game was played out: the Shah had fought his own Turkish wars, and had received not one scintilla of help from Europe. Sherley was dismissed impatiently, and had to face the fact that the grand strategy dreamed up by his brother two decades before had existed in imagination only. He died heartbroken and was buried in Persia, while his widow, now a devout Catholic, ended her days in Rome.

After Robert Sherley's death, a junior member of his party, a young gentleman-adventurer named Thomas Herbert, pursued his own travels from India through Persia, and was one of the first Europeans to describe the ruins of Persepolis. He also left a clear and vivid account of the custom of the 'sky-burial' – the exposure of corpses to be devoured by birds of prey. He was fascinated by the charmed and idle existence of the Persian nobility whom he saw, and their lack of intellectual curiosity about Europe. In conversation with Herbert, they would question only whether Europe's wines were good, her women fair, the horses strong, or the swords well forged. Herbert thought that their fondness for wine and for opium might be responsible for their decadence and superficial tastes, although he noted that, above all, 'Poetry lulls them, that genius seeming properly to delight itself amongst them.' When one gets used to his loose syntax, Herbert is observant, piquant and sometimes bawdy, but highly informative and endlessly readable. Halting in southern Africa on his outward voyage, he noted:

> In dark weather the Lions use subtilty to catch and eat the Savages. In the day time they [the native people] dig pits, cover them with boughs, and train the courageous lions thither, where they receive destruction, eating them today, who perhaps were Sepulchres to their friends or parents the day before.

(*A Relation of Some Yeares Travaile into Afrique, Asia, Indies*, p. 15)

His book was first published in 1634 as *A Description of the Persian Monarchy*, but this title did not do justice to its contents, so it was reprinted in 1634 as *A Relation of Some Yeares Travaile into Afrique, Asia, Indies*.

The texts relating to the Sherleys show one aspect of the world of ambassadorial travel: ill-planned, chancy, sordid, haphazard, unrewarding, leaving several books of memoirs as all that remained when the dust had settled – books of dangerous sea voyages and tedious desert journeys, ending in glimpses of alien cultures, with their exotic courts, exotic courtesans and exotic cruelty. A more elevated picture of official diplomacy emerges from the memoirs of Sir Thomas Roe, selected by the East India Company in 1615 as their first representative to the court of Jahangir, the Great Mogul. The Company's affairs were in some disorder, their position in India had no recognised status, and they faced natural hostility from the Portuguese and from the Jesuits. They needed a genuine ambassador with royal authority to urge their cause, and in Roe this is what they found. An insider at the English court, he was famous for his tact, good breeding and resourcefulness, and was a favourite of the royal children. He had already proved himself a gallant Jacobean by taking a ship to Guiana and becoming the first Englishman to explore the lower reaches of the Amazon. During his four years in India he employed all his diplomatic skills in achieving lasting advantages for his employers, despite being tried to the limit by the pride, cunning, greed and falsehood of the people with whom he had to deal. Roe complained that the only language any of them understood was that of gifts, bribery and secret pacts. He lamented that he was unable to match the gifts of his enemies, although he brought with him from London a luxurious coach for the Mogul, complete with an English coachman, a man named William Hemsell, whose subsequent fate in India we never learn.

Roe's journal, published after his return, is a clear-sighted and colourful record of the Mogul's court, which revealed Jahangir – the name meant 'world-grasper' or 'world-conqueror' – as inheriting few of the qualities of his great father, the Emperor Akbar: he was gracious and courteous to his European suppliants, but he was intellectually languid, given to drink and opium, vain and easily swayed, but a great patron of Mogul art. Above all he was browbeaten and henpecked by his principal wife, Nur Mahal, and the constant victim of her intrigues to advance her family. She was an extraordinarily strong character, who had no intention of ever remaining within the shadows of the harem: she accompanied her husband on hunting trips and was a crack shot with a gun. Eventually Nur and her faction would hold the Emperor under a kind of house arrest, while she and her son, Shah Jehan, ruled the roost. But she was too much for him too, and he had her banished as soon as he acceded to the throne. Some of Roe's descriptions of Indian court behaviour have a bizarre pantomime air about them, such as Jahangir's birthday celebrations:

> Coming to the Palace, I ... went up on the scaffold under him, which Place, not having seen before, I was glad of the occasion. On two trestles stood two Eunuchs with long Poles headed with feathers fanning him. He gave many favours and received many Presents. What he bestowed he let down by a silk string rolled on a turning instrument; what was given him, a venerable fat deformed old Matron, wrinkled and hung with gimbels like an Image, pulled up

at a hole with such another Clue. At one side in a window were his
two Principal wives, whose Curiosity made them break little holes
in a grate of reed that hung before it to gaze on me. I saw first their
fingers, and after laying their faces close now one eye, Now another;
sometime I could discern the full proportion. They were indifferently
white, black hair smoothed up; but if I had had no other light, their
diamonds and Pearls had sufficed to show them. When I looked up
they retired, and were so merry that I supposed they laughed at me.

> (*The Embassy of Sir Thomas Roe to the Court of the
> Great Mogul, 1615–1619*, vol. 2, pp. 320–21)

Here Roe is playing up the familiar image of eastern court life as alien,
absurd, theatrical and ritualised, yet he also has the crucial insight
to recognise that he is being laughed at too, that he is the foreigner.
It is an interesting balance: it justifies Roe's famous reputation as a
diplomat of sense and understanding, and it shows his gifts as an
accomplished writer.

After long, frustrating delays, Roe at last secured the privileges
that he sought for the East India Company. What emerges from his
narrative, however, is the sheer indifference of the Mogul's court to
this European campaign. Jahangir was amused and perhaps a little
flattered to be so wooed by a remote king from the other side of the
world, but he would never have regarded King James as his equal;
only the Sultan in Constantinople or the Shah in Isfahan could be
called 'world-graspers' like himself. In this, of course, time would
prove him to be badly wrong, for Roe, who never visited the country
again, undoubtedly laid important foundations for the future growth
of British power in India. Roe's story was first published in the travel
collection of Samuel Purchas in 1625.

Exactly contemporary with Roe was a much lowlier figure in the
East India Company, but a man who was surely one of the most
remarkable world travellers of the pre-modern age. Peter Mundy was
a Cornishman, who, between 1628 and 1657, spent varying periods of

time as a commercial agent in Turkey, India, China, Japan, Russia and the Baltic countries. Almost from the outset of his career he kept a very full diary, running to thousands of pages and embellished it with dozens of rather crude but charming pen-and-ink sketches – some of them less charming than others, since Mundy took a rather macabre interest in the physical punishments meted out in the countries he visited. Mundy writes clearly and engagingly, but not brilliantly, so that the sheer length of his work becomes daunting, and the volume of detail overwhelming. Exotic travel yarns or fabulous wonders are rather rare in Mundy. A few of his descriptions have become well known, such as his eyewitness account of the building of the Taj Mahal, but since he keeps his own personality rather in the background we do not receive from his pages any real explanation as to why he is writing. His carefully composed manuscript is massive, and it seems reasonable to assume that it was intended for publication, but if so the intention was not fulfilled, and it was published only in the early twentieth century. Had it been published in its own day, Mundy would probably have become as celebrated a figure as Coryate or Lithgow. He calculated, rather whimsically, that he had travelled almost exactly 100,000 miles, and been in serious danger almost exactly 1,000 times.

Jesuit Missionaries

Alongside the ambassadors and the merchants, there was a third class of important professional travellers in the sixteenth and seventeenth centuries: the missionaries. The older religious orders, Franciscans and Dominicans, had followed the navigators of Spain and Portugal into the newly discovered worlds from the very beginning, but the group which embraced overseas missions with the greatest fervour were the newly formed Jesuits. In the Americas North and South, in Africa and in Asia, wherever the conditions were harshest, the task most demanding and the indigenous peoples least approachable, there the Jesuits would be drawn to preach, baptise and, very often, suffer death for their faith. It was clearly no part of their vocation to write travel books, but many of these Jesuits did write reports and letters to their superiors in Europe, descriptive documents which range from Canada to India, and from Central Africa to the Pacific, some of which were made public. Central to the Jesuit enterprise was the vow of obedience, which in practice meant obedience to the command to go wherever one was sent, anywhere on earth, to reclaim some portion of the world for the Catholic Church; this was the overt military ethos which ruled the Society. The supreme, inspirational figure among the Jesuit missionaries was Francis Xavier, one of the original companions of Ignatius Loyola when the order was founded in 1540, and who, within a year, was en route to the East, where he established Christian missions in India, Sri Lanka, the Moluccas, Japan and the periphery of China, where he died in 1552.

It is difficult not to interpret these tenacious, dedicated missionaries as a second wave of conquerors: conquerors of the spirit, setting out to take possession of the world for Christianity, for Europe's religion and culture. This would be especially true of the missions to sophisticated Asian countries like Persia, India and China, where military conquest was impossible. From Portuguese Goa, for example, the Jesuits advanced into Mogul India, so that by 1580 the great Akbar personally invited them to his court to explain the nature of Christianity. Rudolfo Aquaviva fulfilled this role, and was heard politely by the broad-minded emperor. However, Akbar's idea of an ordeal by fire between a Muslim and a Christian, the first to enter the fire holding the Quran, the second holding a Bible, was diplomatically declined. Another Jesuit, Jerome Xavier (unrelated to Francis) later translated the four gospels into Persian for Akbar, and seems to have cherished the wild hope of converting to Christianity both Akbar and Jahangir.

St Francis Xavier has often been criticised on the grounds that his missionary philosophy was narrow, aggressive and single-minded, concerned only with maximising baptisms, and having no interest in indigenous cultures except to change them. This theory finds some support in his own admission that he was a poor linguist who had to rely on interpreters or even sign language, and therefore his understanding of the peoples among whom he worked was necessarily poor. Also, he spent relatively little time in any one country, driven on by ever more ambitious schemes to evangelise new regions. In his letters from India he is scathing in his attacks on the Brahmins and their religion, claiming that the priests' true object was merely to deceive the people into offering food and money to their idols, which they themselves took and enjoyed. A vital part of his strategy was to evangelise the children:

> The fruit that is reaped by the baptism of infants, as well as by the instruction of children and others, is quite incredible. These children, I trust heartily, by the grace of God, will be much better than their fathers. They show an ardent love for the Divine law, and an extraordinary zeal for learning our holy religion and imparting it to others. Their hatred for idolatry is marvellous. They get into feuds with the heathen about it, and whenever their own parents practise it, they reproach them and come off to tell me at once. Whenever I hear of any act of idolatrous worship, I go to the place with a large band of these children, who very soon load the devil with a greater amount of insult and abuse than he has lately received of honour and worship from their parents relations and acquaintance. The children run at the idols, upset them, dash them down, break them to pieces, spit on them, trample on them, kick them about, and in short heap on them every possible outrage.
>
> (*The Life and Letters of St Francis Xavier*, vol. 1, pp. 153–4)

To the modern reader, this sounds uncomfortably close to the children in Orwell's *1984*, and their betrayal of their parents to the Thought Police. Xavier's interest in the Japanese was aroused by hearing reports of them as a highly moral and religious nation, but he asks brutally, 'What good learning can any people possess who know not Jesus Christ?'

If this uneasiness with Xavier's aggressive stance is justified, then the lessons were certainly learned by the Jesuit order at an early stage. An alternative strategy can be seen at its clearest in the career of Matteo Ricci, an accomplished mathematician and astronomer who devoted thirty years to the grand project of a mission to China. His approach to the task was to master the Chinese language, to understand Chinese culture, to adopt Chinese customs, and to direct his efforts to the higher echelons of Chinese society, on the assumption that their power and influence would further his aims far more decisively than large numbers of peasant baptisms. In effect Ricci decided to turn Chinese himself, rather than attempt to change the millions of Chinese into Italians or Portuguese. Western access to China was severely restricted when Ricci first set out in 1582, and he had to proceed slowly in a series of steps, winning his way towards the centre of Chinese life and power. His personal teaching and writing introduced a wide range of western scientific ideas into China, and he became a respected figure first in Canton, then in Nanking and finally in Peking, his ultimate goal. Safely established in the capital for the last ten years of his life, he had the satisfaction of feeling that his intellectual approach to the missionary task had been fully vindicated. He displayed clocks, maps, celestial and terrestrial globes and other scientific instruments before the eyes of his hosts, and translated Euclid and Copernicus into their language; he also brought the name of Confucius to Europe.

In view of his lifelong dedication to China, Ricci was perhaps more of an expatriate than a traveller, one who brought to perfection the art of living among indigenous peoples, but nevertheless his letters and journals have left us a unique picture of Ming China. After his death in 1610, his manuscript history of the Chinese mission, with its descriptive survey of his host nation, was brought to Rome and edited for publication by Father Nicolas Trigault. It took Europe by surprise, and was printed again and again in many languages. Ricci effectively opened European eyes afresh to China, just as they had originally been opened three centuries before by Marco Polo, and the Christian mission he established endured into the twentieth century.

By 1600, although China was firmly on the map and had been seen and visited by many Europeans, there remained a nagging problem: where was Cathay, the fabled land whose marvels had filled the works of Marco Polo and the other medieval travel writers? Access to China had now been established by sea, but only when the overland route had been successfully followed from Persia, or perhaps from India, would it be certain that Cathay was China. This historic task, linking separate geographical empires but also separate eras of history, the medieval and the modern, was the achievement of another Jesuit, Benedict Goes, an Azorean, who with Akbar's blessing left Agra in 1602 planning to cross the mountains and to pursue his way eastwards on the Silk Road.

What did this form of geographical exploration have to do with Christian missions? Apparently, in a late echo of the Prester John legend, there were still rumours of isolated communities of Christians living in or beyond the great mountains in the north of India, and travellers' tales of religious ceremonies that seemed to resemble those of the Christians. These reports fired the Jesuits with visions of restoring these long-lost flocks to the fold of the Catholic Church; this was the background to Goes's mission. After making his way to Lahore, he joined a caravan to Kabul, from where he embarked on the perilous crossing of the Hindu Kush and the Pamirs, the first recorded traverse by a European of these formidable ranges. Only fragments of the diary which Goes kept survived, but he wrote that some members of the caravan died in the high snowfields, and that others suffered from what we can easily recognise as altitude sickness. The party descended the northern slopes to Yarkand, where Goes was detained for almost a year by Chinese officials, and where the priest's patience was sorely tried by the promiscuous women for which the town was notorious. He then spent two more years journeying slowly and through many difficulties as far as Suchow in eastern China, by which time he had become convinced that China was indeed Cathay, but he had also succumbed to sickness. He was able to send word to Ricci in Peking, but by the time help arrived Goes had died. 'In search of Cathay', wrote one contemporary, 'he found heaven.' Ricci was able to piece together the narrative to Goes's travels, and through his own writings Ricci endorsed the view that China and Cathay were one.

No less remarkable were the travels of another Jesuit from the Goa mission, Father Antonio de Andrade, who in 1624 penetrated the central Himalayas by disguising himself and joining a Hindu pilgrimage to the Garhwal, to Badrinath and Nanda Devi. Andrade described for the first time the horrors of severe frostbite, yet he survived well enough to found his own mission in Tsaparang, after he had realised that the supposed Christian rites in the Himalayan kingdoms were mistaken reports of Buddhist ceremonies; his mission flourished for some years before falling victim to local opposition. But despite these pioneering crossings of the Himalayas, still no westerner had retraced Marco Polo's route overland to or from China. It was not until 1661 that two Jesuits, John Grueber and Albert d'Orville, left Peking not to follow the ancient caravan routes along the Silk Road, but to cross the Tibetan plateau to Lhasa, which they entered in October 1661. They were awed by the distant view of the Potala Palace, but, like many subsequent travellers, appalled by the filth and squalor of the fabled and holy city. Thankful to leave Lhasa, Grueber and d'Orville travelled westward beside the Brahmaputra, before crossing the watershed to Kathmandu and relative civilisation. Their journey from Peking to Agra occupied a whole year, but their hardships cost d'Orville his life, leaving Grueber to press on through Persia and Turkey, returning to Rome to make his report to the Pope.

English Eccentrics

The Jesuits were the fiercest, most committed, wide-ranging and purposeful group of travellers in the world; but there were signs that travel without a purpose was becoming increasingly fashionable, and nowhere more so than in England. Back in the previous century, in the great Age of Discovery, the English role on the world stage had not been a major one. Yet by the beginning of the seventeenth century, the English had emphatically caught up in the geopolitical sense, and they had embraced the idea of travel and of travel literature in a manner surpassed by no other nation. An insular people who had experienced a cultural renaissance and defied the might of Catholic Spain, they set out with their new-found self-confidence to taste the flavour of the world beyond their own shores, often in a spirit of humour, condescension or even arrogance. They set the fashion of travelling for no other reason than to please themselves, to survey the non-English world, and to test what 'Italy' or 'Greece' or 'The Levant' or 'Egypt' – names continually encountered in intellectual discourse – really meant. It could be argued that the English writers of this period inaugurated travel literature proper, because they travelled for no purpose but to satisfy their own wanderlust, and because their own egos are very much to the fore in all their writing.

But although men like Fynes Moryson, Thomas Coryate and William Lithgow may have written for pleasure, they cannot all be read with equal pleasure today. Between 1591 and 1596, Moryson made two extensive journeys which took him first through Holland, Germany, Poland, Austria, the Alpine countries and Italy, and then to the eastern Mediterranean, the Holy Land and Constantinople. His aim seems to have been to build up a plain, accurate survey of the countries of Europe and the Near East, concentrating very largely on the appearance of their cities, their institutions, and the civilised or uncivilised manners of the people. Moryson was a well-educated

Cambridge scholar, judicious in his approach, but dry and bloodless in his writing, with the result that his painstakingly composed book, *Itinerary*, published in 1617, resembles a rather dusty guidebook. Moryson lacked almost all trace of an aesthetic sense, and he could make nothing of the famed beauties of the Italian cities, although perhaps this may be forgiven him because, in the south of the country at least, the Inquisition was then very active, and as a visiting Protestant he was in considerable danger. Of the Vatican frescoes by Michelangelo and Raphael, he notes only that the walls and ceilings are 'adorned with many fair pictures gilded all over'. Like most men of his time, he had no eye for the glories of mountains, lakes and rivers, but a more personal note appears in his reaction to continental inns, where he found 'gross meat, sour wine, stinking drink and filthy beds' – the beginning of a long tradition of English invective on this subject. Jerusalem he found to be inhabited by 'the scum of divers nations ... as wicked as they were when they crucified our Lord, gladly taking all occasions to use Christians despitefully'. There are many such generalisations in Moryson, but there is no incident, no drama, no adventure, no philosophy and no humour. After his return to England he devoted three years to piling up a manuscript report of his journeys so vast that even he realised it would be unpublishable, and the text that we now have, immense as it still is, is an abbreviation.

What Moryson's writing lacked in personal charisma was supplied with a vengeance by his exact contemporary Thomas Coryate: whimsical, attention-grabbing, egotistical, his curious work of 1611, *Coryat's Crudities*, introduced an entirely new note of intellectual slapstick into English travel literature. Coryate was a university wit of the 1590s who cultivated aristocratic friends and became a hanger-on of the Jacobean court. He knew Ben Jonson and John Donne and seems to have been one of the luminaries of the Mermaid Tavern, where he may have encountered Shakespeare himself. His skill in wordplay and repartee was said to be unrivalled, but he poured his energy also into buffoonery and practical jokes. Perhaps he should have become an actor, but chose instead to make a drama of his life by doing something entirely novel and irrational – travelling on foot across Europe. The full title of his famous book of 1611 is worth quoting for its true Coryate flavour:

> *Coryat's Crudities Hastily gobbled up in five Moneths travells in France, Savoy, Italy, Rhetia commonly called the Grisons country, Helvetia alias Switzerland, some parts of high Germany and the Netherlands; Newly digested in the hungry aire of Odcombe in the County of Somerset, and now dispersed to the nourishment of the travelling Members of this Kingdome.*

Behind this elaborate joke lay Coryate's exploit of walking most of the way to Venice and back again, distilling from it a far more personal account than Moryson's. Coryate was a passionate traveller who enjoyed and admired much of what he saw, laughed at a good deal of it, and yet generally despised foreigners. His first view of Venice he freely confesses took his breath away, for it 'yeeldeth the most glorious and heavenly show upon the water that ever any mortal eye beheld, such a show as did even ravish me both with delight and admiration.'

As he passes through scores of towns and cities in a half-dozen countries, Coryate makes original notes on their architecture, social life, food and drink, churchgoing, trade and sources of wealth. But amidst all this he parades his own personality and opinions: he describes his own seasickness all too graphically; he tells how he was carried over the Alpine passes in a kind of cradle; how he climbed proudly onto the Great Tun at Heidelberg; how he visited a courtesan in Venice – but only (he claims) to convert her from her way of life; his discovery of the joys of eating with a fork, then apparently unknown in England; how astonished he was to see actresses on the stage in Italy; how he pilfered grapes from the vineyards; how disgusted he was in a synagogue by the wailing and roaring of the cantor; his shock

The exuberant title page to Thomas Coryate's *Crudities* of 1611, showing some of the author's adventures and misadventures between the English Channel and Venice.

at seeing respectable women bathing more or less naked in public at Baden-Baden, and so on. His prose is sometimes ornate and facetious, but more often he is direct and lively, so that his book became an overnight success, a handbook to western Europe, and its author achieved what he had set out to do – he became a celebrity, presenting his book personally to the King and the Queen. Coryate's travels involved almost no adventures or picaresque incidents, as Pinto's did; instead the humour is in the angle, the viewpoint of the foursquare Englishman, his eyebrows more or less continuously raised at what he sees. A year after establishing his fame with *Crudities*, Coryate left England again, bound for India via Constantinople, Jerusalem and Persia. Crossing the Persian desert, he had a chance encounter with Robert Sherley and his Persian wife, who were travelling west from India, and who shared their refreshments with the eccentric pedestrian. Coryate reached his destination, but died there in India in 1617, without writing a full account of his journey. He may be said to have introduced the travel writer as wit, as his own impresario, his writing an entertainment, designed to show how amusing conflicting cultural values can be.

If there is a traveller who equals or surpasses Coryate as a character whose eccentricity is paraded as a feature in his writing, it is William Lithgow. A wealthy Scot who spent his life indulging in his passion for travel, Lithgow was known as 'cut-lugged Willie', having as a young man suffered the bizarre fate of having his ears cut off by three brothers who had caught him in flagrante with their sister. Lithgow was not a man to let this darken his life, however, for, as his later ordeals show, he remained tough, adventurous and fiercely independent through experiences that would have shattered most men. Between 1609 and 1621 he made three extended journeys through Italy, Greece, Turkey, the Holy Land, Egypt, Morocco and eastern Europe. He shared with Coryate the conviction of the superiority of British civilisation, although in Lithgow's case this was coloured by his fervent Calvinism and his rabid anti-Catholicism; he repeats many times his conviction that the Muslims he encountered in the East were more civilised and devout than the inhabitants of Catholic Europe. Even Paris he found 'a mass of poor people, for lackeys and pages a nest of rogues, a tumultuous place, a noctuall den of thieves and a confused multitude'; yet this pales into nothing beside his disgust with Rome, where he quotes St Catherine on the 'abomination, profanation and irreligious living', whenever she thought of 'the filthiness of the Pope's Palace, the beastliness of Rome ever stunk in my nose'. Never the diplomat, Lithgow had to go into hiding and then leave the city in a hurry, having 'hardly escaped from the hunting of blood-sucking Inquisitors'. Having made his way to Venice, Lithgow was delighted by the gruesome spectacle which greeted him on his arrival:

> perceiving a great throng of people and in the midst of them a great
> smoke, but we begun to demand a Venetian what the matter was; who
> replied there was a grey friar burning quick at St Mark's pillar, of
> the reformed Order of St Frances, for begetting fifteen young noble
> nuns with child, and all within one year – he being also their father
> confessor.
>
> (*The Rare Adventures and Painful Peregrinations*
> *of William Lithgow*, p. 39)

But throughout the land of 'Papistry' Lithgow saw little that impressed and much that disgusted him, including the fashion for 'beastly sodomy', which was

> rife here as in Rome, Naples, Florence, Bologna, Venice, Ferrara,
> Genoa – Parma not being excepted, nor yet the smallest village of
> Italy. A monstrous filthiness, and yet to them a pleasant pastime,
> making songs and singing sonnets of the beauty and pleasure of their
> *bardassi*, or buggered boys. (p. 43)

In Greece Lithgow could find nothing to correspond to the images of nobility and beauty which had made the name of Greece unique; time and the barbarousness of the Turks had, he concluded, destroyed all the monuments of antiquity. Lithgow was a natural writer, a moraliser driven by a grim contempt or fury at much that he saw. He was also something of an adventurer, whose travels are punctuated by encounters with robbers, pirates, swindlers and rascally priests. His sightseeing among the shrines and hallowed places of the Holy Land he sums up in a few passionate words:

Now thou bottomless gulf of Papistry, here I forsake thee: no winter-blasting furies of Satan's subtle storms can make a ship-wreck of my faith on the stony shelves of thy deceitful deeps.   (p. 129)

Lithgow's idiosynscracies made his book *A most delectable and true Discourse of a Peregrination in Europe, Asia, Africa* (1614) immensely popular, yet barely a year later he was again en route for more adventures. Given that violent anti-Catholicism dominated much of his thought, there was perhaps a certain tragic inevitability about the most terrible event in Lithgow's life, which came in the course of his third journey. In 1619 he planned the most ambitious of his adventures, to see the dominions of Prester John in Ethiopia. Only Lithgow would have set out for Ethiopia by way of Ireland, where he spent six months before embarking for France, and travelling onwards to Madrid. He formed a poor opinion of Spain and its miseries, and it is likely that he again made trouble for himself through his outspokenness. In Malaga, while on the point of taking ship for North Africa, he was suddenly seized in the street, dragged before the governor and accused of spying. All his money was taken from him and he was thrown in chains into a dungeon. As a 'Lutheran son of the Devil' he was deemed to be subject to the laws of the Inquisition. He was beaten and tortured, racked almost to death, and threatened with burning as a heretic; yet the indomitable Scot held fast and refused to submit. By sheer good fortune his plight became known to the English consul and ambassador, and he was released just days before he was due for execution. Slowly and painfully he was conveyed back to England, where he exhibited his 'martyred anatomy' to the king, the court, and all who wished to see it.

Incredible as it seems, Lithgow recovered sufficiently to undertake more travels, although to less exotic destinations. He produced

William Lithgow attacked by robbers in Moldavia, one of the many experiences
in which he found himself the victim of treachery and violence.

a number of miscellaneous works, including some undistinguished
poetry. Towards the end of his life he noted that his painful wanderings through kingdoms, continents and islands had amounted
to thirty-six thousand odd miles, 'which draweth near to twice the
circumference of the whole earth: and so farewell'. Why he travelled
or what he gained from it he never really explained, but he was a
genuine original, the travel writer as his own hero, a man who sets out
to challenge the world, who redefines the experience of travel, whose
narrative is entirely shaped by the uniqueness of his own personality;
a thousand other men might have travelled exactly where he did, and
not produced a book remotely like his.

Travel

Captives and Castaways

And yet in one sense Lithgow belongs very firmly within the special subgenre of travel that focused on the suffering of the traveller, and especially on shipwreck and captivity overseas. Captivity may appear to be diametrically opposed to travel, but there must have been thousands of unfortunate men who were compelled as captives to travel against their will. There were several dozen such narratives by Englishmen relating to events between 1560 and 1620. There was Edward Webbe, who sailed to Russia as a gunner under Captain William Borough, and found himself in Moscow in 1571 when the city was attacked by Tartar hordes, who captured and enslaved him. He was ransomed and returned home, but his misfortunes continued, for just one year later at sea off Tunis he was taken by the Turks, and was forced to serve them for fifteen years, first as a galley slave, then as a master gunner. He was again ransomed home, and published a memoir of his harrowing experiences in 1590. A similar story appeared in 1595 from the pen of Richard Hasleton, who was also forced to fight in the Turkish galleys, but not before he had been tortured by the Spanish Inquisition. Hasleton resolutely defied his tormentors' demands that he become a Catholic or a Muslim, and his Protestant and patriotic fervour resembles that of Lithgow.

Given the historical situation at this time, Spain played the part of the malignant power in most of these captivity narratives. One of the best known and most pitiful of these memoirs was that of Job Hortop, who was one of the men lost during the disastrous Hawkins–Drake Caribbean voyage in 1567. Held captive by the Spanish in Mexico for two years, he was then shipped to Seville, and sentenced to ten years in the galleys. After that he was held for a further ten years as virtually a slave in Spain's royal mint. He finally escaped and returned to England in 1590, after enduring twenty-three years of slavery and cruelty. Another ordeal which originated with Drake was that of Peter Carder, whose pinnace became separated from Drake's fleet in a storm in the Magellan Strait. On reaching land, the men were attacked by Indians, and most of them were killed. Carder somehow stayed alive and even won the respect of the Indians, before setting off on an adventurous solo journey from the River Plate to Bahia in Brazil, eventually finding his way back to England after nine years, where he was brought before Queen Elizabeth to tell his story. The problem with Carder's adventure was that there could be no corroboration whatsoever for it, and it has been thought by many to be almost entirely fictitious.

The theme of enforced travel emerges even more clearly in the cases of Andrew Battell and Anthony Knivet. Battell was shipwrecked on the Brazilian coast in 1589, captured by Indians and handed over to the Portuguese, who sent him in chains across the Atlantic to work in Angola. Here he fell into the hands of a savage tribe, with whom he lived, travelled and traded for fifteen years. Knivet's fate was the reverse: another survivor of a failed expedition cast up in South America, he stowed away to Angola, where he was seized and sent back to Brazil. Both men wrote interesting descriptions of their African 'hosts', which were the first such accounts in English, and which not surprisingly dwell on alien customs like cannibalism, infanticide and widow-sacrifice, although these are described with great coolness. Battell had a certain acuteness of observation:

> These people will suffer no white man to be buried in their land, and
> if any stranger or Portugal come thither to trade, and chance to die,
> he is carried in a boat two miles from the shore, and cast into the sea.
> There was once a Portugal gentleman that came to trade with them,
> and had his house on shore. This gentleman died, and was buried
> some four months. That year it did not rain so soon as it was wont,
> … so that they lacked rain for some two months. Then their *mokisso*
> [witch-doctor] told them that the Christian, which was buried, must
> be taken out of the earth, and cast into the sea; and within three days
> it rained; which made them have a great belief in the devil.
>
> (*The Strange Adventures of Andrew Battell*, p. 51)

Knivet claimed to have spoken personally with the great King of the Congo, and to have amazed him with his stories of Queen Elizabeth, the king being fascinated by the idea of a virgin queen who ruled her people through peace. Knivet called central Africa 'the infirmest country under the sun' for its heat and diseases, for here, he remarked, 'the Portugals die like chickens'.

Probably the best known and most unusual of these captivity stories is that of William Adams, the navigator who shipped with a Dutch fleet from Rotterdam in 1598 bound for the Far East via the Pacific. The voyage was a disastrous one, with men and ships lost through sickness, storm, attacks at sea by the Spanish and attacks on land by native peoples. In desperation the survivors, having passed the Magellan Strait, made boldly for Japan, where the remnants of the crew arrived in the last stages of starvation and sickness. They were humanely treated, and were received in Osaka by the Shogun Iyeyasu, who took a special liking to Adams. The Englishman taught him mathematics, geography and shipbuilding, and was rewarded with an estate and many gifts, including a Japanese wife. But one favour was always refused him – permission to return home, so that Adams was held for twenty years in his open prison, his accounts of which reached England through various intermediaries, and were published in 1625, five years after Japan's solitary Englishman had died.

The more conventional captivity texts are very different in kind from that of Lithgow: they are brief and reveal little of the writers' personalities; in fact the most striking aspect of them is the amazingly stoical and matter-of-fact way in which intense personal suffering is described, almost as if it would be un-English to complain overmuch of a little imprisonment, forced labour, starvation and torture. The texts seem to have been ghostwritten, wholly or in part, to fill out and vary their subject matter. Webbe, for example, describes the sights of Egypt and the Holy Land as if he were an ordinary sightseer, instead of a galley slave who had been forcibly pressed into the Turkish army.

Hortop too spices the record of his sufferings with notes on the exotic beasts, birds, fishes, plants and natural wonders he saw, as if to conform to some antiquated idea of what a travel narrative should be.

No one could call these captivity narratives great literature, but, like the memoirs of Mendes Pinto, they represent the underside of history, the stories of the casualties of overseas exploration, trade and warfare. They revived the ancient paradigm of travel as ordeal, and they served to remind contemporary readers of the extreme danger of travel even within Europe, where the bitter antagonism between Catholic and Protestant might plunge the innocent traveller into a prison or a torture chamber, while the Mediterranean was still plagued by violence and piracy. In spite of this, the extent of private travel seems to have been rather remarkable: in Lithgow's book, for example, it is striking how often he will encounter fellow Britons, in far-flung corners of Italy, Greece, the Levant or Egypt, sometimes travelling as he was, but often engaged in settled trade in these places, far removed from the relative safety zone of northern Europe. Coryate was unusual in his jokey approach to travel, and in his prevailing attitude that abroad is – usually – funny.

Scholarly Travellers

There were also serious scholarly men, who travelled out of a deliberate intellectual curiosity, and whose written works were offered not as mere adventures but as considered responses to other cultures. George Sandys, son of an Archbishop of York, sailed for the Levant from Venice in the summer of 1610, and what he saw and recorded in Egypt made him probably the first genuine Egyptologist of the modern era. Even at this early date Sandys opens his book with the words, 'France I forebear to speak of, and the less remote parts of Italy, daily surveyed and exactly related: at Venice I will begin my journal.' Sandys was never a good sailor, and, leaving Venice, he made frequent stops among the islands of the Adriatic and the Aegean. Before reaching Constantinople, he went ashore to contemplate what he was told were the ruins of Troy, although what he can have seen is something of a mystery. He laments that what was left of the fabled city was 'lessened daily by the Turks, who carried the pillars and stones unto Constantinople, to adorn the buildings of the great bazaar.' He rhapsodised over Constantinople even more than over Venice, writing:

> Than this there is hardly in nature a more delicate object, if beheld from the sea or adjoining mountains: the lofty and beautiful cypress trees so intermixed with the buildings, that it seemeth to present a city in a wood to the pleased beholders. Whose seven aspiring heads (for on so many hills and no more they say it is seated) are most of them crowned with magnificent mosques all of white marble, round in form and coupled above, being finished on the top with gilded spires, that reflect the beams they receive with marvellous splendour.
>
> *(A Relation of a Journey Begun An; Dom: 1610...*
> *Containing a description of the Turkish Empire etc*, p. 24)

As Sandys was leaving the city, after a stay of several months, he witnessed the sad fate of some Christian slaves escaping from the marble quarries of Marmara in a captured galley: while attempting to pass the Gallipolli Straits, they were fired on by the shore batteries, and all were drowned. On reaching Alexandria, Sandys found few relics of its ancient past, except a few 'hieroglyphical obelisks' – perhaps those which later found their way to London and New York. He proceeded to the Nile and interspersed his sight-seeing notes with lofty descriptions of the wisdom and science of its former inhabitants, although some of these were obviously derived from Herodotus, two thousand years before. He also affirms that the Egyptians first taught the adoration of the gods, the immortality of the soul and 'the transmigration thereof into another body, either of man or beast, clean or unclean, as it had behaved itself in the former'. He was delighted with the Pyramids and the Sphinx, in spite of calling them 'barbarous

A party of Europeans before the pyramids of Egypt, possibly the first ever picture of tourists on a sightseeing trip, from George Sandys's *Relation of a Journey...*, 5th edn, 1652.

monuments of prodigality and vainglory'. He climbed to the top of the Great Pyramid, whose building, he confidently reports, occupied 366,000 men for twenty years. He went into the interior, but found it cramped and the atmosphere poisonous, but, again like Herodotus, he was fascinated by the practice of mummification. Sandys then travelled overland to Jerusalem, but in between his cultural observations he had many unpleasant encounters with the locals, being several times robbed, threatened and humiliated. His enthusiasm for the Levant waned rapidly, and he made for home, although his return journey was again disrupted by seasickness, and by the need to dodge the pirates infesting the Eastern Mediterranean. His feelings may be guessed from his remarks on leaving the coast of Palestine:

Now shape we our course for England. Beloved soil, as in site 'wholly from the world disjoined,' so in thy felicities. The summer burns thee not, nor the winter benumbs thee; defended by the sea from wasteful incursions, and by the velour of thy sons from hostile invasions ...
Our sails now swelling with the first breath of May, on the right hand we left Cyprus, sacred of old unto Venus who (as they say) was here first exhibited to mortals.   (p. 218)

Sandys's *Relation of a Journey... Containing a description of the Turkish Empire* was published in 1615, and it included perhaps the first picture of a party of culture-hungry tourists, seen on horseback with the Pyramids and the Sphinx in the background. Sandys showed no desire ever to return to the Near East, turning his attention instead to the New World, and spending the decade of the 1620s as a leading member of the Jamestown colony of Virginia.

A couple of decades after Sandys, a second Englishman sailed out of Venice into the Adriatic, but Sir Henry Blount's first objective was the largely untravelled regions of eastern Europe under the dominion of the Ottoman Turks. Blount was open in stating that the purpose of his journey was intellectual, to discover whether Turkish culture was 'absolutely barbarous, or rather another kind of civility, different from ours'. The Turkish Empire had invaded the world, he says, and an understanding of its principles and its conduct was imperative. He was determined to investigate this subject not through books but through unprejudiced eyes, in person, in Turkey itself and among the peoples who lived subject to them. Landing at Spalato, Blount toured the remains of the Palace of Diocletian, then crossed the Dinaric Alps into Turkish territory, dressed as a Turk, but wearing a cross on his turban. He was more than once confronted by bandits, but he hit upon a pose of bravado and good humour in dealing with them that won their respect and ensured his own safety. Arriving in Sarajevo he was astounded by the giant-like stature of the men, whom he thought must be descendants of Teutons described by Caesar and Tacitus. From

Sarajevo he moved on to Belgrade, where he found himself surprisingly free to roam around the castle and fortifications. He was given a sharp insight into the deep ethnic hatreds of this region when he befriended a brutal and embittered Serbian eunuch in the garrison:

> I, going to visit him in his house, nigh the River Danubius, found
> him alone, very drunk; he out of that heat, and experience of my
> engagement, fell to rail against the Turks, and withal showing me
> how they had marred his game, well, (quoth he) do you see that
> River, there seldom hath past week since I have been in this city
> (which was half a year) but some night or other, I have thrown some
> of their children therein, and he told me that formerly in other places,
> he had done many such secret revenges, for their gelding of him.
>
> <div align="right">(<i>A Voyage into the Levant</i>, p. 133)</div>

Blount also found a surprising number of Christian renegades who had taken service with the Turks, and who now professed themselves atheists. For safety, Blount left Belgrade for Sofia among a huge army of 50,000, and he was amazed at the strict discipline that prevailed among such a powerful host, at the plentiful supplies of food, and the deafening Turkish war music of drums, brass and woodwind that accompanied them. Sofia he found a delightful city, which had not yet lost its old Grecian civility, replete with stately homes, exquisite baths and fountains. At Sofia he parted from the army and moved south-east towards Constantinople into classical landscapes, at least of his imagination:

> Sixteen, or eighteen miles Eastward of Sofia, we passed over the Hill
> Rhodope where Orpheus lamented his Eurydice ... In the lowest
> of those descents runs a little Brook, of which I conjectured, and a
> learned Jew, (to whom I owe most of my information) confirmed, that
> the old Poets had made the River Strymon, where the disconsolate
> Orpheus was torn in pieces by the Thracian Dames.   (p. 18)

Even more so than Sandys, Blount was moved to elegiac thoughts when he sought for the remains of Troy, for 'that famed town hath now put on immortality, having no existence but in poetry'. Blount retraced Sandys's footsteps to Cairo and the Nile, and was enchanted with the rich houses that he visited in the city, with their cool inner courts, their fountains and pools, their orange and lemon trees, and the ceremonious drinking of sherbet and coffee. Then he too entered a pyramid, 'tied by a cord, descending as into a well, ten or twelve fathoms, leaving a Janissary and two of our company at the top to awe the Arabs, who often leave strangers within, and return when they are starved to rifle them'.

Blount travelled upwards of 6,000 miles overland through the many divisions of the Turkish Empire, and his *Voyage to the Levant*, published in 1636, rightly established him as the foremost authority in England on all things Turkish. In view of the image of Turkey as a malevolent, barbaric threat to Christian civilisation poised on Europe's doorstep, his estimation of the Turkish way of life is remarkably open-minded. He thought their public buildings and institutions far superior to those of the west – their hospitals, colleges, highways, bridges, roadside fountains for travellers, and so on. He sensed that the foundation of their empire lay in the demand for 'exact obedience', enforced with 'exemplary severity'. He contrasted this with the countries of the west, whose lenience in judicial matters meant that they were always full of rebellions, conspiracies and civil troubles. He found the Turkish character much misunderstood, for it was 'generous, loving and honest, so far from falsifying his promise that if I had an hundred lives I durst venture them upon his word'. The personal habits of the Turks were also pleasing, as 'he or she who bathe not twice or thrice a week are held nasty'; few if any Europeans in the seventeenth century could match this record of cleanliness.

How can we sum up these first English sightseers, the first gentlemen travellers, the first writers on travel for its own sake? The obvious quality of their work is its innocent curiosity: these writers saw themselves as engaged in a kind of reconnaissance of the world beyond

England, and what interested them above all was men, manners and morals, the tangible fabric of life in the social, almost the physical, sense. How do men dress; what do they eat; how do they treat their wives; what is their legal system; how do they worship; how are they governed; are they poor or wealthy; what are their dwellings like; are their towns well ordered or filthy; are they civilised or barbaric? In each country, these are the things that they notice and comment on. For the beauties of a region, the landscapes and the natural grandeur, they seem to have no eye whatsoever. Even the love of knowledge is not their primary concern, for historical and cultural analysis is largely beyond them, except on the anecdotal level. Consequently we gain almost no feel of a country, no real sense of place; the poetry of travel is evidently something still entirely unknown to them. Allied to this, the process of travel itself is left entirely vague: how did they overcome the language barriers; did they travel alone or with a retinue of servants; what did they use for money; how did they procure horses or boats when they needed them; did they possess maps to plan their journeys; did they employ local guides? About such things we learn almost nothing. Perhaps we are meant to see these things as unworthy of comment, understanding that an English gentleman with money in his pocket will always find those who will serve him and guide him to his destination.

And this is the central point about these narratives, that they are permeated by a sense of superiority, a faint contempt for whatever is foreign, their eyebrows raised at the strange pantomime of life abroad. The writer is portrayed as if stirring the waters of some exotic pool and revealing bizarre life forms in its depths. The purpose of the travel writer was to investigate these alien regions and bring back reports on them to England, the land of sanity and sense. The traveller juggles with familiar and unfamiliar environments, crossing over from the known to the unknown, the familiar to the bizarre, and probing the differences between them. This was the stance pioneered by Coryate, through which he made himself a personality, a wit, a pundit, a comedian. The captivity narratives of course reverse this stance, and show abroad as a place of cruelty, injustice or even horror. When this framework of contempt for what is alien, whether comic or tragic, is missing, we notice it immediately, as in the works of Sandys or Blount, where we find considered attempts to do justice to foreign cultures. But the supreme opponent of foreignness was surely Matteo Ricci, the Jesuit who sensed that the only way to understand China was to cease to treat it as a foreign land, and become part of it. This is the great gateway of imagination through which the traveller must pass – to recognise that there is no foreign land, for he is the foreigner.

Buccaneers and Satirists

These gentlemen-travellers concentrated their attention on the old world, but in the seventeenth century the new world gave birth to a very different species of traveller – the buccaneers, who were the seaborne heirs of the conquistadors, to whom the waters of Central America were a kind of free frontier land where, in pursuit of wealth and adventure, men made their own laws. This wild, brawling subculture was chronicled in one undoubted classic, *The Bucaniers of America: or a true account of the most remarkable assaults committed of late years upon the coasts of the West-Indies, by the Bucaniers of Jamaica and Tortuga, both English and French*. This was the work of a French Huguenot, Alexander Olivier Esquemelin, and it became a European best-seller, appearing in many languages from 1678 onwards. Esquemelin had sailed as a servant of the French West Indian Company, but found himself held as a virtual slave by several masters until he was able to buy his freedom, and join the buccaneers as a surgeon's apprentice. He had personal acquaintance with the legendary Henry Morgan at the time of his attack on Panama. Esquemelin returned to Europe and practised as a surgeon in Amsterdam, where his book was first published in a Dutch version. It offered fascinating insights into the political context of the buccaneers' activities, and the way they were authorised by the British and French governors to harass the Spanish in Central America, just as Drake had been a century before. In the popular imagination, Esquemelin single-handedly put the Caribbean on the map, and created the image of the swashbuckling, law-breaking but heroic adventurer. This work spawned an entire subgenre of pirate literature well into the eighteenth century, much of it half-fact and half-fiction, which attracted writers such as Defoe, so that the seafaring adventure and the picaresque tale together became very much implicated in the development of the English novel.

The borderland between piracy and honest commerce, and between fiction and fact, appears very clearly in the career of William Dampier, an enigmatic figure who has entered the history books as an explorer – discoverer of the rather insignificant Dampier Strait off Papua New Guinea – but who spent a dozen years learning his seafaring skills as a buccaneer, plundering his way around a good part of the world's oceans. He wrote up his experiences, most of them plausibly disguised as exploration, in his *A New Voyage Round the World* of 1697, to such good effect that he was appointed to command a government reconnaissance expedition to Australia and the Pacific. This was the first party of Englishmen to set foot in Australia, many decades before Cook, but Dampier made the crucial mistake of focusing his attention on Australia's barren north-western coast, where the indigenous people were, in his view, 'the miserablest people in the world'. This somewhat chaotic voyage ended with Dampier's being court-marshalled for misconduct and cruelty, after which he wrote his second work, *A Voyage to New Holland* (1703), then returned to privateering, but with no very great success.

Dampier managed to keep diaries during most of his travels, in which he was very concerned to describe carefully all that he saw, while not attempting to conceal his own moods or opinions. The result is a lively narrative which combines maritime adventure with a form of bluff rationalism about the people and places of the world; indeed Dampier sought to promote himself as above all an apostle of geographical knowledge, not a mere adventurer, and certainly not a coarse buccaneer. Dampier's originality of approach as a travel writer lay in his passion for information: he seems reluctant to omit any detail of the people and places he saw. Physical characteristics, costume, food and drink, money, houses, social habits, ceremonies, laws, beliefs – all these things pour out in a kaleidoscopic flow of information that tends to daze the reader of today, although it appealed strongly to the early-eighteenth-century public; indeed in some ways it pointed forward to the taste of the Augustan age. Yet every now and then we get a flash of off-beat humour, whether intended or not is sometimes hard to say, such as this, thrown in apropos of nothing:

> The Chinese are very great gamesters, and they will never be tired
> with it, playing night and day till they have lost all their estates; then
> it is usual with them to hang themselves.

(A New Voyage Round the World, vol. 1, p. 405)

Like Esquemelin's, Dampier's book had a strong influence on writers like Defoe, Swift and Smollett; fittingly, it was Dampier who rescued Alexander Selkirk, the original of Robinson Crusoe, after he had been marooned for four years on Juan Fernandez Island.

Jenkinson, Roe, Coryate, Lithgow, Sandys, Esquemelin, Dampier – all these show the growth of a literature of travel in the obvious sense, but there is clear evidence that the idea of travel as a theme was beginning to enter the mainstream of imaginative literature too. As early as 1594 Thomas Nashe published *The Unfortunate Traveller*, a prose fiction which follows the fortunes of young Jack Wilton, a page at the court of Henry VIII, in his travels through Europe. In Germany he witnesses the Anabaptist revolution in Münster, and he hears Luther disputing at Wittenberg. At various time he meets celebrated scholars including Erasmus, More, Agrippa and Aretino.

He visits Florence and Rome, the latter in the grip of plague and civil chaos, where he marries an Italian courtesan and returns to the court of King Henry. Brief as it is, *The Unfortunate Traveller* can fairly be seen as the first picaresque adventure novel in English, anticipating the works of Defoe and Fielding. It is written in an exuberant, ironic style, suggesting *Candide* rewritten by James Joyce, a riot of language that culminates in several scenes of revolting cruelty. It cannot strictly be called a travel book, for so far as we know Nashe never set foot in any of the places that Jack Wilton visited, but it is figurative travel: it shows an English author for the first time seizing the theme of travel as a fantasy framework on which to hang a narrative that could not possibly take place in England, and through which he can give his imagination free rein.

A decade later, Joseph Hall, a future bishop of the Church of England, published an elaborate parody of the discovery narrative, in which he mocks unmercifully the fashion for exotic travel, maintaining that human nature is the same all over the world. This cynical standpoint explains his title, *Mundus Alter et Idem* ('Another World, Yet The Same') of 1605, for his chief protagonist voyages in search of the unknown southern continent, and, finding it, discovers to his chagrin that its people are all too familiar in their vices, for they inhabit kingdoms such as Gluttonia, Letcheritania and Hungerland. The model for Hall's satire is obviously More's *Utopia*, and it looks forward to Swift's satirical use of the travel device. Hall's book contains nothing about the actual experience of travel, and it is all rather obvious burlesque humour; yet it is striking to find at this date such a thoroughgoing and scornful attack on the travel vogue.

Verbal echoes from a number of travel texts can be heard in Shakespeare, but it was only late in his career that the great dramatist seems to have been awakened to the possibility of using travel as a metaphor for suffering and transformation in the lives of his protagonists. In the late romances, *Cymbeline, Pericles, The Winter's Tale* and *The Tempest*, journeys are first ordeals then turning points, causing the destruction of the character's old life, and offering the first stage of regeneration into a new. The metaphors of storm and shipwreck are used to symbolise the loss of a former identity, but it may also become the means of reconciliation between those who have long been parted. It seems virtually certain that Shakespeare had pondered over contemporary travel narratives, including the many stories of captivity or exile, and had recognised in them a device that he could use to explore in vivid and dramatic ways his chosen themes of parting, suffering and reconciliation. Travel in this view is a search for knowledge, but the destination is incidental, for it is knowledge of the self that is the true gift of travel.

This is emphatically not true of the most celebrated use of the travel symbol to appear in this whole period – Bunyan's *The Pilgrim's Progress*, which was published in 1678. Here the apparatus of the travel adventure – difficulties, dangers, friends, enemies, hope, despair – are given a real physical setting: hills, valleys, rivers, plains and castles, although we have no exact sense of where we are, and we seem to be always in England. But here the destination is the supreme feature of the story: to reach the Celestial City is the driving force behind the entire narrative. The personality of the Pilgrim is not delineated, for it is not important, except that he remains true and valiant as he threads his way through the perils of his journey, pressing onwards towards his longed-for heaven. The concept of the journey of life receives here its classic expression. It could be argued that *The Pilgrim's Progress*, with its swamps, mountains, rivers and monsters to be conquered, is an archetypal model for that form of physical adventure narrative that is overlaid with moral symbolism, for example in mountaineering literature, where reaching the summit is the overarching goal whose achievement transfigures the climber's life: all the suffering of the journey towards it becomes an allegory of life's struggle, like Christian's journey towards the Celestial City.

FOUR

The Eighteenth Century: Travelling for Knowledge

Curiosity is seldom so powerfully excited, or so amply gratified,
as by the faithful relations of Voyages and Travels. The different
Appearances of Nature, and the various Customs of Men, the gradual
Discovery of the World, and the Accidents and Hardships of naval
Life, all concur to fill the Mind with Expectation and Wonder.

Samuel Johnson
(Advertisement to John Newbery's *The World Displayed*, 1760–61)

I have always thought ... that we possess at this time very great
advantage towards the knowledge of human nature. We need no
longer go to history to trace it in all stages and periods. History from
its comparative youth, is but a poor instructor ... But now the great
map of mankind is unrolled at once, and there is no state or gradation
of barbarism, and no mode of refinement which we have not at the
same moment under our view.

Edmund Burke (Letter to Dr Robertson, 1777)

THE NEW PARADIGM that enters travel literature in the eighteenth
century is travel as the pursuit of knowledge. In the age of reason and
science this was natural enough. It was inevitable that the 'curiosity'
which inspired the seventeenth-century traveller should be heightened,

transformed into something more deliberate and formal, something dignified with the aura of 'knowledge'. The panorama of the world outspread before the traveller must now be considered, analysed and interrogated in search of answers, and the question that lay behind so much eighteenth-century travel literature was always the nature of humanity. The proper study of mankind was man, and in the context of travel this meant asking the question: was the European way of life the only possible form of civilisation? If so, was it God-given, or had we invented it ourselves? Was civilisation a necessary development of nature, or a contradiction of it?

The two characteristic but very different sites of eighteenth-century travel where these problems came into focus were the Pacific and the Grand Tour of Europe, the latter always culminating in Italy. The aim of the Grand Tour was to expose the insular Englishman to the seeds and the fruits of European culture at its highest development, in the lands where it had its birth in the classical era. Greece had long been in decay and, under Turkish control, was regarded as unfriendly, if not completely inaccessible. Italy, however, was the ideal destination for the educated and enquiring tourist, with its classical past and its Renaissance splendours. By approaching this shrine through either France or Germany, both the essence and the gradations of European culture could be experienced and weighed. So the Grand Tour posed the question about civilisation in a refined and agreeable way.

But, as the great naturalist Sir Joseph Banks remarked scornfully, 'Any blockhead can go to Italy.' Banks's idea of a grand tour was the Pacific, and for all practical purposes to cross the Pacific meant circumnavigating the world. The Pacific became the 'new world' of the eighteenth century, the last expanse of virgin space on the surface of the globe, and home to a bewildering variety of scattered peoples. Only here could the more profound questions of nature and civilisation be studied. The very fact of their isolation posed tantalising questions about their origin, their alien customs and their place within the human family.

The Pacific

The first generation of world explorers, the generation of Columbus, Vespucci and Magellan, when they first encountered the people of the new world, had all been struck by the overwhelming fact that they were naked – that is, they were outside the norms of civilised humanity. Why? Where had these people come from? Were they in fact human at all? The entire early history of the new world unfolds under the shadow of this problem, this encounter between people who cannot recognise each other as human. But in the scramble for new lands, for gold, for colonies and for slaves, this issue as an intellectual problem had been shelved for almost two centuries. It was in the age of the Enlightenment, and in the Pacific rather than in the Americas, that it was at last to be fully explored.

The Pacific had of course been crossed a number of times since Magellan, but its incomparable vastness meant that two centuries of piecemeal exploration had, when the eighteenth century opened, left it still a realm of mystery. On its charts ghostly outlines of coasts might appear based on a single mariner's report and on theoretical conjecture, while islands were found, named, lost, refound and renamed, during which time they might drift a thousand miles or more, according the map-maker's imagination. The Pacific of the imagination had indeed been taking shape in parallel with the Pacific of reality – it became the place to site a long and growing line of imaginary kingdoms, some intellectual and utopian, some places of ordeal, and some absurd. Thomas More sited his Utopia in the South Sea (as the Pacific was originally called); Francis Bacon followed suit with his New Atlantis; Hall's rather laboured satire *Mundus Alter et Idem* was set in a southern continent which was popularly supposed to fill the ocean's unexplored southern expanse; the two seminal works of English travel fiction, *Robinson Crusoe* and *Gulliver's Travels*, are both located in the South Sea, as were a whole family of French fantasy novels.

The idea of a great, undiscovered southern continent was passionately adopted by many armchair geographers of the eighteenth century, when it acquired a strong political resonance, especially in Britain and France, for by then the Pacific was evidently the last great blank upon the map of the world, the last opportunity to establish a new overseas empire to rival that of Spain. Thus there was a many-sided fantasy-Pacific which had put down deep roots in the European imagination, and which explorers of the Age of Enlightenment set out to probe. This desire became still more urgent after the end of the Seven Years War in 1763, when France had lost Canada and India, and therefore turned her attention to the Pacific, seeking with great determination a new empire to replace the one she had lost. Britain was equally determined to forestall her, and to this end both countries furnished large, carefully planned voyages of exploration, manned by skilled, scientifically trained officers to solve the Pacific problem once and for all.

For political reasons, therefore, the Enlightenment Pacific project really got under way only after 1760. Before that there were several ventures into the Pacific, one of the most interesting being the last Dutch expedition under Jacob Roggeveen in 1721–22, who had the distinction of becoming the discoverer of Easter Island and its unique monoliths. Roggeveen and his men noticed several strange and unexpected features about the Easter Islanders: that there was evidence of a form of writing in existence there, although it appeared to be ancient, and no longer practised; that the indigenous people showed extraordinarily long ear lobes, pulled down towards their shoulders and pierced to take ornate and heavy ear-rings; and above all the gigantic, quasi-human, stone figures that were set up near the seashore:

> we merely observed that they set fires before some particularly high
> erected stone images, and then sitting down on their heels with bowed
> heads, they bring the palms of their hands together, moving them

up and down. These stone images at first caused us to be struck with astonishment, because we could not comprehend how it was possible that these people, who are devoid of heavy thick timber for making any machines, as well as strong ropes, nevertheless had been able to erect such images, which were fully 30 feet high and thick in proportion.

(*The Journal of Jacob Roggeveen*, pp. 97–8)

The object of Roggeveen's expedition was to search for the supposed southern continent, so he did not linger to investigate; this was a pity because the island was not visited again for fifty years and the island cult had apparently changed by then, so that it seems Roggeveen missed a valuable opportunity to probe the meaning of these mysterious statues.

For the British, the landmark first Pacific voyage of the century was the circumnavigation of Captain George Anson in 1740–44. This took place in the context of the war with Spain, and it was in fact a military expedition on the old pattern, with the capture of the great bullion ship that ran from Panama to Manila as its overriding object. It was not a scientific voyage of exploration, but it did result in 1748 in a published account (*Voyage Around the World*) edited from Anson's own journals and recollections, which was printed over and over again, and which made him a national hero. As a narrator Anson had a crisp, readable stiff-upper-lip style, which gave his book a long life as a kind of schoolboy classic down to the 1930s, this in spite of the fact that the voyage had been disastrous for many, with three-quarters of the crew dying from disease. This was overlooked at the time, when Anson's Spanish plunder was carried in triumphant procession through the City of London. Anson was hailed, rather obscurely, as a Ulysses, and, more understandably, as a second Drake.

Anson's was the first in a series of British and French circumnavigations in which the Pacific was the real centre of interest. The second was that of John Byron, grandfather of the poet, who had sailed with Anson's squadron, but whose ship, the *Wager*, had been wrecked on the coast of Chile. Many years later Byron published a memorable account of the subsequent adventures and ordeals of the crew, which recalled the castaway and captivity narratives of the previous century, but the texture of Byron's narrative is richer. His description of the wreck of his ship is as dramatically coloured as a novel, portraying with great honesty the terror of the men when the ship first struck:

> Particularly one [man], in the ravings despair brought upon him, was seen stalking about the deck, flourishing a cutlass over his head, and calling himself king of the country, and striking everybody he came near, till his companions, seeing no other security against his tyranny, knocked him down.
>
> (*The Wreck of the Wager: the narratives of John Bulkeley and the Hon. John Byron*, p. 165)

As the ship became stuck fast among the rocks and became stable, the men grew less frantic, but, the captain lying injured in his cabin, discipline now broke down completely:

> The scene was now greatly changed; for many who but a few minutes before had shown the strongest signs of despair, and were on their knees praying for mercy, imagining they were not now in that immediate danger grew very riotous, broke open every chest and box that was at hand, stove in the heads of casks of brandy and wine, as they were borne up to the hatch-ways, and got so drunk, that some of them were drowned on board, and lay floating about the decks for some days after. (p. 167)

These shocking scenes are probably not what we would expect of men of the British Navy in a crisis, but it is worth remembering that Byron was just 17 years old when he witnessed this, and much later, back in England, there was considerable debate as to whether the events that followed the wreck constituted a mutiny; Byron was in no doubt that they did. Having abandoned the ship and reached land, the men quarrelled violently; some of them rejected the captain's

Captain John Byron in Patagonia in 1764, reigniting the controversy about the
supposedly gigantic inhabitants of the region.

authority and determined to make their way in a longboat back
through the Magellan Strait, which they succeeded in doing. Byron
himself remained in the smaller, loyal party, and thereby found
himself condemned to spend the next five years of his life in the
struggle to get back to England. First he had to endure the misery
of the coast of southern Chile, 'the most unprofitable spot on the
globe of the earth', bitterly cold, provided with almost no natural
food, and inhabited by the most primitive of people. Nevertheless it
was with the help of some of them that Byron and the others were
finally able to find their way out, struggling north mainly by sea
some 800 miles to Santiago, and by a series of stages, as prisoners
of the Spanish, back to England. No one involved was ever tried for
mutiny, for the case turned on the interesting point that, from the
moment of their ship's destruction, the men were no longer in the
paid service of His Majesty, and therefore they argued they could not
in justice be subject to the discipline of the officers. Byron's text is
only one of the documents, but certainly the most absorbing, in this
confused odyssey, for he writes of his hardships with honesty and

imagination. At one point the little group was so beaten down with hunger and suffering that he remarked, 'the preservation of life had now in great measure lost its actuating principle upon us' – a dignified way of saying that they no longer cared if they died.

Byron's own later circumnavigation in 1764–66 was remarkable in three very odd respects. First, it reignited the legend of the giants of Patagonia. Byron claimed that he and all of his crew encountered these people and were astounded by their stature. Rather strangely, he did not trouble to give precise measurements, but contented himself with saying that a man of 6 foot 2 inches was 'a mere shrimp' beside them, and that 'the stoutest of our grenadiers would appear nothing to them'. This is all the stranger seeing that after his first landfall twenty years earlier, following the wreck of the *Wager*, Byron had given no hint of anything odd about the native people whom he met. These reports split the worlds of science and of travel into two camps, one side avowing that they too had seen these titans, the other side pooh-poohing them. Some reports had them as 'wild and gigantic cannibals' as much as four yards high, while others vowed they had met in Patagonia only 'a harmless, civil, inoffensive people, of mid-dling stature, and well-shaped'. The thinnest rationalisations were produced: the Patagonians must have been wrapped in huge blankets; they must have been seen on horseback; there must be something abnormal there about the refraction of the light, and so on. When Louis de Bougainville, surely the most reasonable and civilised of travellers, encountered them just a few years after Byron, and got out his tape measure, he was unable to find one who stood more than 5 foot 10 inches tall. Is it possible that the whole story was an elaborate hoax, a kind of trap for travellers? Perhaps there existed an inner circle who were in on the joke, so that those who claimed to have seen the giants were immediately known to be frauds. If this was the case, it has never reached public knowledge, leaving the whole episode of the Patagonian giants simply inexplicable.

The second oddity was that Byron discovered a fine harbour in the Falkland Islands, where 'all the navy of England might safely ride', and he took possession of it for the nation. What was so odd about this? Simply that the French under Bougainville had claimed possession of the Falklands nine months earlier, and that at that very moment a colony of French settlers were living on the other side of the island; Byron sailed away blissfully unaware of this fact. Byron's official commission, once having passed the Straits of Magellan into the Pacific, was to sail far to the north, to find Drake's 'New Albion', and from there to search for a passage into Hudson Bay – the fabled Northwest Passage in reverse. Byron completely ignored these instructions, and crossed the Pacific on the usual course, north and then due west. His blatant disregard of his orders he justified by blaming continual and severe storms and the poor state of his ship. This account contributed to his later naval nickname of 'foul-weather Jack', but this was the third oddity, for, in spite of all these claimed hardships, he made the swiftest circumnavigation then on record, and discovered precisely nothing en route. Perhaps Byron possessed the same gift of imagination that would emerge in his grandson; certainly the poet knew his grandfather's text and claimed to have been inspired by it when writing the shipwreck scenes in *Don Juan*.

Only a couple of months after Byron stepped ashore in 1766, the next English squadron, under Samuel Wallis and Philip Carteret, set sail for the Pacific, with instructions to sail due west from the Magellan Strait for more than 100 degrees of longitude, in search of the great southern continent. Soon after emerging from the Strait, their two ships became parted, with the result that two separate circumnavigations entered the historical record. There is undoubtedly a certain sameness about the narratives of these maritime adventures – endless variations on the themes of foul weather, sickness, unreliable charts, landfalls that are delayed until death or disaster threatens, all this narrated with a great deal of nautical jargon and a stiff upper lip. The impression given is that all will come right in the end, that stoicism and tenacious seamanship will be vindicated. Generally speaking – and this emerged strongly from Byron's castaway account – it is only when these voyagers touch land that their narratives find the opportunity to become truly novel or original. This was above all the case with Wallis's voyage in HMS *Dolphin*, for to him fell the honour of being the first European to discover Tahiti, and thus to inaugurate a process of cultural encounter, bafflement, comedy, tragedy, myth and misunderstanding that reverberated for half a century and became the cardinal event in Pacific history. It is with the controversy over Tahiti that the records of travel in the Pacific become the literature of travel.

After taking the tape measure to Byron's Patagonian giants and finding them of perfectly normal size, Wallis steered his ship through the Straits, but then like all navigators he was faced with adverse winds from the west, and he was desperate to get into warmer waters; consequently he disregarded his instructions, setting a course north by west, bringing him to the Tuamotus. On 17 June 1767 he sighted the volcanic cone of Mehetia, and the next day he lay off what was plainly a much larger well-populated and significant island, which he felt might well be an outlier of the great southern continent, and which he promptly named King George III's Island, but which was known to its inhabitants as Otaheite. This historic first contact was not all innocence and bliss: the beauty of the island and its people were unmistakable, and their friendly disposition was striking when compared to the savagery of many Pacific island peoples; but they were too friendly for comfort, swarming over the ship, attempting to steal whatever they could, and hostility inevitably followed. Ship and crew were stoned, and the large gun had to be fired to drive off the marauders. The Tahitians' introduction to European power was swift and deadly, and respect was established. When Wallis took possession 'by right of conquest', and hoisted a British pennant near the shore, the Tahitians were seen piling propitiatory offerings around it.

Captain Samuel Wallis's ship, the *Dolphin*, arrives in Tahiti in June 1767, initiating one of the most intriguing clashes of culture in the history of travel.

Thereafter relations became cordial, and a mutual affection sprang up between Wallis and the woman whom he took to be the Tahitian queen, Purea. The captain was not alone in his admiration of the Tahitian women, who seemed to prize the ship's iron nails above all else, and who inspired fierce competition for their favours. Finally Wallis recorded that 'To preserve the ship from being pulled to pieces, I ordered that no man except the wooders and waterers, with their guard, should be permitted to go on shore.' This was clearly not enough to deter the excited seamen, who considered a flogging a price well worth paying for the pleasures offered by the women of Tahiti. Refreshed after five weeks in this enticing but disturbing environment, Wallis decided it was time to press on, leaving Queen Purea and many others weeping for them on the shore.

Wallis's official record of this encounter was published in 1773, but a more informal journal kept by the ship's master, George Robertson, was not published at the time. However, Wallis and his seamen were not immediately responsible for the flowering of the Tahiti myth – that was due more to the work by the French explorer, Louis de Bougainville, which appeared in French and in an English translation before Wallis's work was published. Bougainville was a very different figure from Wallis, or Byron or Anson: an experienced soldier, man of action and a tenacious explorer, he was also something of a scholar and a philosopher, a humorous man and a more consciously graceful writer. Dispatched with two ships to the Pacific to seek new lands for colonisation, this was a well-resourced expedition, with scientists and artists on board to study and interpret what they saw. The naturalist was Philibert Commerson, who took with him a valet named Jean Baret, who happened to be a woman in disguise. When this fact came to light in the course of the voyage, Commerson, a reserved and serious man, was mortified, but the amused Bougainville remarked lightly that if the ship had happened to be wrecked on a desert island, Baret's fate would indeed have been an interesting one.

Bougainville's little fleet dropped anchor off Tahiti in April 1768, just ten months after Wallis had left, but he remained unaware that he had been forestalled in his discovery; he evidently did not find Wallis's pennant, nor did he mention seeing Queen Purea. Instead the ships were boarded by a chief named Ahu-toru, who was apparently curious to see European women, and some instinct attracted him to Commerson's valet, who swiftly escaped in confusion. After this unfortunate beginning, the romantic traffic was all the other way – European men and Tahitian women.

Bougainville remained in Tahiti only for ten days, but the Tahitians evidently made a deep impression on him. The contacts that he and his men had with the people, especially the women, confirmed Wallis's experience, so that back at his desk in France two years later he let loose his imagination as he prepared to write his account of those few days, an account which included this brief but hugely influential passage:

In spite of all our precautions, a young girl came on board, and placed
herself upon the quarter-deck, near one of the hatch-ways, which was
open, in order to give air to those who were heaving at the capstern
below it. The girl carelessly dropt a cloth, which covered her, and
appeared to the eyes of all beholders, such as Venus shewed herself to the
Phrygian shepherd, having, indeed, the essential form of that goddess.

(*A Voyage Round the World*, pp. 218–9)

This was the classic image of Tahitian beauty and innocence, the seed
from which the island myth was to grow. Apparently a brief, sharp,
photographic moment, Bougainville overlays it with such a sense of
natural grace that this young girl overturns centuries of European
moral codes and sexual stereotypes, revealing not simply her body, but
a culture that lived in the state of nobility and dignity that the Ancient
Greeks had enjoyed. Bougainville bestowed on the island the far more
imaginative name of 'Nouvelle Cythère', the island of love, the Greek
island where the goddess Aphrodite was said to have risen from the
sea. In a further classical image, Bougainville wrote that wandering
over Tahiti 'one would think oneself in the Elysian fields'. But it was
not merely a matter of imagery; he quickly perceived the philosophical
implications of what he saw. As Captain Cook expressed it:

Upon the whole these people seem to enjoy liberty in its fullest extent,
every man seems to be the sole judge of his own actions and to know
no punishment but death, and this perhaps is never inflicted but upon
a public enemy.   (*Captain Cook's Journal*, p. 100)

This response was shared by other members of the expedition, like
Commerson, who was evidently a good Rousseauist, and who gave
his own judgement that in Tahiti they had at last discovered

the state of natural man, born essentially good, free from all bias, and
following without suspicion as without remorse, the gentle impulses
of an instinct which is always sure because it has not degenerated into
reason.

(*The Quest and Occupation of Tahiti
during the Years 1772–1776*, pp. 461–6)

So in the strong impression which Tahiti made, there was this curious blend of the sensuous, the thinly disguised sexual excitement, with the philosophical appeal of nature in its glory – nature which in Enlightenment thought was the true revelation of divine rule over the universe. From classical imagery and rational philosophy, Bougainville moves to the final tribute to Tahiti, now voiced in biblical terms:

> I thought I was transported into the garden of Eden; we crossed a turf covered with fine fruit-trees, and intersected by little rivulets, which keep up a pleasant coolness in the air, without any of those inconveniences which humidity occasions. ... We found companies of men and women sitting under the shade of their fruit-trees ... everywhere we found hospitality, ease, innocent joy, and every appearance of happiness amongst them.
>
> (*A Voyage Round the World*, p. 228)

Thus, two and half centuries after Europeans first ventured into the new worlds beyond the oceans, they had at last found a part of the earth not filled with savagery, with hostile people living in hostile surroundings, fit only to be conquered or exploited, clinging to their barbaric gods, but a kind of paradise. It was unquestionably not civilisation, but nor was it something dark and brutal that threatened civilisation; rather it was something that went back before civilisation, before laws, before conflict, before intellect, before guilt. Could these people be the 'noble savages' of the philosophers, the true descendants of mankind before the Fall, and their island cast away in time, the peaceful land sought and described by so many travellers through so many generations? This was the question debated in the salons of Europe over the next two decades, but Bougainville's parting deed was decidedly more down to earth: he claimed possession of the island for France by the slightly underhand means of writing a deed in the King's name and burying it in a bottle at the dead of night when no indigenous people could witness it. He then departed, taking with him Ahu-toru, who lived the life of a celebrity in Paris for two

Bougainville and his officers exultantly take possession for France of a tiny island in the Magellan Strait.

years, before setting out to return to Tahiti; sadly he died during his homeward voyage. Bougainville's account of his adventure was well received, his wit and his graceful writing being everywhere as evident as his skilful seamanship. His wanderings after leaving Tahiti were difficult and dangerous, and the sufferings of the men were extreme, he and his high-born officers being forced to share rats for their dinner. Of one particularly trying period, starving and sick in the equatorial heat off New Guinea, unable to land because of shoal waters or hostile indigenous people, Bougainville wrote: 'There has been much dispute on where hell is, but the simple truth is: we have found it.'

Of all the responses to the Tahiti experience, the most celebrated came from Diderot, who at once foresaw the tragic destruction which Europeans must inevitably bring with them to this island paradise. He wrote in melodramatic terms imploring the navigators of the future to leave Tahiti in peace untouched in its innocence:

Ah, Monsieur de Bougainville, steer your vessel far far away from the shores of these innocent and fortunate Tahitians. They are happy and

you can only bring harm to their happiness ... You took possession
of their country as if it did not belong to them. It is as unjust and
senseless for you to write on your metal plaque, 'This country belongs
to us,' as it would be for a Tahitian to land on our shores and carve
on one of our mountains, 'This country belongs to the inhabitants of
Tahiti' ... At length you sailed away from Tahiti. These good and
simple islanders bade you farewell. Oh that you and your compatriots
and all the other inhabitants of Europe might be engulfed in the
depths of the ocean rather than see them again! As dawn broke and
they saw that you were setting sail, they rushed forward, embraced
you and wept.

Weep, ill-fated Tahitians, weep! But weep for the arrival and not
the departures of these ambitious, corrupt and wicked men. One day
you will know them better. One day they will come with crucifix in
one hand and dagger in the other to cut your throats or to force you
to accept their customs and opinions: one day under their rule you
will be almost as unhappy as they are.

(*Supplément au Voyage de Bougainville*, p. 120)

Diderot of course was absolutely right in his predictions that the
shock to the Tahitians of this encounter was one which their way of
life could not possibly survive. But was the issue as simple and clear-
cut as Bougainville had suggested, or was there a darker side to life
on Tahiti which the Europeans had not yet been made aware of? The
third expedition to Tahiti was under the greatest of all Pacific explorers, James Cook, whose four visits greatly increased the numbers of
eyewitness accounts and intensified the argument. On his first voyage
of 1769, Cook spent three months on Tahiti, far longer than Wallis
and Bougainville combined. The object of the expedition was to search
for the great southern continent and to chart the Pacific. To this end
a group of scientists and naturalists sailed on board the *Endeavour*,
headed by the young, rich and ebullient Joseph Banks, who had partly
financed the whole trip; Cook's job was merely to sail the ship. The
call at Tahiti had the specific purpose of observing the transit of Venus
on 3 June, for which the island's position was ideal.

In spite of the full records that he kept throughout his career, Cook is a difficult man to know. He was highly intelligent, a first-rate navigator and surveyor, a leader who commanded universal respect, but there always remains something hidden about him: there is a sense of reserve, a lack of charisma and idiosyncracies. He was so constantly correct in all that he did that we feel an air almost of infallibility. As a writer he is lucid, observant and informative, yet he conveys a sense of impersonality, in his role as a commander and as a writer. James Boswell, a sharp judge of character, met Cook in London and found him 'a grave, steady man', and his wife 'a decent plump Englishwoman'.

Having anchored and been surrounded by the indigenous people in the usual way, the first cloud in the sun-filled skies of Tahitian warmth and friendship appeared in the form of stealing. The islanders, wrote Cook, were 'prodigious experts' in picking pockets; they simply could not keep their hands off the Europeans, their belongings and their equipment. The Europeans were at first amused, then annoyed, then outraged; again and again hostility would erupt, and peace and friendship had to be restored. In a culture where artefacts, possessions or intricate things simply did not exist, the contents of the *Endeavour* and the complex belongings of its men proved absolutely irresistible. But when a gun was snatched from a marine, things became serious: an officer ordered his men to open fire, and the thief was shot dead, to the shock of both sides. Even the quadrant, without which the transit of Venus could not be observed, was stolen from the special encampment built to house the scientists. Cook was preparing for possible battle, when Banks and a well-disposed Tahitian chief succeeded in cornering the thief and reclaiming the quadrant. The other thing that they noticed fairly quickly was that Tahitian society was certainly not classless, not egalitarian. The chiefs had many servants, whose duties included placing the food in their superiors' mouths; this level of servility should surely have cast a shadow over the island's idyllic image.

But still, in spite of the theft problem, Banks was in ecstasies over the beauty of freedom of life on Tahiti, and especially of its women. 'Such the Grecians were, from whose model the Venus of the Medicis was copied'; their physical beauty 'might even defy the imitation of the chisel of a Phidias or the pencil of an Apelles'; Tahiti was 'the truest picture of an Arcadia of which we were going to be kings that the imagination can form'. This admiration was not only intellectual, for Purea, now referred to as Obarea, had reappeared, and she and her handmaidens became favourites of Banks and the other officers; Parkinson, the artist, thought her 'a fat, bouncing, good-looking dame', and Banks described her as 'about forty, tall and very lusty, her skin white and her eyes full of meaning'. Banks is circumspect about what took place between them, but he spent many nights ashore in the Tahitians' huts and there does not seem to be much doubt that he succumbed, if not to Obarea then to the girls in her entourage. What struck the Europeans perhaps more than anything else was that the Tahitians regarded it as perfectly natural for sex to take place in public. Even the rough sailors found this extraordinary and disconcerting. The most explicit reference to this in Cook's journals came in a passage that later became notorious when published back in England:

> this day closed with an odd Scene at the Gate of the Fort where a young Fellow above 6 feet high lay with a little Girl about 10 or 12 years of age publickly before several of our people and a number of the Natives. What makes me mention this, is because, it appear'd to be done more from Custom than Lewdness, for there were several Women present particularly Obarea and several others of the better sort and these were so far from shewing the least disapprobation that they instructed the girl how she should act her part.
>
> (*The Journals of Captain James Cook*, vol. I, pp. 93–4)

It is noticeable that Cook recorded this scene without any other comment or sign of being shocked. The *Endeavour* experienced exactly the same vanishing-nail problem that Wallis's *Dolphin* had done, and while Cook made no attempt to prevent his men going to the women, he had no hesitation in ordering a flogging when for example one seaman stole a large quantity of nails from the store, thus endangering the ship and its mission. Cook did hint at disapproval of the *arioi*, a class of people who formed a kind of priesthood, but whose chief public function was to organise dances and exotic semi-theatrical entertainments. One of these dances he saw performed by a company of young girls – 'a very indecent dance which they call Timorodee, singing the most indecent songs and using the most indecent actions, in the practise of which they are brought up from the earliest childhood.' He also noted that 'both sexes express the most indecent ideas in conversation without the least emotion, and they delight in such conversations beyond any other.' All the witnesses agree that Cook remained aloof from any close female contact.

The most extraordinary fact about the *arioi* was that their religious function forbade them to reproduce, but since celibacy was evidently impossible they resorted to infanticide, a practice viewed with inexpressible horror by all Europeans. So the evidence that Tahiti had a darker side was mounting steadily: thievery, licentiousness and infanticide. When Cook and the *Endeavour* departed in mid-July, the observation of the transit of Venus completed, he and colleagues took with them a considerable enigma as to the truth about Tahiti. That departure had to be delayed as two seamen deserted during the last night: Cook was told that they 'were gone into the mountains and that they had got each of them a wife and would not return'. Cook's response was ruthless: he took half a dozen chiefs hostage, including Obarea, until the missing men should be found, which they soon were. They were given two dozen lashes and confined below decks until the ship was well out to sea. Cook was besieged by young Tahitians wanting to sail away with him, and he chose a chief named Tupaia with his servant boy. Tupaia was clever, proud and unpopular, while the boy, Tayeto, was the reverse and became a well-loved cabin boy; both died of sickness during the voyage.

The *Endeavour* did not reach England until July 1771, having charted New Zealand and the Eastern coast of Australia but having failed to find the great southern continent. It is not too much to say that Cook's return, and that of Bougainville to France, were the signal for the emergence of a 'Pacific industry' in the intellectual and social life of both countries. Since the 1740s, Rousseau had been expounding the idea of the noble savage, and the dream of the biblical Eden or the classical Arcadia had intrigued the philosophers. Now apparently they had been found, the preconceived idea had become a reality. To European eyes, the most striking impression left by the islanders was that they lived without guilt, and any wrong that they did was soon forgiven; they possessed a child-like innocence that has long been lost from 'civilisation'. Combined with the search for the southern continent, and the political rivalry between England and France, this intellectual problem placed the Pacific high on the cultural agenda. Never before had travel and travel writing been of such deep and popular interest, an interest undoubtedly stimulated by the tantalising stories of sexuality in Tahiti. Banks, with his elite social connections, became a definite celebrity, while Cook played a secondary role.

In its wisdom, the Admiralty handed Cook's journals to an established literary figure, John Hawkesworth, together with the records of Byron, Wallis, Carteret and Banks, to be published jointly as a record of British activity in the Pacific. This book, *An Account of the Voyages undertaken by the order of His Present Majesty...* was published in 1773, and attracted enormous attention, partly because Hawkesworth, encouraged by Banks, tended to play up the picture of the so-called noble savage. Tahiti and the Pacific became topics of popular discussion, but there was an equally strong reaction, especially as Hawkesworth published verbatim Cook's description of sex in public. The moralists were out in force, complaining of 'an attack upon religion and an outrage against decency', while the satirists joined the fray with poems mocking what they saw as a philosophical veil cast over mere sensuality. Hawkesworth died just six months after the book was published in 1773, his memory defended by his friends as a pious and virtuous man, destroyed by this controversy and the malice of his critics. But Parkinson's illustrations in the book had already begun to fix in the public mind an idealised image of Tahiti and the Pacific which would be difficult to alter.

As to the philosophical argument about the noble savage, the jury was still out: was immorality to be dignified as innocence, and applauded? In France the Diderot position was fashionable, but realistically there was no question of halting further voyages of exploration as Diderot had urged: once the quest for knowledge and territory had begun, it was, like all other aspects of progress, unstoppable. In England, more insular and more attached to religion and traditional morality, there were many sceptics, who laughed scornfully at the idea of primitive peoples representing some ideal form of humanity. Further evidence was needed, and it would be provided by Cook's second and third voyages, from 1772 to 1775, and from 1776 to 1778.

During these voyages Cook called at Tahiti three times, each time gathering fresh impressions and noting many changes. On the first of these visits he learned that the island has experienced a civil war and a great deal of bloodshed, the aftermath of which was everywhere to be seen; without ascertaining the causes in detail, this was clearly a fatal blow to the paradise image. Subsequently he was also invited to witness part of a ceremony of human sacrifice. This was not quite what it sounds, for the victim had been swiftly dispatched the previous day, and the ceremony consisted of his burial as an offering to the Tahitians gods. Nevertheless it too was an experience which could not fail to change the European view of island culture. To counterbalance these two shocks, Cook and his men experienced their first contact with cannibalism, not in Tahiti but far away in New Zealand, and

Cook discovered that the Tahitians abhorred the practice. In European eyes, the issue of cannibalism proved to be the final dividing line between civilisation and savagery, and it seemed that the Tahitians fell well on this side of that line. Europeans could scarcely claim that their own culture was free from theft, from sexual immorality, from war, or even – given the thousands of lives extinguished by judicial execution – from human sacrifice; but cannibalism was simply beyond every standard of morality, a crime that condemned the perpetrator as a monster rather than a man. When the men on Cook's ship witnessed a Maori act of cannibalism during the second voyage, there was an islander named Oediddee who had been taken on board, and this is how Cook described his reaction:

> [He] was so struck with horror at the sight that he wept and scolded
> by turns, before this happened he was very intimate with these people
> but now he neither would come near them or suffer them to touch
> him, told them to their faces that they were vile men and that he was
> no longer their friend. (*Journals*, vol. II, p. 293)

So the balance sheet on the Pacific was becoming complicated, and the fact was emerging that there existed profound differences among the Pacific peoples, their appearance, their languages and their way of life. When Cook returned to Tahiti for the last time, he watched pessimistically as the islanders were preparing their war canoes for a great military offensive against the neighbouring island of Moorea. Cook had become harsher after all his years at sea under extreme conditions of deprivation, danger, and the need to maintain discipline; he ordered the ears to be cut off from one persistent thief on the island. Almost his last word on Tahiti was to express his opinion that it would have been better if these people had never known the Europeans. Cook himself does not seem to have expressed an opinion on the 'noble savage' controversy – he was content to leave that to the armchair philosophers and the scribblers.

Ironically the final item on the balance sheet was to be his own violent death at the hands of the people of the Pacific. True, his killers were not Tahitians, they were Hawaiians, but perhaps this was a distinction that was lost on people in England. This was by no means the first fatal clash in the Pacific, but Cook's death was certainly the most famous, and as such it became part of the Pacific Industry, the subject of narratives and reflections, first-hand and second-hand, of many paintings, and even of dramatic stage productions in London, Paris and elsewhere.

The general attitude to the Pacific was swayed by another high-profile public event: the mutiny on HMS *Bounty* which took place in 1789 but whose reverberations continued for many years thereafter. The *Bounty*, captained by the single-minded, irascible William Bligh, spent five months anchored off Tahiti, gathering breadfruit seedlings for transport to the West Indies. This long wait proved fatal to the expedition, for there is no doubt that the luxurious life of Tahiti, in contrast with the fierce discipline on board the *Bounty*, provided the real fuel for the mutiny. The mutineers did indeed return to Tahiti, to the women they had left behind, before dividing into two groups, one deciding to take their chance there on the island, the other escaping to the tiny, remote Pitcairn Island, where they lived out their lives, becoming part of Pacific legend. One of the mutineers who waited on Tahiti was James Morrison, and he was duly taken back to England to be tried. He was pardoned, but during the long period between the mutiny and the trial he composed a thoughtful narrative of the dramatic events, in which he highlights the distinction between the cruel, tyrannical regime of Bligh's *Bounty* and the land of beauty, harmony and plenty which they found on Tahiti. This account was not published at the time but it was submitted during the trial and was instrumental in securing Morrison's pardon. It seems entirely reasonable to believe that if the ship had not spent those long months on Tahiti, the men would not have mutinied. But this was clearly a two-edged argument, for God-fearing disciplinarians in England would say that the men had succumbed to immoral luxury, that they represented an extreme case of what was dismissively termed 'going native' – that is, adopting the same way of life as the indigenous people. The fact that the mutiny occurred in the same year as the French Revolution added to its impact: effectively it was seen as a miniature revolution against civilised English values. Bligh himself returned to Tahiti in 1792, and he was struck by the pace of social change and decline. Whaling ships had begun to call, and had corrupted the population, many of whom were now addicted to drink. Their own culture had proved too fragile to withstand exposure to that of Europe, and their traditional way of life had been fatally damaged.

This sense of disillusion was shared by the great French successor to Bougainville in the Pacific, Jean-François La Perouse. The records which La Perouse made of his great voyage show him to have been a humane and civilised man, and also a brave and determined seaman. His voyage, scientifically equipped and backed by official, royal sanction, lasted three years from 1785 to 1788 and covered a huge expanse of ocean, from Australia and the South Pacific to the seas of China, Japan and Alaska. Wherever he went he observed and wrote with great perception, whether it was of the insufferable boredom of the lives the Spanish colonists lived in Concepción in Chile, the incorrigible thievery of the Easter Island people, the potential paradise that was California, where he saw the mission gardens at Monterey rich with fruits of all kinds, or the desolation of the farthest coasts of Asia at the Sea of Okhotsk; here he saw deer and bears but no people, at least none living, but he did come upon a mysterious tomb which contained two bodies wrapped in bear skins, and surrounded by tools, artefacts and food for their journey into the next world; who knows how long they had lain there in that cold dry air?

In Petropavlosk on the Kamchatka Peninsula, La Perouse was told by the Russians that the climate was so mild that they regarded

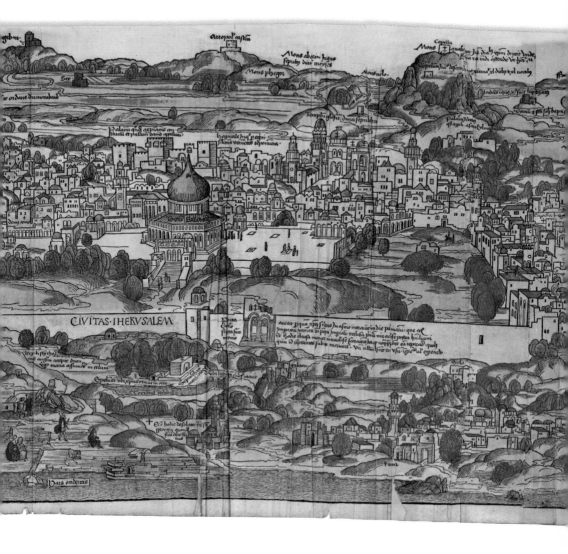

Detail from map view of the Holy Land from Breydenbach's pilgrimage itinerary of 1483. This very accomplished work of art has been weighted to give a dominant place to Jerusalem.

Detail from a map of the Holy Land from the second half of the fourteenth century. This unique map is full of colourful vignettes of the towns and fortresses of Palestine.

(*opposite*, *top*) Marco Polo handing a letter to the Great Khan on his arrival in China, from a French manuscript of the fourteenth century.

(*opposite*, *bottom*) No manuscripts of Ibn Battuta's travels include illustrations, but this lively picture from a fourteenth-century manuscript shows Arab travellers of the Middle Ages.

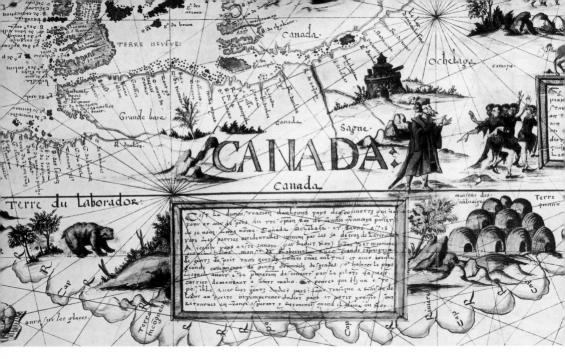

(*above*) Canadian Indians fleeing in fear at their first sight of Jacques Cartier, from the Desceliers world map of 1550. South is at the top, with Newfoundland and the St Lawrence clearly charted.

(*below*) Probably the first depiction of the Amazon, in an anonymous chart of 1548, drawn shortly after news of Orellana's historic first voyage reached Europe.
© Bibliothèque nationale de France.

Utopia: the map of Sir Thomas More's fictitious island. More's book, the first truly intellectual response to the Age of Discovery, describes an imaginary society in the Pacific more rational than any in Europe.

Europeans in their black hats, lower left, at a *durbar* (court) of Sa'dallah Khan,
not long after Sir Thomas Roe's important diplomatic mission in 1615.
From a seventeenth-century album of Indian paintings.

(*opposite*) Sir Robert Sherley, diplomatic traveller to Persia during the reigns of
Queen Elizabeth and King James, portrayed in Persian dress by Van Dyck (1622).
© NTPL/Derrick E. Witty.

La Perouse discussing Pacific exploration with King Louis XVI in 1784, by
Nicolas André Monsiau (1754–1837). © RMN (Château de Versailles)/Gérard Blot.

The Piazzetta, Venice, by Carlevarijs, *c.* 1720: tourists and booksellers
in the foreground, the Marcian Library in the background.
© Ashmolean Museum, University of Oxford.

(*above*) Tischbein's celebrated portrait of Goethe in an Italian setting, 1787.
Goethe's journey of 1786–88 resulted in a deeply felt romantic narrative, which
was published some years later. © U. Edelmann – Städel Museum/ARTOTHEK.

(*opposite, top*) Print of Wood and Dawkins discovering the ruins of Palmyra in
1751. This superb neoclassical painting by Gavin Hamilton, with the two Englishmen
dressed in togas, reminds us that aesthetic travel in the eighteenth century did not
have to end in Southern Italy. Photo © Victoria and Albert Museum, London.

(*opposite, bottom*) Lord Macartney's embassy to China, 1792, by Gillray. Lord
Macartney with his diplomatic mission kneels and cringes before a bored and
contemptuous-looking Chinese Emperor, presenting rather tawdry gifts with their
request for trading concessions, which they failed to obtain. Macartney's mission was
big news in England, but Gillray's cartoon showed what most people felt about it.
© Trustees of the British Museum.

Portrait of Byron in Albanian costume. With *Childe Harold's Pilgrimage*,
Byron created the persona of the romantic wanderer. Replica by Thomas Phillips,
c. 1835 (1813) © National Portrait Gallery, London.

(*above*) An officer of the British East India Company smoking his hookah during an audience with an Indian ruler, *c.* 1760. © Ashmolean Museum, University of Oxford.

(*below*) Colonel James Tod, historian of Rajasthan, hunting in magnificent style on an elephant, *c.* 1820. Photo © V&A Images/Victoria and Albert Museum, London.

Vignettes by Turner illustrating Samuel Rogers's poem *Italy* (1822).
The gift of this book while still a child was one of the formative events of
Ruskin's life, instilling passions for Turner and for Italy.

'Morning in spring with north-east wind, Vevey', watercolour by Ruskin, *c.* 1849. To Ruskin the Alps were the supreme revelation of natural beauty, and the perfect setting for Turner-inspired art. © Ashmolean Museum, University of Oxford.

Petra by David Roberts, from *The Holy Land*, 1842.
The breathtaking rock-cut temples of Petra, discovered by Burckhardt,
became a favourite subject for European artists of the picturesque, of whom
Roberts was the outstanding master. © Trustees of the British Museum.

A scene on Easter Island in 1786, drawn during the visit by La Perouse and his party. This is one of the series of fine charts and pictures sent overland by La Perouse from eastern Siberia to France, before his entire expedition vanished without trace in the Pacific.

this region as the French regarded Provence, which, in the falling September snow, he rather doubted. We get some insight into the loneliness of both the explorers and the European settlers whom they met, for La Perouse and his colleagues had had no contact with France for more than two years when they received a great consignment of mail while they were in Petropavlosk: it arrived while the officers were attending a ball given in their honour by the Russians, and the joyful celebrations continued long into the night. The question now arose of returning their own reports and letters to France: Petropavlosk would soon be isolated for the winter and no ships would call. One of the French party, Barthélemy de Lesseps (a relative of the builder of the Suez Canal) was selected to travel overland to St Petersburg, and his journey turned into a subsidiary epic in its own right. With his precious mailbags, he travelled on horseback, by sledge and by riverboat through the entire breadth of

Siberia, arriving in St Petersburg in 1788 after a full year's journey, his account of which filled a two-volume work.

His surveys of America's Pacific coast convinced La Perouse that the old idea of river passage from the interior of Canada, from the Great Lakes, was merely a myth. He turned his attention to his other commissions, which lay in the South Seas and Australia. But in Samoa he suffered a tragic blow: a party going ashore for fresh water was attacked and twelve men were killed. It is typical of La Perouse that he would not permit the revenge which his colleagues urged him to wreak on the native people, but sailed away, naming the place on the island of Tutuila 'Massacre Bay'. La Perouse had been a pragmatic man before, impatient with armchair intellectuals and their talk of 'noble savages', but this experience embittered him. He wrote that, 'Man when almost savage and in a state of anarchy, is a more evil being than the wolves and tigers of the forests', and he warned that men living in such primitive conditions could never be trusted, however idyllic their surroundings might appear. La Perouse cherished no personal hatred for the islanders, but he believed that they were following savage instincts, and he was scornful of those Europeans who denied those instincts. During his earlier landing in the Hawaian Islands, he had refused to claim possession of Maui, even though he knew that no other Europeans had landed there. He saw his task as scientific exploration and surveying, and he regarded it as ridiculous and immoral to claim ownership of territories where native populations had lived for centuries.

La Perouse made for the eastern coast of Australia, where he had been asked to report on the rumours of a penal colony to be planted there by the British. This he did, and had friendly contacts with Captain Phillips and his men, leaving more mail to be sent back to Europe. The French resisted the covert approaches of British convicts seeking to escape, although one prisoner, who happened to be a Frenchman, was later found to be missing, and may have been quietly smuggled aboard. On 10 March 1788, La Perouse and his two ships sailed out of Botany Bay, bound eventually for Mauritius and Cape Horn, but they were never seen again by European eyes. Over their fate a veil of mystery descended, which was not to be lifted for forty years. Back in France, King Louis XVI became much concerned, and continued to enquire for any news of the men, even in the final days before his execution. Major rescue expeditions searched long and hard without result. Finally in the 1820s evidence was found on one of the Santa Cruz Islands in the Solomons that both La Perouse's ships had been wrecked there, and that all the men had been either drowned or killed by the inhabitants. It was a desperately sad end for a humane and courageous explorer who was in the final stages of his momentous voyage. A large numbers of records and artefacts must have been lost with the ships, but the reports sent from Petropavlosk and Botany Bay were enough to furnish a full account of his travels and his reflections. Ironically, when the faithful Lesseps at last arrived with his mailbags in St Petersburg in September 1788, his former comrades were already dead, and he was, without knowing it, the sole survivor of the expedition.

La Perouse did not visit Tahiti because he felt it had already attracted enough attention. A new and transforming phase in the island's story began in 1797 with the arrival of the first group of Christian missionaries from England. The second wave of reports, the deeper knowledge of the reality of Pacific life, the reports of cannibalism and the death of Europeans at the hands of Maoris and islanders – all this meant that English admiration for a society of noble savages was fading rapidly, in favour of moral intervention. One of the founders of the London Missionary Society launched the campaign with a sermon in which he spoke of 'the innumerable islands which spot the bosom of the Pacific Ocean, where savage nature still feeds on the flesh of its prisoners, appeases its gods with human sacrifices, whole societies of men and women live promiscuously, and murder every infant born among them'. As with the work of Francis Xavier in India, the missionaries had no intellectual interest in the rites and customs of the Pacific islanders except to suppress them and to save their souls.

Twenty-nine missionaries and settlers arrived aboard the ship *Duff* in March 1797, and a comprehensive account of the establishment of the mission was published two years later by William Wilson, who served as first mate of the ship. *A Missionary Voyage to the Southern Pacific Ocean* is, however, a composite work based on the journals and recollections of several of the participants, and does not give a single, personal and consistent point of view. What emerges from it is the very great difference in the approach of the missionaries from that of the earlier visitors, and their overwhelming need to regulate the forms of social and personal contact between Europeans and islanders. Sexual contact of any kind was obviously completely taboo, but so too was commerce, and even friendship was seen as dubious, for the missionaries were very uneasy at the formalised signs of *tayos*, the bond of friendship sealed through the exchange of names, communal meals and gifts of clothing. The identity and integrity of the Europeans were clearly paramount, and their relationship to the islanders must be that of teachers and taught. They were disturbed to find that their role in this respect was in danger of being undermined by the presence of certain other Europeans – beachcombers and other renegades. The worst example of this kind of thing came from among their own ranks, although mercifully not in Tahiti itself but in Tonga.

George Vason had arrived with the *Duff* as one of the group of 'practical' missionaries: he was not an ordained minister but a builder, a bricklayer, who was to assist in educating the islanders in useful arts and crafts, instilling a new order, discipline and practicality into their lives. But instead Vason learned the language of the islanders and went to live with them on their own terms, adopting their dress, drinking *kava*, the local liquor, and taking a wife, a relative of one of the chiefs. He left his former identity behind, merging himself entirely in his adopted environment. Before very long, however, he was caught up in civil strife on the island, and was soon living in fear of his life. He was picked up by a ship, and became a sailor, eventually returning to England and experiencing a spiritual reawakening: he became a respectable Christian again, and was appointed governor of Nottingham jail. His narrative was published in 1810 as coming from his mouth, although it was edited by a local clergyman.

There would be no going back on the missionary enterprise once it had begun, and the official European view of the Pacific Islands would be deeply influenced by it. Looking back in the 1840s, John Sterling, Christian philosopher and friend of Carlyle and Mill, would sum up the rather stern early Victorian view of this subject:

> The missionaries have done a great deal for us in clearing up our notions about savage nations. What an immense deal of harm Captain Cook's *Voyages* did in that way! Sailors, after being a long time at sea, found a fertile island, and a people of lax morals, which were just the things they wanted; and of course there never were such dear, good, kind, amiable people. We know now that they were more detestably licentious than we could have imagined.... There scarcely ever existed such a set of blood-thirsty barbarians.
>
> (*Essays and Tales*, vol. 1, pp. xx–xxi)

It would be hard to conceive of a more scornful epitaph for the idea of the noble savage than that. The great Enlightenment debate concerning innocence and civilisation, which had occupied European thinkers since the first Pacific contacts, was now being dismissed by the robust self-confidence of the Victorians.

The Grand Tour

Pacific travel had taken Europeans into a remote and alien environment, into places of great beauty and perceived great savagery, whose way of life challenged for a time the intellectual and moral laws laid down by their own culture. The other great paradigm of eighteenth-century travel, the Grand Tour of Europe, was in some ways related in its motivation, for it too had knowledge as its avowed object. Yet the reality was vastly different, or at least it became so, for the Grand Tour was largely undertaken not for exploration, geographical or intellectual, but for social pleasure, and for the identification of the traveller as a member of the elite. Ostensibly, the goal of the Grand Tour was to tread upon classical ground, to visit the shrine of Europe's classical past in Italy: the protagonists of Europe's new Augustan age felt they must take inspiration from the soil on which Roman civilisation had flourished. Samuel Johnson put this idea succinctly when he proclaimed:

> A man who has not been in Italy is always conscious of an inferiority, from his not having seen what it is expected a man should see. The grand object of travelling is to see the shores of the Mediterranean. On those shores were the four great empires of the world; the Assyrian, the Persian, the Grecian and the Roman. All our religion, almost all our laws almost all our arts, almost all that sets us above savages, has come to us from the shores of the Mediterranean.
>
> (*Boswell's Life of Johnson*, p. 505)

The Tour was undoubtedly a form of cultural pilgrimage, obviously taking in the classical architecture and sculpture of Rome, but also the second great wave of Italian artistic glory – that of the Renaissance. This would include the paintings of Raphael and Titian, Carracci and Reni, and Palladian and baroque architecture. In this sense the culmination of the pilgrimage probably lay in Florence, in the Tribuna gallery of the Uffizi, which housed the gems of the Medici art collection.

But, as with the earlier, religious forms of pilgrimage, the route and the destinations of the Tour were predetermined and conventionalised; the sights and the experiences became conventionalised, and so too did the responses to them. France, regarded as home to all that was fine in style and manners, was the subsidiary goal, reached by the brief purgatory of a Channel crossing. A month in Paris was followed by another in some provincial city, before Italy was reached, commonly via the Mont Cenis pass. Mountain scenery did not suit eighteenth-century tastes; rather it was an ordeal which formed an essential part of the Grand Tour experience. Florence, Venice, Rome and Naples were the great cities which must be visited, before the homeward journey via Switzerland, Germany and the Netherlands. Occasionally this itinerary would be reversed, making Paris the climax of the Tour. Young aristocrats would be accompanied by tutors to act as both guides and guards, to ensure that they paid due reverence to the classical sites and learned what they were supposed to learn. This was the 'finishing school' theory of the Grand Tour, that it exposed the youthful traveller to the culture and manners of continental Europe, giving him social style and intellectual perspective. It was to make him a citizen of Europe, conscious of his social bond to the elite of foreign nations, but also of his distinction as an Englishman.

Within this rigid framework, the promise of great travel literature would appear to be slight, and there is undoubtedly a sameness about the records of the Grand Tour. The skill of the writer was to ring innumerable variations on a few basic themes, to infuse personal colour, life, adventure or eccentricity into the conventionalised experience. A competitiveness quickly arose among writers as to who could bring back the most colourful stories, the most whimsical, eccentric or bizarre. As a result, the artistic beauties of Florence, Venice and Rome almost invariably came second to stories about the roads, the inns, the local characters and villains, the grand parties, the loose morals, and – if the traveller was of the elite – the life of the European courts which he visited. Thomas Gray, who made the Grand Tour in 1739–41 in the company of Horace Walpole, even wrote a satirical 'Outline for a Book of Travels', which makes it perfectly clear what he thought of the typical literature of the Tour:

CHAP 8: Proceeds to Lyons. Vastness of that city. Can't see the Streets for the houses. how rich it is, & how much it stinks. Poem upon the confluence of the Rhône & the Sâone by a friend of the author's; very pretty!

CHAP 9: Makes a journey into Savoy, & in his way visits the Grand Chartreuse; he is set astride upon a Mule's back & begins to climb up the Mountain. Rocks and Torrents beneath; Pine-trees & Snows above; horrours & terrours on all sides. The Author dies of the Fright ...

CHAP 15: Arrival at Florence. is of opinion, that the Venus of Medicis is a modern performance, & that a very indifferent one, and much inferiour to the K: Charles at Charing-Cross. Account of the City & manners of the inhabitants ...

And here will end the first part of these instructive & entertaining voyages. the Subscribers are to pay 20 Guineas; 19 down, & the remainder upon delivery of the book. NB A few are printed on the softest Royal Brown paper for the use of the Curious.

(*Letters of Thomas Gray*, pp. 52–5)

Gray's lampoon was not published of course, and in fact a great deal of the most evocative and best-remembered writing on the Grand Tour took the form of letters and journals, which did not reach the reading public for decades or even centuries. John Evelyn, James Boswell, William Beckford, Gray and Walpole, Mary Wortley Montagu and Edward Gibbon – all these major figures filled their private pages with images of the Grand Tour, pages which have become literature to us, but which originally formed, if not exactly a 'secret history' of the Grand Tour, then at least an informal, and sometimes subversive, account of it. But these private pages were sometimes known about among the literary elite in England.

A pioneer of the Grand Tour was John Evelyn, one of the many royalists who spent the Civil War and its aftermath travelling on the Continent. Evelyn was an imaginative, precise and evocative recorder of all that he saw, which included some grim scenes of torture in a Paris prison, and a moving account of galley slaves in Marseilles:

The spectacle was to me new and strange, to see so many hundreds of miserably naked persons, their heads being shaved close, and having only high red bonnets, a pair of coarse canvas drawers, their whole backs and legs naked, doubly chained about their middle and legs, in couples, and made fast to their seats, and all commanded in a trice by an imperious and cruel seaman ... there was hardly one but had some occupation, by which, as leisure and calms permitted, they got some little money, insomuch as some of them have, after many years of cruel servitude, been able to purchase their liberty. The rising-forward and falling-back at their oar is a miserable spectacle, and the noise of their chains, with the roaring of the beaten waters, has something of strange and fearful in it ... They are ruled and chastised by strokes on their backs and soles of their feet, on the least disorder, and without the least humanity, yet are they cheerful and full of knavery.

(The Diary of John Evelyn, vol. 1, pp. 124–5)

Yet Evelyn was also capable of a strain of pensive poetry, as when he wandered through Venice:

Hence I passed through the Mercera, one of the most delicious streets in the world for the sweetness of it, and is all the way on both sides tapestried as it were with cloth of gold, rich damasks and other silks, which the shops expose and hang before their houses from the first floor ... to this add the perfumes, apothecaries' shops, and the innumerable cages of nightingales which they keep, that entertain you with their melody from shop to shop, so that shutting your eyes, you would imagine yourself in the country, when indeed you are in the middle of the sea. It is almost as silent as the middle of a field, there being neither rattling of coaches nor trampling of horses.

(pp. 195–6)

It seems to have been a chance accident that made one of these unpublished journals into an influential guidebook. Richard Lassels was a Catholic divine resident in France, who supplemented his income by accompanying wealthy young aristocrats on the Tour; indeed it is Lassels who is credited with coining the phrase 'The Grand Tour'. He died in 1668, but a friend saw through the press his manuscript notes which became *The Voyage of Italy* (1670), which was still being used and admired a hundred years later as one of the best accounts of the curiosities of Italy.

It was a far more celebrated writer than Lassels, Joseph Addison, who did much to establish the status of the Grand Tour. His *Remarks on Several Parts of Italy* (1705) is both a personal response to his travels between 1699 and 1703, and a superior guidebook. Addison's progress through Italy, which included the ascent of Vesuvius and a visit to Capri, is presented overtly as a form of pilgrimage, in the footsteps of the classical Latin poets. The sights he sees constantly recall passages from Ovid and Virgil, while the antiquities of Rome serve to illuminate Seneca, Juvenal and Manilius. In a separately published poem, *A Letter from Italy*, Addison gave rapt expression to his sense of this classical inheritance:

> For wheresoe'er I turn my ravish'd eyes,
> Gay gilded Scenes and shining Prospects rise;
> Poetick Fields encompass me around,
> And still I seem to tread on Classic ground.   (verse 2)

Although he was a sincere Christian, Addison had little admiration for the post-classical Christian culture of Rome and Italy; indeed a strong anti-Catholic sentiment coloured his view of modern Italy, and added an important dimension to his travel writing. In his view, popery and arbitrary power had made the Italy of his day a barren land of backwardness and injustice, in contrast to the far more invigorating life of the Protestant nations of northern Europe, and he even considered the desolate landscape of the *campagna* to be the product of misgovernment. This contrast between the classical golden age and the contemporary decay of Italy was to be immensely influential. It gave an added philosophical and political point to the travels of the young aristocratic tourist, as he was encouraged to meditate on the differing national characters and cultures of the lands he visited; in these meditations, of course, it was expected that the verdict would always come down in favour of England. Addison's approach – the classical footsteps and stern judgement – had all the more impact, coming as it did from one of the acknowledged arbiters of eighteenth-century taste; his travel writing showed learning, judgement and elegance – all qualities supposedly nurtured by the Grand Tour.

What became effectively the definitive guidebook to the Grand Tour was written by Thomas Nugent and published in 1749, with a volume each devoted to France, Italy, Germany and the Netherlands. Almost nothing is known of Nugent except that he was a productive writer in London's Grub Street, with translations of Montesquieu's *The Spirit of the Laws* and Rousseau's *Émile* to his credit. He had a good personal knowledge of Germany and Holland, but there is no evidence that he ever visited France and Italy; indeed he openly acknowledges several other published works as sources of his own; by definition therefore Nugent must have a peripheral place in the history of travel writing. Yet his approach is of great interest because it determinedly occupies the Addisonian high ground. From the remotest times, he argues in his Preface, it has only been through travel that the human understanding improves and culture spreads. It enables one nation, one culture and one form of government to be compared with another, thus contributing to the progress of civilisation. Travel enriches the mind, sharpens the judgement, and forms the character and intellect of a gentleman; it is moral and educational. Nugent's guidebook was filled with a mass of practical information on roads, inns, distances, currencies, and so on, as well as careful lists of what the traveller should see in any particular place. But he evidently regarded this pragmatic kind of writing as serving a higher intellectual purpose: his job was to speed the traveller on his way to the most important destinations, not to re-create his own subtle or dramatic personal experience of travel. His style therefore has little literary showmanship about it. Armed with Nugent's book, anyone could plan their own Grand Tour, and his book therefore represents an important step towards the democratisation of travel.

Voltaire made a Grand Tour in reverse, as it were, recording in his *Lettres Philosophiques* of 1734, his two years' residence in England from 1726 to 1728. The letters discuss various aspects of English life and culture, always to the detriment of their French counterparts. In religion, social freedom, government, science and literature, Voltaire finds the English model superior to the French, a fact which caused the book to be banned and burned when it appeared.

The intellectual and cultural experience was the avowed ideal of travel, but it was seldom or never realised, at least not by English writers. Instead we have the self-conscious style of mock-grandeur in which figures such as Walpole, Gray and Beckford all sought to glamorise their own experiences, to display a sensitivity far above the common ruck, and above the class of people who might be guided by Nugent's book. Walpole — exquisite and waspish — wrote in a high camp style that lightly mocked almost everything that he saw, including the absurd grandeur of the rococo mansions of Paris:

> Yesterday I dined at La Borde's, the great banker of the court. Lord! Madam, how little and poor all your houses in London will look after his! In the first place, you must have a garden half as long as the Mall, and then you must have fourteen windows, each as long as t'other half, looking into it; ... You must have a first and second antechamber, and they must have nothing in them but dirty servants. Next must be the grand cabinet, hung with red damask, in gold frames, and covered with eight large and very bad pictures, that cost four thousand pounds ... I cannot afford them you a farthing cheaper. Under these, to give an air of lightness, must be hung bas-reliefs in marble. Then there must be immense *armoires* of tortoise-shells and *or moulu*, inlaid with medals — and then you may go into the *petit cabinet*, and then into the great *salle*, and the gallery, and the billiard-room, and the eating-room; and all these must be hung with crystal lustres and looking-glasses from top to bottom; and then you must stuff them fuller than

they will hold with granite tables and porphyry urns, and bronzes, and
statues, and vases, and the Lord or the devil knows what...

(*The Letters of Horace Walpole*, vol. 6, p. 374)

The effeminate note in Walpole is strongly in evidence in his descriptions of his Alpine crossing, when he and Gray were carried over the
passes by porters in a form of sedan chair:

> So, as the song says, we are in fair Italy! I wonder we are; for on the
> very highest precipice of Mount Cenis, the devil of discord in the
> similitude of sour wine, had got amongst our Alpine savages, and set
> them a-fighting with Gray and me in the chairs: they rushed him by
> me on a crag, where there was scarce room for a cloven foot. The
> least slip had tumbled us into such a fog, and such an eternity, as we
> should never have found our way out of again. We were eight days
> in coming hither from Lyons; the four last in crossing the Alps. Such
> uncouth rocks, and such uncomely inhabitants! My dear West, I hope
> I shall never see them again! At the foot of Mount Cenis we were
> obliged to quit our chaise, which was taken all to pieces and loaded
> on mules; and we were carried in low arm-chairs on poles, swathed
> in beaver bonnets, beaver gloves, beaver stockings, muffs, and
> bear-skins.   (vol. 1, pp. 40–41)

It was on this crossing that there occurred the much-quoted episode,
where Walpole's little spaniel – 'the prettiest, fattest, dearest creature'
– was seized by a wolf which emerged from the forest and darted
away with him in its jaws. 'It was shocking', lamented Walpole, 'to see
anything one loved run away with to so horrid a death.' Gray's letters
home assumed a similar air of fastidious mockery, although he could
not quite match Walpole's impulsive wit. Thirty years after Walpole,
however, a second Gothic novelist, William Beckford, surpassed even
Walpole in his virtuoso evocations of Italy. This is Beckford on the
Italian passion for the opera:

> their rage for theatrical spectacles ... This passion they seem to inherit
> from the ancient Romans, and the bequest has lost nothing in their

hands. In the fashionable world, the morning is spent in a slovenly dishabille, that prevents their going out, or receiving frequent visits at home. Reading, or work takes up a very small portion of this part of the day; so that it passes away in a yawning sort of nonchalance. People are scarcely wide awake, till about dinner-time. But, a few hours after, the important business of the toilette puts them gently into motion; and, at length, the opera calls them completely into existence. But it must be understood, that the drama, or the music, do not form a principal object of theatrical amusement. Every lady's box is the scene of tea, cards, cavaliers, servants, lap-dogs, abbés, scandal, and assignations; attention to the action of the piece, to the scenes, or even to the actors, male, or female, is but a secondary affair. If there be some actor, or actress, whose merit, or good fortune, happens to demand the universal homage of fashion, there are pauses of silence, and the favourite airs may be heard. But without this cause, or the presence of the sovereign, all is noise, hubbub, and confusion, in an Italian audience. The hour of the theatre, however, with all its mobbing and disturbance, is the happiest part of the day, to every Italian, of whatever station; and the least affluent will sacrifice some portion of his daily bread, rather than not enjoy it.

(*Travel Diaries of William Beckford of Fonthill*, vol. I, p. 252)

In the atmosphere of Italy, Beckford confessed himself transported, aware that the locals must often have thought him distracted. 'I was stalking proudly about like an actor in an ancient Grecian tragedy', he wrote, identifying an important aspect of the Grand Tourist: he *was* indeed an actor, striding across a recognised stage, playing a part, registering sights and emotions, and sending reports back to England which were obliged to echo those of his predecessors. Beckford assembled his impressions into a book, *Dreams, Waking Thoughts and Incidents* (1783), but when his personality and career became mired in scandal, the entire edition was destroyed under pressure from his family, and only a handful of copies now survive. Beckford introduced a note of poetic reverie, and even rapture, into his reminiscences that was quite new, so that he seems to belong to an era of Romantic travel. This is his response to the Coliseum in Verona:

When I paced slowly across it, silence reigned undisturbed amongst
the awful ruins; and nothing moved, save the weeds and grasses
which skirt the walls, and tremble with the faintest breeze ...
Throwing myself upon the grass in the middle of the arena, I enjoyed
the freedom of my situation; and pursued the last tracks of light, as
they faded behind the solitary arches, which rise above the rest. Red
and fatal were the tints of the western sky; the wind blew chill and
hollow, and something more than common seemed to issue from
the withering herbage on the walls. I started up; fled through a dark
arcade, where water falls drop by drop; and arrived, panting, in the
great square before the ruins.   (p. 139)

A Walpole or a Beckford might use all their resources of style
and fantasy to create the persona of a traveller who was sparkling,
theatrical or poetic; but occasionally a traveller would emerge whose
response to Italy and the classical past reached another plane entirely,
and such was Edward Gibbon. Gibbon was always a precocious scholar
with a highly developed sense of his own destiny as a historian, but
he freely acknowledged that it was his own Grand Tour in 1763–65
which brought all his intellectual passions into focus and inspired *The
Decline and Fall of the Roman Empire*. In his memoirs, Gibbon lists
his astonishing preparatory studies made before commencing his Tour,
grinding conscientiously through scores of the most authoritative
works, ancient and modern, on the history, topography and character
of Italy. 'Perhaps I might boast', he remarks complacently, 'that few
travellers more completely armed and instructed have ever followed
the footsteps of Hannibal.' He was brief in his general account of the
Tour, and had no time for social or theatrical distractions, yet his acute
intelligence is always in evidence: having spent some weeks devouring
'the various treasures of art, of learning and luxury' to be found in
Paris, he adds judiciously that

An Englishman may hear without reluctance that in these curious and
costly articles Paris is superior to London, since the opulence of the
French capital arises from the defects of its government and religion.

In the absence of Louis XIV and his successors, the Louvre has been left unfinished: but the millions which have been lavished on the sands of Versailles and the morass of Marli could not be supplied by the legal allowance of a British king.

(Memoirs of my Life, pp. 138–9)

Venice, with its absence of any classical architecture or associations, held few attractions for Gibbon: 'Old and in general ill-built houses, ruined pictures, and stinking ditches dignified with the pompous denomination of Canals'; to him, the spectacle of Venice 'afforded some hours of astonishment' and some days of disgust. Naples was more rewarding, with its ancient remains and its modern decadence; its 'luxurious inhabitants seem to dwell on the confines of paradise and hell-fire', he wrote. But it was 'the miracle of Rome' which had drawn him to Italy, and he was not disappointed:

> I can neither forget nor express the strong emotions which agitated my mind as I first approached and entered the *eternal City*. After a sleepless night I trod with a lofty step the ruins of the Forum; each memorable spot where Romulus *stood*, or Tully spoke, or Caesar fell was at once present to my eye; and several days of intoxication were lost or enjoyed before I could descend to a cool and minute investigation. (p. 146)

And it was here a few days later that he conceived his plan of writing the history of Rome's decline, inspired by the sight of Franciscan friars singing vespers in the former temple of Jupiter. Twenty-three years later he brought his great conception to a triumphant conclusion in what amounted to a history of European civilisation, bridging the ancient and modern worlds. For Gibbon's title was actually a profound paradox: ancient Rome may have fallen to the barbarians, but it rose again as the centre of the spiritual empire of Christianity, to dominate Europe for a further thousand years. The literary memorial which Gibbon erected to his Grand Tour was unlike any other, severe, majestic and impersonal; yet without those emotions which so agitated his mind when he saw Rome, perhaps it would never have been written.

After Gibbon, it would be hard to imagine a more different Grand Tour journal than James Boswell's. Comic, nervous, fast-moving and completely unbuttoned, these journals show the unofficial underside of the Grand Tour, the strutting and social scrambling, the squalor of the inns and the hardship of the roads, and above all the sexual adventures. Boswell was a shamelessly ebullient, self-dramatising, self-promoting character, but he was also a frequent prey to angst and depression, and his travel journals are more personally revealing than those of any other writer. Who else would record receiving the news that his young illegitimate child, born to a serving girl back in Scotland, had died while he was on the Continent? The plain truth is that Boswell, aged 23 when he left England, was a sex tourist whose burning desire, wherever he went from the Netherlands to Southern and Italy and back to Paris, was to lure into bed almost any available woman. He besieged many *grandes dames*, usually without success, and so fell back on dancers, chambermaids and prostitutes, filling his notebooks with the records of the shillings for the *filles charmantes*, the pleasures he received in exchange, and, not infrequently, the subsequent consultations with doctors concerning the visits of 'Signor Gonorrhoea'; over his three-year tour, these encounters ran into hundreds. Museums, art galleries, studies in history and Latin, all were a poor second for Boswell. He was certainly breaking new ground as a Grand Tour writer in setting all this down graphically and honestly, but of course his very honesty made his journals unpublishable; indeed their very existence was unknown until the twentieth century. The writing is colourful, colloquial and non-literary, suggesting that Boswell might have become an outstanding novelist had he turned his talents that way.

Boswell's journey acquired a more respectable and serious weight when he visited Corsica, and became a personal friend of the Corsican patriot Pasquale Paoli, who was fighting for the island's freedom from its Genoese overlords. On his return Boswell published *An Account of Corsica*, and became known as the British expert and spokesman on all things Corsican. The other experience on his Grand Tour of which Boswell certainly made no secret was his meetings with Voltaire and Rousseau, for upon both of these celebrities he had thrust himself with shameless persistence, although without receiving any words of profound wisdom from either. Passing through Paris en route for England, Boswell met Horace Walpole, and later Walpole reported that a 'strange being' with 'a rage for knowing anybody that ever was talked of … forced himself upon me at Paris.' Boswell found Walpole 'a lean, genteel man', but he did not give him his undivided attention, for he was busy pursuing no less a quarry than Thérèse Le Vasseur, Rousseau's long-standing mistress, who happened to be in Paris too. So, within sight of England, Boswell's European odyssey ended in characteristic style, enjoying both the arts of love and a slightly bizarre intimacy with the great and famous; in the eighteenth-century literary world, there was really nobody quite like Boswell.

Whether their passion was art, history, culture, the social whirl or simply sex, all these Grand Tourists had experienced their own form of inspiration during the travels. But there was one visitor who, when he sat down to record his Tour, seemed scarcely able to find enough vitriol in which to dip his pen. Tobias Smollett, an unsuccessful Scots physician and a controversial writer of picaresque novels, published his *Travels Through France and Italy* in 1766, a work so bitter and ferocious that one has to suspect the author's mental balance. Smollett's novels may be compared to Hogarth's pictures, delineating the sordid reality that lay beneath the surface of the Augustan age. The same spirit informs his travel writing, for everything that Smollett saw of the social life and personal character of France and Italy disgusted him, so that he becomes a caricature of the bluff, honest, non-nonsense Briton assailed by degeneracy, corruption and falsehood on every side.

He admits some charms to the landscape of southern France and to the architecture of the Italian cities, but the people and their way of life are universally flayed in his pages:

> [In northern France] The *noblesse* are vain ... They allow their country-houses to go to decay, and their gardens and fields to waste, and reside in dark holes in the upper town of Boulogne, without light, air, or convenience. There they starve within doors, that they may have the wherewithal to purchase fine clothes, and appear dressed once a day in the church, or on the rampart. They have no education, no taste for reading, no housewifery, nor indeed any earthly occupation, but that of dressing their hair, and adorning their bodies. They hate walking, and would never go abroad, if they were not stimulated by the vanity of being seen. I ought to except indeed those who turn devotees, and spend the greatest part of their time with the priest, either at church, or in their own houses ... their religion affords a perpetual comedy. Their high masses, their feasts, their processions, their pilgrimages, confessions, images, tapers, robes, incense, benedictions, spectacles, representations, and innumerable ceremonies, which revolve almost incessantly, furnish a variety of entertainment from one end of the year to the other.
>
> (*Travels through France and Italy*, pp. 31–3)

In Italy, his fury was vented not merely on the Italians but on the English tourists:

> I have seen in different parts of Italy a number of raw boys, whom Britain seemed to have poured forth on purpose to bring her national character into contempt: ignorant, petulant, rash, and profligate, without any knowledge or experience of their own, without any director to improve their understanding or superintend their conduct. One engages in play with an infamous gamester, and is stripped, perhaps, in the first party; another is poxed and pillaged by an antiquated cantatrice; a third is bubbled by a knavish antiquary; and a fourth is laid under contribution by a dealer in pictures. Some turn fiddlers and pretend to compose, but all of them talk familiarly of the arts, and return finished connoisseurs and coxcombs to their own country. (p. 288)

Smollett seems here to be bitterly resisting the accepted eighteenth-century idea of travel as improvement, as a pathway to knowledge, culture or pleasure, fighting against the very notion that foreign countries and peoples have anything to teach us. Interestingly, the book was a popular success, having apparently tapped into a vein of suppressed resentment which many Grand Tourists felt for the countries of Europe whose culture they were supposed to admire. Smollett, with his sour and caustic reaction to all things foreign, found himself caricatured by his fellow novelist Laurence Sterne, in the latter's novel *A Sentimental Journey* of 1768. Sterne declared that the aim of his book was 'to teach us to love the world and our fellow creatures', an ideal put into practice by the amiable fictitious narrator, Parson Yorrick, in a series of sentimental encounters with all manner of men and women. Sterne was the most ambiguous of novelists, and readers have never been able to agree whether his guiding principle was serious or ironic, and whether the book embodies actual reminiscences of his own Tour, which took place in 1765. In this enigmatic fantasy novel, Sterne plays his usual games with truth and fiction, teasing, manipulating and laughing at the reader. *A Sentimental Journey* has somehow become part of the history of travel literature, but we learn nothing at all about France from its pages, and the episodes that he describes evidently took place only in his imagination. Smollett's book, however, seems to have been part of a growing disillusionment with the Grand Tour, a feeling that it was becoming standardised and vulgarised, and that it was time someone told the truth about it.

One record of the Grand Tour deserves special mention because it was undertaken as a very specific quest for knowledge. Sir Charles Burney's *The Present State of Music in France and Italy* (1771) represented the written-up journals of his tour to collect materials for his famous *History of Music*. Burney's motives are very plainly stated: books on the history of music are, he says, such faithful copies of each other that he who reads two or three, has the substance of as many hundred. In hopes, therefore, of stamping on my intended history some marks of originality, or at least of novelty, I determined to allay my thirst of knowledge at the source, and take such draughts in Italy, as England cannot supply. It was there I determined to hear with my *own* ears, and to see with my *own* eyes; and, if possible, to *hear* and *see* nothing but *music*. ... Learned men and books may be more useful as to ancient music, but it is only *living* musicians that can explain what *living music* is.

(*Dr Charles Burney's Continental Travels*, p. xvii)

Unfortunately for Burney, his Tour was rather badly timed: in Italy Corelli, Scarlatti and Vivaldi were all long dead, as were Bach and Telemann in Germany, while the classical school of Haydn and Mozart was not yet born. Therefore Burney's pages are full of names which now mean little to anyone but the specialist. But he was able to gather some fascinating stories which have become invaluable to music historians, including that of the origin of Tartini's 'Devil's Trill' sonata: that Tartini in a dream made a Faustian compact with the Devil, and gave the Devil his violin to find out what manner of musician he was; the famous sonata was Tartini's faint recollection, written on waking, of the superb piece which the Devil played. He gives a wonderful account of the ethereal singing of Allegri's *Miserere*:

This piece, which, for upwards of a hundred and fifty years, has been annually performed in Passion Week at the Pope's chapel, on Wednesday and Good Friday, and which, in appearance, is so simple as to make those, who have only seen it on paper, wonder whence its beauty and effect could arise, owes its reputation more to the manner in which it is performed, than to the composition: the same music is many times repeated to different words, and the singers have, by tradition, certain customs, expressions, and graces of convention, which produce great effects; such as swelling and diminishing the sounds altogether; accelerating or retarding the measure at some particular words ... the candles of the chapel, and the torches of the balustrade, are extinguished, one by one; ... the *Maestro di Cappella* beating time slower and slower, and the singers diminishing or rather *extinguishing* the harmony, by little and little, to a perfect point. (p. 54)

Burney is very revealing on the social context of music, whether on the 'barabarous noise and indecorum' of Italian opera audiences, or the lowly status of musicians at the small royal courts. Frederick II's musical staff in Berlin were treated to the same rigid discipline as his soldiers – they had to produce exactly and only what the king wished to hear; there was no scope for novelty or originality. In consequence music stagnated in these courts; this is one of the most significant pictures that we receive from Burney's work.

But the Grand Tour was not the exclusive province of the English, and the freshest, most thoughtful and captivating of the Tour journals was that of Goethe. Goethe travelled in 1786–88, but his *Italian Journey* was not published until 1816, a lapse of almost thirty years. This gulf of time might lead us to expect that he had rewritten his experiences, but, from the evidence of the surviving manuscripts, this does not appear to have happened to any great extent. In 1812–13 he had been working on his autobiography, *Poetry and Truth*, and it seems that he turned naturally to this record of another phase of his life, and decided to publish it. The writing is sensitive and poetic, while always remaining simple and direct. Goethe writes of his deeply felt need for Italy, its warmth, freedom and beauty, after his years in Germany, especially the closed-in years at the court of Weimar. He apparently escaped Weimar virtually in secret, at night, so that no one could attempt to dissuade him, and travelled with all possible speed south to Munich and the Brenner Pass, where he writes:

Now it grew darker and darker, details merged, the masses became larger and more imposing, but at last, when everything was just moving before me like a mysterious, murky picture, I suddenly saw the high, snowy peaks again, illumined by the moon. Now I wait for the morning to brighten this rocky gorge that hems me in, here on the boundary between south and north ... The fact is that I am taking an interest in the world again, am trying my powers of observation, and testing the extent of my knowledge and scientific training. Is my eye clear, pure, and bright, how much can I grasp in passing, can the creases be eradicated that have formed and fixed themselves in my mind?

(*Italian Journey*, pp. 25–6)

At Lake Garda Goethe sits by the shore with the draft of his tragedy *Iphigenia* and begins to rewrite a new version of it, inspired by the sense of reawakening that now possesses him. His mind and his writing move on several levels at once – personal, aesthetic and intellectual, conveying a sense that everything is open and non-stereotyped, in complete contrast to the normal standard of Grand Tour writing. He achieves what is perhaps the greatest aim of the travel writer, that his personality blends with the world he is describing. When entering Venice for the first time, he suddenly recalls a toy gondola he possessed as a child, and as he steps into the real gondola that now awaits him, he relives his long-forgotten childhood pleasure – an almost Proustian moment. Much of the writing seems to belong to an era later than that of the 1780s, more reflective and personal, without ever descending into self-conscious fine writing:

Unless a person has walked through Rome in the light of the full moon he cannot imagine the beauty of it. All individual details are swallowed up in the great masses of light and shadow, and only the largest, most general images present themselves to the eye. For three days we have been thoroughly enjoying the brightest and most splendid nights. The Coliseum offers a particularly beautiful sight. It is closed at night, a hermit lives there in his tiny little church, and beggars nest in the dilapidated archways. They had laid a fire on the level floor, and a quiet breeze drove the smoke first toward the arena, so that the lower part of the ruins was covered and the huge walls above jutted out over it darkly. We stood at the grating and watched the phenomenon while the moon stood high and clear in the sky. Gradually the smoke drifted through the walls, holes, and openings, looking like fog in the moonlight. It was an exquisite sight. This is how one must see the Pantheon, the Capitol, the forecourts of St.

Peter's and other great streets and squares illuminated. And so the
sun and the moon, just like the human spirit, are quite differently
employed here than in other places, here, where their gaze meets huge
and yet refined masses.   (p. 137)

Goethe would affirm throughout his life that Italy had been for him
a rebirth, the most decisive experience of his creative career, placing
before him new standards of beauty and clarity, and the letters and
journals which lay behind the *Italian Journey* were the first fruits of
this transformation, forming a work which reached out beyond its
own time.

Of course the Grand Tour and the Pacific were not the only subjects
for travel writers of the eighteenth century. One of the earliest women
travellers was the brilliant, mercurial Lady Mary Wortley Montagu,
the outstanding female figure in the men's world of Augustan English
letters. She cannot be claimed as a pioneer of the lone female traveller,
for her journey to Constantinople took place in the company of her
husband, who had been appointed ambassador to the Turkish Court
in 1716, and her stay there was brief, for her charmless husband was
recalled within in a year because of his utter incompetence. The letters
she wrote from Turkey were not published for forty years, but they
were well known among her elite friends, and when they did find their
way into print they caused a considerable sensation, for they glowed
with heartfelt admiration for a non-European, non-Christian civilisation. She pleaded that the Turkish reputation for cruelty and sensuality
was a myth, and that life in Constantinople was more gracious and
free than in European high society. In particular she claimed that
Turkish women were privileged and contented, and that the European
fascination with the seraglio was mere prurience. Against her view,
it must be stated that she moved only in the highest circles of the
Turkish capital, and had little or no contact with any other. She took
delight in contrasting the exotic, sensuous world of the east with the
insular coldness of English life:

The first sofas were covered with cushions and rich carpets, on which sat the ladies, and on the second their slaves behind 'em, but without any distinction of rank by their dress, all being in the state of nature, that is in plain English, stark naked, without any beauty or defect concealed, yet there was not the least wanton smile or immodest gesture amongst 'em. They walked and moved with the same majestic grace which Milton describes of our General Mother. There were many amongst them as exactly proportioned as ever any goddess was drawn by the pencil of Guido or Titian, and most of their skins shiningly white, only adorned by their beautiful hair divided into many tresses hanging on their shoulders, braided either with pearl or riband, perfectly representing the figures of the Graces.

I was here convinced of the truth of a reflection that I had often made, that if 'twas the fashion to go naked the face would be hardly observed.

(p. 97)

Lady Mary would later fall decisively out of love with England and chose to live abroad, writing hundreds of racy letters about her strange and unhappy life, mainly in Italy. Proud, opinionated and highly gifted, she was the female equivalent of Walpole as a painter in letters of eighteenth-century life.

The Grand Tour conventionally ended somewhere near Naples, for Greece and its Turkish overlords then inspired mistrust or even fear. Nevertheless for those sufficiently determined there was no official ban on travel there, and in 1750–51 Robert Wood and James Dawkins undertook a memorable journey through the lands of the Eastern Mediterranean, taking in Asia Minor, Syria, the Holy Land and Egypt. This was a consciously aesthetic tour, whose object was the classical remains to be seen throughout the region. The highlights of the tour were the discoveries of the ruined cities of Palmyra and Balbec, where Wood made many sketches, which he published back in England. Discovery is not strictly accurate here, for these sites had never been entirely lost or forgotten, but Wood certainly placed them definitively before European eyes, and the 'discovery' was immortalised in a fine neoclassical painting by Gavin Hamilton. Wood declared his classical passions when he wrote that the whole object of his travels had been 'to read the Iliad and the Odyssey in those countries where Achilles fought, where Ulysses travelled, and where Homer sang'.

It was in 1774 that London was enthralled by another travel narrative, that of James Bruce and his journey to Abyssinia, in the course of which he claimed to have discovered the source of the Nile – at least of the Blue Nile. Bruce was an eccentric Scots laird, a physical giant of a man with an ego to match. His journey was indeed a remarkable one, for he travelled from the Red Sea coast to reach the exotic and bloodthirsty court at Gondar, from which he returned with some outlandish stories. The most grotesque of these was ridiculed by Horace Walpole in his inimitable style:

> Africa is, indeed, coming into fashion. There is just returned a Mr.
> Bruce, who has lived three years in the court of Abyssinia, and
> breakfasted every morning with the Maids of Honour on live oxen.
> Otaheite and Mr. Banks are quite forgotten; ... Oh yes; we shall have
> negro butchers, and French cooks will be laid aside.
>
> (*The Letters of Horace Walpole*, vol. 9, p. 16)

Bruce had asserted that steaks of beef were cut from live cattle and eaten raw on the spot, a statement which provoked both disgust and disbelief. Poor Bruce became a laughing stock, and found that other episodes in his story, including the discovery of the Nile source itself, were now dismissed as an invention, like the medieval fables in Mandeville. He withdrew in anger from London society and returned to his estate, where he finally published his *Travels to Discover the Source of the Nile* in 1790, in which he attempted to rescue his reputation as a serious explorer and writer. Bruce may undoubtedly have found one of the springs in the Abyssinian highlands from which the Blue Nile arises, but he later travelled downstream to the site where Khartoum would be built, and observed the confluence of his river with the larger White Nile, yet still insisted on his claim. Bruce was perhaps more like a figure from an earlier age of travel, that of Coryate or Lithgow, than a fastidious observer of the Age of Reason.

A very different kind of expedition in the 1790s became the basis of another travel classic – Lord Macartney's embassy to China. China had wrapped itself in seclusion for centuries, and had permitted only limited trade with the west, mainly with the Dutch, while the British had been largely frozen out. Macartney was the most senior diplomat of his era, having previously carried out negotiations with the Russian court and with the Indian princes, and much was expected from his large and well-financed expedition. Yet the journal he kept throughout his six-month visit is filled with frustration at the mystery of the Chinese mind, and the lack of response that he met with. 'The Chinese are such puffs and exaggerators', he wrote, 'and so given to lying where even they have no motive … that everything I give as from them must be received … with prodigious abatements.' They refused to be impressed by the gifts and novelties the British had brought with them, so that the grand project of launching an air balloon to show off western science was abandoned. 'Superstitious and suspicious' was Macartney's verdict on the people, while the state itself was doomed in his view:

> The Empire of China is an old, crazy First rate man-of-war, which
> a fortunate succession of able and vigilant officers has contrived to
> keep afloat for these one hundred and fifty years past, and to overawe
> their neighbours merely by her bulk and appearance, but whenever
> an insufficient man happens to have the command upon deck, adieu
> to the discipline and safety of the ship. She may perhaps not sink
> outright; she may drift some time as a wreck, and will then be dashed
> to pieces on the shore; but she can never be rebuilt on the old bottom.
>
> (*An Embassy to China*, pp. 212–13)

Of course Macartney was writing when he knew his embassy was failing: no trading agreements were reached, and the state of Anglo-

Chinese relations was exactly the same when he left as when he arrived. There was great public interest in his trip, and the feeling that perhaps China might even become another India for Britain, but his pessimistic account of the Chinese as isolationist and inscrutable was to remain the standard one throughout the nineteenth century.

Fictional Travel

It was in the eighteenth century that travel became an important theme in fiction, sometimes in the form of real travel to real places, sometimes as a philosophical idea or device through which the imagination of both writer and reader can be released. Some of the most famous literary works of the age are based on the premiss that travel may reveal some form of truth about humanity, about society or simply about the individual traveller. In Defoe's *Robinson Crusoe* (1719) the narrator is thrown back into a state of nature and of complete isolation, and he proceeds to rebuild a civilisation for himself. Part of the charm of the book lies in the pin-sharp, down-to-earth realism with which Defoe describes Crusoe's life on his island, but there are passages bewailing its terrible loneliness, when Crusoe questions God's plan and purpose in inflicting this ordeal. Both these elements, the harsh realism and the mental anguish, seem to link Crusoe with the tradition of narratives which drew on seafaring hardships and captivity. Crusoe's island could easily be a real island; indeed his story is known to have been based on that of Alexander Selkirk, marooned for five years on Juan Martinez. Defoe's other novels, *Moll Flanders*, *Roxana*, and so on, all use travel to give spice to his narratives, making the equation between foreign travel and adventure, while *Captain Singleton* is a romance of piracy and exploration in Africa and the West Indies, surely drawing on Esquemelin's book as a source. There is absolutely no idealisation in Defoe: abroad may be a place to get rich, a place to suffer, a place of pleasure, or a place to die; in this sense, abroad is indistinguishable from Defoe's England, and to the question of human nature as revealed by foreign cultures, the writer attempts no answers. *Captain Singleton* had such an air of authenticity that apparently it was regarded by some as a genuine narrative of an East–West crossing of Africa.

Swift's *Gulliver's Travels*, published in 1726, uses travel in a very different way, tracing its descent ultimately from More's *Utopia*, but turning its idealism upside down. The islands visited by Lemuel Gulliver exist only in Swift's imagination, and he uses them to construct fantasy versions of eighteenth-century society, ruled by folly, blindness and absurdity. It may be significant that *Gulliver* was written after the bursting of the South Sea Bubble, after it became clear that the image of the Pacific held by English minds was little else but a form of madness. The precise targets of Swift's satire have been much debated but never identified, for *Gulliver* is not an allegory of Swift's England; instead he attacks ignorance, vanity and pride in general; indeed in the final sections of the book he appears to descend into a kind of horror at human nature itself, which is far removed from the light-hearted humour of the earlier sections. It is remarkable that two such books were published within the same few years; that both depended on the current interest for maritime exploration, especially in among the Pacific Islands; that both were destined, in abridged form, to be seen as children's classics; but that both contained depths of meaning which have puzzled readers and scholars for centuries.

A third philosophical travel story was more easily understood by readers in Augustan England, and Samuel Johnson's *Rasselas* now appears a rather quaint period piece. Rasselas, the Prince of Abyssinia, leaves his life of ease and pleasure to travel in search of knowledge, but after surveying human life and society in various places concludes that ideal happiness is unobtainable. Wherever he looks, among rich or poor, kings, serfs or philosophers, there is always some cause for discontent, and a constant desire for something other than what they have. Resignedly, the prince and his companions return home, convinced of the vanity of human desires and ambitions. Calm and reflective in its tone, Rasselas is in a way an anodyne version of a far zanier and more challenging novel, the outrageous *Candide*, which tears both eighteenth-century rationality and the conventions of the travel narrative to pieces. As fate tosses Candide to and fro in Europe, South America or the Near East, chaos and violence engulf him, in the world of nature – the Lisbon earthquake – or in the world of men – the bands of soldiers and pirates who swarm over the face of Europe. Voltaire himself was no great traveller, but, on a lesser scale than Candide, had been harried around several countries in flight from his enemies; he once remarked than if he wished to travel he would open a book and travel in the mind. *Candide* makes a mockery of the central principle of much eighteenth-century travel writing – that the traveller is in control, a superior, rational being, gathering facts and impressions about alien ways of life.

In the world of English narrative realism, it is perhaps surprising that a full-length novel built around the Grand Tour did not emerge from the picaresque school of Fielding, Smollett and company. Their domestic novels depend on movement from place to place within Britain as an essential part of the plot mechanism – travel to named places obviously anchors a narrative within social reality and brings a novel to life. Later, with the Gothic fashion of the 1790s, the theme of danger had moved centre stage in the Gothic novel, where foreign countries, especially those of southern Europe, become the setting for all conceivable manner of wickedness. So, on the evidence of Swift, Johnson and Voltaire, most fiction of the eighteenth century still regarded foreign travel as an intellectual device, rather than as providing realistic settings for a narrative; Defoe's interesting lead in this matter was not widely followed.

The Grand Tour began as an avowed quest for knowledge and for civilised values, based on the equation of Augustan England with ancient Rome, but it became in time more like an extended party, with fresh characters arriving while others were leaving, as though through constantly revolving doors. The great paradox of the Grand Tour was that everything abroad was awful – the manners, the morals, the religion, the food, the roads, the government, the laws, everything – but the Englishman had to see it. Why? As part of his education, to reinforce his Englishness, his sense of superiority over an alien world. For the English the Tour formed strong and stereotyped images of the countries of Europe: the effeminate French; the sturdy peasant Swiss; the avaricious Dutch; the lazy, decadent Italians; the cold, militaristic Germans. There was of course a profound ambiguity in worshipping Italy's past while despising contemporary Italy, but this was explained by the oppression of unjust government and corrupt religion. This also explained why the Grand Tourist could return home laden with Italian works of art, ancient and modern, to beautify his country house, which might well have been rebuilt in the Palladian manner. Likewise the mature travel writer on the Grand Tour had to balance what he saw with what he knew; effectively he had to take possession of the sights he saw, and present them as things of his intellect and his imagination. Sometimes this was done in a defensive mode, in the waspish satire of Walpole or the brutal invective of Smollett; sometimes, but rarely, it was a supremely intellectual response like Gibbon's; in Boswell's case the written record was a secret, personal possession which remained unpublishable for years; but in Beckford's breathless emotion and Goethe's aesthetic serenity, we see two pointers to the future, to the Romantic age when the purpose of foreign travel was not to confirm one's existing identity, but to take one outside it.

FIVE

The Nineteenth Century:
The Theatre of the World

'Like all great travellers,' said Essper, 'I have seen more than I
remember, and remember more than I have seen.'

Benjamin Disraeli (*Vivian Grey*)

Journeys may have secret destinations, of which the traveller is
unaware.

Martin Buber

FOR NINETEENTH-CENTURY Europe, travel became a dimension
through which many of the historic forces of the age expressed themselves. Travel writing could be romantic, scientific, military, aesthetic,
imperial, scholarly, religious, commercial, patriotic, heroic or merely
whimsical. The historic position of Europe vis-à-vis the rest of world
demanded that Europeans travel as part of a vast programme of intellectual reconnaissance and political domination. Nor did one motive
necessarily exclude another. The British in India, for example, had
large commercial and military interests; but individuals sent there for
that purpose might respond by developing scholarly interests in the

country's history and culture, while others would be romantically and artistically inspired by it. Whatever the avowed motive, behind all the major travel texts of the century lay the interaction of the self with the outside world, as the European psyche refined itself, seeking knowledge and power, but also self-understanding, through this deliberately sought encounter with the world.

Romanticism and Travel

In England, the most revolutionary travel text from the early years of the century is an epic poem, which links the old, Augustan world of the Grand Tour with the more passionate form of search that would totally supersede it. Byron's *Childe Harold's Pilgrimage* was the work which made its author the most famous poet in Europe, creating the figure of the Byronic hero, the outcast bearing his burden of pain and loneliness, seeking escape and self-understanding through travel. Written in 1810–11, when France and Italy were inaccessible through war, the first parts of the poem re-create Byron's journey to Portugal and Spain, and then on by sea to Greece and Albania. There had never been a travelogue like this before: colourful, dramatic, emotional, its language heightened to a poetic intensity, and the whole thing permeated by an intoxicating sense of the writer's rebellious individuality. Byron's physical journey had been reshaped in his imagination: it had become a romanticised work of art.

Yet it was also a travelogue in the stricter sense, filled with local colour and reflections on the culture and history of Spain. The bullfight he sees as expressing a spirit of ritualised revenge, while the cruelty of the French occupation, which he witnessed in person, he interprets as a historical retribution for the Spanish decimation of the peoples native to Central America. In Greece, Byron's persistent theme is obviously his bitter sadness at finding the home of classical beauty and learning under Muslim power. Addison's enthusiasm for Italy a century before seems tame compared with Byron's rapture at treading 'the haunted, holy ground' of Greece, the 'vast realm of wonder' that makes his senses ache. He vents his fury on modern British travellers like Lord Elgin for pillaging Greece's classical heritage, stealing 'what Goth and Turk and Time hath spared'. In Albania, remote and little known to westerners, he was equally delighted by reminders of its classical past and the oriental luxury of its present rulers.

Four years passed before Byron resumed work on *Childe Harold* in 1816, having now left England with his reputation tainted and his life in turmoil. He was, as he says, 'half mad ... between metaphysics, mountains, lakes, love unextinguishable, thoughts unutterable', and once again he projects himself in the persona of a Cain-like outcast. With the Napoleonic threat lifted, he was now able to retrace the original route of the Grand Tour, although, omitting France and travelling down the Rhine to the Alps, after devoting much space to the field of Waterloo, now become a magnet for tourists. Byron's famous evocation of the battle itself – 'There was a sound of revelry by night' – is followed by a long meditation on Napoleon's nemesis, the poet clearly seeing himself as a mirror image of the fallen emperor, his ambition and his past glories now shattered. Some of the most novel passages of *Childe Harold* come in Byron's response to the Alps, in whose majestic power, especially at night or in storms, he finds a reflection of his longing to escape from the corrupt world of men into a more intense form of existence. This is archetypal romantic nature poetry, offering a paradigm for all future travel writers.

In the Italian section of the poem, the range of cultural reference is very wide – writers, artists, the history of Rome – and throughout Byron is clear that what he finds in Italy is memory, both personal and collective: as he travels he is not merely walking through cities and landscapes, but is lost among images and ideas he already possessed. Even for the arch romantic rebel and outcast, the centrality of classical learning is still absolute. Between the cultural meditations, he returns repeatedly to the beauties of nature, as if the whole poem is a meditation on the conflict between the violence and transience of human history, and the pull towards the deeper life of the mind and the imagination. While travelling through the real landscapes of Europe, *Childe Harold* is essentially a psychological epic. The poem ends in Rome, reminding us that it is entitled a pilgrimage rather than a grand tour; but a pilgrimage to what? Not to conventional religious faith, but to the self, and to a new conception of the self as travelling through and seizing new worlds of experience, in which nature is as important as the study of mankind:

> There is a pleasure in the pathless woods,
> There is a rapture on the lonely shore,
> There is society where none intrudes,
> By the deep Sea, and music in its roar:
>   ... I steal
> From all I may be, or have been before,
> To mingle with the Universe, and feel
> What I can ne'er express, yet can not all conceal.
>
>   (Canto IV, verse 178)

Of course Byron was not the first writer to pay homage to mountain scenery, for this had already become a cliché among the Gothic novelists. In works like Ann Radcliffe's *The Mysteries of Udolpho* (1794) full use is made of atmospheric landscapes: mountains, gorges, forests, waterfalls – all serve to create the settings in which the characters are solitary, tragic, helpless or threatened. Radcliffe exploited the same scenery in her account of her travels through Germany in the 1790s, especially in her descriptions of her Rhine journey. But her style, though effective enough, is picturesque; there are constant evocations of 'the romantic' and 'the tremendous' – 'the fiery sunset', 'the roaring chasm', 'the fading gleam', and so on. This is external, these are staged scenes, passages of fine writing rooted in the eighteenth-century cult of the sublime. Byron's merging of the self with the landscape, his heart-on-sleeve histrionics, are things of a different order, still rhetorical no doubt, but they have what the Gothic novelists lacked, namely passion. For all Byron's easily mocked effusions in *Childe Harold*, they were not easily copied. Samuel Rogers, a competent and highly popular poet, also travelled in the post-Waterloo years, and published in 1822 his own long poem, *Italy*. Part travelogue, part collection of melodramatic Italian stories, Rogers's verse is mildly readable, but beside Byron it feels quaint and passionless. His book is remembered now for the charming vignette illustrations by Turner.

Byron's experience of travel in the eastern Mediterranean gave him the material and the inspiration for his exotic verse tales *The Giaour*, *The Corsair, the Bride of Abydos*, and so on, but he eventually tired of this play-acting. The final work of his life was another travel epic, *Don Juan*, but a work of a very different kind, in which the vision shifts from the heroic to the comic. The innocent young Don Juan is fortune's plaything, tossed around from Spain to Greece, Turkey, Russia and England; he is seduced, shipwrecked, enslaved, embattled or lionised. This is a picaresque novel in verse, owing something to *Candide*, portraying all the ideals and conventions of European society as a veneer covering a pantomime of folly, intrigue, lust and absurdity, but the tone is kept light and farcical; if Fielding had placed a novel in a European setting, it would surely have been rather like *Don Juan*. Had Byron lived, *Don Juan* would certainly have been much longer, visiting more countries, including those beyond Europe. Byron's own life on the Continent, as revealed in his letters, was almost as colourful as Don Juan's, and he used his new epic to express his characteristic philosophy that the great object in life is 'to feel that we exist': the three experiences that he believed gave life's richest rewards were gambling, battle and travel. By the time he arrived at this definition he had clearly outgrown the youthful romanticism of *Childe Harold* and had constructed a more suave, cynical, man-of-the-world persona.

Even if he had not started it, he had certainly fuelled the romantic revolution, then apparently turned his back on it.

Byron used travel as a poetic strategy, a symbolic escape from the restrictions of traditional poetry and the restrictions of English life. Shelley was another renegade aristocrat, who spent much time with Byron in Italy and elsewhere. In *Julian and Maddalo*, he penned an atmospheric portrait of the two poets riding at sunset along the shoreline opposite Venice. To Shelley, Italy was the 'paradise of exiles', and in his preface to *Prometheus Unbound* he wrote passionately:

> This Poem was chiefly written upon the mountainous ruins of
> the Baths of Caracalla, among the flowery glades, and thickets of
> odoriferous blossoming trees, which are extended in ever winding
> labyrinths upon its immense platforms and dizzy arches suspended in
> the air. The bright blue sky of Rome, and the effect of the vigorous
> awakening spring in that divinest climate, and the new life with which
> it drenches the spirits even to intoxication, were the inspiration of this
> drama.   (p. 6)

By the time we come to the Swinburne of the 1850s, the noble, classical south, admired and worshipped by Addison and Gibbon a century earlier, has been replaced by an uninhibited pagan south, where Italy and Greece are places of passion, bringing intoxicating and very un-English images of freedom and abandonment. The history of the poetic imagination is not the same thing as the history of travel literature; but poets obviously influence how we approach and perceive the world. Byron's Alpine romanticism extended and deepened the kind of writing that Ann Radcliffe had popularised – the rapturous word-painting on the beauties of nature. Thackeray called this 'letterpress landscape', and noted that it had become an expected feature of fictional and non-fictional travel writing.

One of the founders of European romanticism, Chateaubriand, had already introduced this style to French readers in both fictional and non-fictional form. His short novel *Atala* is a Rousseauesque tale of love and tragedy set in the wilds of America; the author had gathered his local colour during his journey in 1791 to the region of the Great Lakes and the Mississippi, which he evoked in several autobiographical writings:

> During my travels among the Indians of America, I left behind me the dwellings of the Europeans and found myself for the first time alone in the midst of the ocean of the forests. In the species of delight which seized me I forsook all paths, wandering from tree to tree, saying to myself, 'Here there are no more paths to follow, no more cities, no more confining houses, no presidents, republics or kings, and above all no laws and no men...'
>
> Who shall describe what one feels as one penetrates into these forests that are as old as the world! They alone give an idea of Creation, as it issued from the hand of God. The light, coming from above, slanting through a veil of foliage, spreads through the interior of the forest a changing and shifting twilight.... Soon the forest grows dark again, the eye can discern only the trunks of oaks and walnut trees in close array; the further off they are, the closer they appear to draw together. I am confronted with the notion of endlessness.
>
> (*Chateaubriand's America*, p. 32)

All Chateaubriand's experiences in the American wilderness take him further from his civilised background, and deeper into a new sense of himself: the storms, the nights in which silence follows silence, the gloom of the forests, moonlight and clouds, the roar of rivers – all these make the solitary traveller a stranger to himself. He broods over a grief that is causeless and nameless, and cannot recognise his former self. Chateaubriand is credited with first articulating the *mal du siècle*, the romantic melancholy which would become so typical of the nineteenth century. But he was very unusual in being a Christian romantic, because, he believed, man's desire for the infinite is absolute, and only religion can satisfy that desire; his was an aesthetic religion, discovered not in the churches of France but in the forests and wilderness of foreign places.

'Letterpress landscape' is perhaps too scornful a term for any and every piece of impassioned nature writing. Proof of this comes from a slightly unexpected source, from John Ruskin, stern Victorian critic and moral teacher. At the age of 12 he was given a copy of Samuel Rogers's *Italy*, with the illustrations by Turner, which, he said, fixed 'the entire direction of my life's energies'. Only two years later he was en route through Europe with his family, and this is the older Ruskin recalling his first glimpse of the Alps from a garden in Schaffhausen:

> There was no thought in any of us for a moment of their being clouds. They were clear as crystal, sharp on the pure horizon sky, and already tinged with rose by the sinking sun. Infinitely beyond all that we had ever thought or dreamed, – the seen walls of lost Eden could not have been more beautiful to us; not more awful, round heaven, the walls of sacred Death.
>
> It is not possible to imagine in any time of the world, a more blessed entrance into life, for a child of such a temperament as mine. True, the temperament belonged to the age: a very few years, – within the hundred, – before that, no child could have been born to care for mountains, or for the men that lived among them, in that way. Till Rousseau's time there had been no 'sentimental' love of nature; and till Scott's no such apprehensive love of 'all sorts and conditions of men,' not in the soul merely, but in the flesh. ... But for me, the Alps and their people were alike beautiful in their snow, and their humanity; and I wanted, neither for them nor myself, sight of any thrones in heaven but the rocks, or of any of spirits in heaven but the clouds.... I went down that evening from the garden-terrace of Schaffhausen with my destiny fixed in all of it that was to be sacred and useful.

> (*Praeterita*, pp. 103–4)

Of all nineteenth-century prose writers, Ruskin was perhaps to be the most influential in linking aesthetics with morality, and these inspirational qualities of nature could also be found, if rarely, in certain man-made landscapes, ideally in the Italian cities. We do not perhaps think of Ruskin as a travel writer, but much of his aesthetic and moral thought would have been impossible without the lessons he learned from Switzerland and Italy. In his great work *Modern Painters*, he attempted to make seeing into a spiritual and not merely a physical act, while *The Stones of Venice* is an extended prose-poem on an idealised past. To Ruskin, Venice was a many-layered palimpsest of medieval, Renaissance and Baroque art and history. To look and to see as a tourist is not enough, one has to understand and reconstruct in imagination what went into the creation of that city and its art in all its various phases: what were the moral and political ideals, what were the social structures the artist was called upon to serve? Out of this exercise Ruskin evolved his creed of selfless craftsmanship, of medieval art as a sacramental activity, based on wholeness of life, before it became, with the Renaissance, perverted by commerce. Whatever we may now think of this thesis, it became a creed which deeply influenced nineteenth-century art and thought, and it demonstrates a response to Venice as profound as that of Gibbon to Rome:

> Thank God I am here! It is the Paradise of cities and there is a moon enough to make half the sanities of earth lunatic, striking its pure flashes of light against the grey water before the window; and I am happier than I have been these five years ... I feel fresh and young when my foot is on these pavements.
>
> (*The Diaries of John Ruskin*, vol. 1, p. 183)

This kind of response, whether to paintings, to the Alps or to cities, he succeeded in conveying to others through his writing; Charlotte Brontë said of one of his books, 'I feel now as if I had been walking blindfold: the book seems to give me eyes.' Could any travel writer ask for more heartfelt praise? Ruskin was the archetypal creator of the purple-prose descriptive style, with his immensely long sentences, full of imagery and alliteration, that seem to rise up like fountains, and cascade through the mind. Still immensely impressive in short bursts, it is a language that, for the modern reader, usually ends by losing touch with reality.

South America: The Scientific Motive

Yet Ruskin was not only an aesthetic traveller, he was a scientific one. To him, geology, crystallography, botany and meteorology were all the studies of nature's various forms, all revealing incomparable beauties of pattern, and all essential to the artist. Ruskin may have remained essentially an amateur in these fields, but serious professional science as a motive had entered the realm of travel at the beginning of the century, with the great Alexander von Humboldt. Humboldt's intellect was formed on the cusp of Enlightenment rationalism and romanticism: he believed in Nature with a capital N, not as a cold inert mechanism, but rather as a living force which mankind could approach and comprehend on the plane of aesthetics. He longed for an unexplored virgin land in which to test this philosophy, and he found it in South America, spending five years from 1799 to 1804 exploring and recording the geography and life-forms of Venezuela, Colombia, Ecuador, Peru and Mexico, accompanied by the French botanist Aimé Bonpland. These regions had been Spanish colonies for almost three centuries, virtually sealed from the eyes of any other Europeans, and von Humboldt had received a unique dispensation from the Spanish Crown to enter and explore them. On his return to Europe he spent almost three decades writing up his vast store of scientific notes and journals, and adding a more informal *Personal Narrative* of his travels.

The catalogue of Humboldt's achievements in a dozen different fields of sciences is truly impressive: he found and mapped the Casiquiare channel, which links the Orinoco basin with that of the Amazon; he discovered and dissected electric eels; he devised the technique of isobars to map places of equal temperature, rainfall, humidity and so on; he brought back to Europe the first samples of curare poison and guano; he correctly analysed the cool ocean current (later named after him) which made the coast of Peru an arid desert, while further north the coast of Ecuador was clad in steamy jungle; he calculated the decrease in the earth's magnetic force from the pole to the equator; he climbed the great Andean mountain Chimborazo to within a thousand feet of its summit; he conceived the plan of cutting a channel between the Atlantic and the Pacific, where the Panama Canal would eventually be built; he had the first precise drawings made of ancient American antiquities, including the Aztec Calendar or Sunstone; and he collected thousands of specimens of flora and fauna, rocks and minerals. His characteristic concern was to relate different phenomena, to find connections between life-forms, climate, geology, terrain, water distribution, and so on, and in this sense he virtually founded the science of ecology. The effect of his travels and his writing was twofold: it was to place South America on the scientific map of the world, but also it was to initiate a new form of scientific travel. He and Bonpland were not conquering, trading or evangelising; they were observing, measuring and analysing. This was a new form of travel discourse, although arguably they were still taking possession of the land in a subtle, intellectual way; they were integrating South America within the European models of earth and life sciences.

The *Personal Narrative* complements the scientific achievement by showing us the human face of the two explorers. When they were not collecting specimens or recording scientific data, they were – despite the torments of heat, insect bites and a sometimes nauseating diet – enjoying themselves; they were revelling in this treasure house of nature, and in their position as the first men of science to explore it. Humboldt once described himself as 'a man spellbound, insect-fashion, to the earth and the endless variety of natural phenomena', and in his narrative he shows himself fully alive to the poetry and drama of nature. Shortly after observing an eclipse at Cumuna, he experienced his first earthquake:

> On the 4th of November, about two in the afternoon, large clouds of
> peculiar blackness enveloped the high mountains of the Brigantine
> and the Tataraqual. They extended by degrees as far as the zenith.
> About four in the afternoon thunder was heard over our heads, at an

immense height, not regularly rolling, but with a hollow and often interrupted sound. At the moment of the strongest electric explosion ... there were two shocks of earthquake, which followed each other at the interval of fifteen seconds. The people ran into the streets, uttering loud cries. M. Bonpland, who was leaning over a table examining plants, was almost thrown on the floor. I felt the shock very strongly, though I was lying in a hammock. ... Slaves, who were drawing water from a well more than eighteen or twenty feet deep, near the river Manzanares, heard a noise like the explosion of a strong charge of gunpowder. The noise seemed to come from the bottom of the well...

The sunset presented a picture of extraordinary magnificence. The thick veil of clouds was rent asunder, as in shreds, quite near the horizon; the sun appeared at 12 degrees of altitude on a sky of indigo-blue. Its disk was enormously enlarged, distorted, and undulated toward the edges. The clouds were gilded; and fascicles of divergent rays, reflecting the most brilliant rainbow hues, extended over the heavens. A great crowd of people assembled in the public square. This celestial phenomenon – the earthquake – the thunder which accompanied it – the red vapour seen during so many days, all were regarded as the effect of the eclipse. ...

When the shock of an earthquake is felt, when the earth which we had deemed so stable is shaken on its old foundations, one instant suffices to destroy long-fixed illusions. It is like awakening from a dream; but a painful awakening ... we mistrust for the first time the soil we have so long trod with confidence.

(*Personal Narrative*, pp. 347–9)

Humboldt's prestige and influence were immense, and all those working in the earth and life sciences realised that travel and field work must form the basis for any advances in data collection and conceptual theory. Among those inspired by Humboldt's example was Charles Darwin, whose voyage around the world on HMS *Beagle* was as important for mankind's intellectual history as that of Columbus had been for man's political history. Even before he received the offer to become naturalist on the *Beagle*, Darwin's head was filled with dreams of following Humboldt across the ocean to South America:

in the morning I go and gaze at Palm trees in the hot-house and come
home and read Humboldt: my enthusiasm is so great that I can not
hardly sit still on my chair ... I never will be easy till I see the peak
of Teneriffe and the great Dragon tree.

(Letter to Caroline Darwin, 28 April 1831)

We have in truth the world before us. Think of the Andes; the
luxuriant forest of the Guayaquil; the islands of the South Sea
and New South Wales. How many magnificent and characteristic
views, how many and curious tribes of men we shall see, what fine
opportunities for geology and for studying the infinite host of living
beings; is this not a prospect to keep up the most flagging spirit?

(Letter to Catherine Darwin, 22 May 1833)

Like Humboldt, Darwin published his official scientific reports,
his detailed results in the field of geology and natural history, but like
his master Darwin also wrote his own more informal account, which
became known as *A Naturalist's Voyage Around the World*, telling
the human story of this remarkable journey. What emerge from this
account are Darwin's acute power of observation and his outstanding
gifts as a writer: he is able to weave masses of detailed factual information into a narrative style that always remains richly textured and
engaging. The ultimate outcome of his voyage on the *Beagle* was of
course *On the Origin of Species*, but had he never written that uniquely
important work, Darwin would still be remembered as a notable travel
writer. His primary focus is obviously on his observations of nature,
but what intrigues us most of all is Darwin's attention to human subjects, and his very perceptive sketches of the people he encountered on
his journey, aboard the *Beagle* and among the indigenous populations.
Standing out from among the first group are the three inhabitants
of Tierra del Fuego whom the ship's captain, Robert Fitzroy, had
previously taken back to England to be educated at his own expense,
and was now planning to repatriate. There was 'York Minster', a big,
powerful, surly man, whom Darwin sensed to be untrustworthy. He

was clearly jealous of any attentions paid to the young girl named 'Fuegia Basket', and he had clearly determined to marry her as soon as they were back at home; she was 'a nice, modest, reserved young girl, with a rather pleasing but sometimes sullen expression, and very quick at learning anything, especially languages'. The favourite of the three was 'Jemmy Button', a short, fat young man, who delighted in dressing as a dandy. He was popular with all, cooperative and kind-hearted, and he would comfort Darwin during the latter's bouts of chronic seasickness, murmuring at his bedside, 'Poor, poor fellow.'

Like many visitors to Tierra del Fuego, Darwin mused on the life of the Fuegians in this desolate land:

> Whence have they come? What could have tempted, or what change compelled a tribe of men to leave the fine regions of the north, to travel down the Cordillera or backbone of America ... and then to enter on one of the most inhospitable countries within the limits of the globe? There is no reason to believe that the Fuegians decrease in number; therefore we must suppose that they enjoy a sufficient share of happiness, of whatever kind it may be, to render life worth having. Nature, by making habit omnipotent, and its effects hereditary, has fitted the Fuegian to the climate and the productions of his miserable country.
>
> (*Voyage of HMS Beagle Round the World*, vol. 1, p. 278)

Darwin evidently conceived a certain affection for them, finding that they had a sense of humour, and a few strange skills:

> After we had presented them with some scarlet cloth, which they immediately tied round their necks, they became good friends. This was shown by the old man patting our breasts, and making a chuckling kind of noise, as people do when feeding chickens. I walked with the old man, and this demonstration of friendship was repeated several times; it was concluded by three hard slaps, which were given me on the breast and back at the same time. He then bared his bosom for me to return the compliment, which being done he seemed highly pleased. The language of these people, according to our notions, scarcely deserves to be called articulate ... with so many hoarse, guttural, and clicking sounds.

They are excellent mimics: as often as we coughed or yawned, or made any odd motion, they immediately imitated us.... They could repeat with perfect correctness each word in any sentence we addressed them, and they remembered such words for some time. Yet we Europeans all know how difficult it is to distinguish apart the sounds in a foreign language. Which of us, for instance, could follow an American Indian through a sentence of more than three words?

(vol. 1, pp. 264–5)

In his mind, the bare existence of these people, possessing virtually no traces of civilisation in their bleak land, contrasted strongly with the lives of the mounted herdsmen of the pampas, the Gauchos, with whom Darwin spent much time while Fitzroy was surveying aboard the *Beagle*. Although a poor sailor, Darwin was a fine horseman who relished his time with these men, whom he found proud, self-reliant, almost heroic in their elemental contact with nature. They seemed to him to transcend civilisation, unlike the Fuegians who stood outside it.

But perhaps Darwin's most powerful impression of the people of South America was recorded when he left Brazil:

I thank God I shall never again visit a slave-country. To this day, if I hear a distant scream, it recalls with painful vividness my feelings, when, passing a house near Pernambuco, I heard the most pitiable moans, and could not but suspect that some poor slave was being tortured, yet I knew that I was as powerless as a child even to remonstrate.... Near Rio de Janeiro I lived opposite to an old lady who kept screws to crush the fingers of her female slaves ... I have seen a little boy, six or seven years old, struck thrice with a horsewhip (before I could interfere) on his naked head for having handed me a glass of water not quite clean; I saw his father tremble at a mere glance from his master's eye.   (vol. 2, pp. 302–3)

Darwin, it seems, was as sensitive in observing his fellow men as he was in observing nature, and he could evidently have become an outstanding pioneer anthropologist. He was fascinated by the diversity of human societies, as with biological forms, and he realised that they too were the results of complex processes of development, which were then little understood. Thanks to Humboldt and Darwin, the scientist became a familiar figure in travel literature: the geologist, the botanist, the ornithologist and the lepidopterist criss-crossed Asia, Africa and the Americas, writing up his field-journals, from which a personal narrative would later emerge. Scientific travel and description became a principal medium through which the nineteenth-century mind mapped – both figuratively and literally – environments beyond Europe, building their results into a world-picture whose elements were comprehensively described, named and understood.

North America: Taming the Wilderness

The natural panorama of South America was explored and analysed by scientists from Europe, the Spanish colonists lacking any intellectual or political motivation to begin the process. In North America, however, the process of opening the continent west of the Mississippi took an entirely different course, beginning with the celebrated expedition led by Lewis and Clark from 1804 to 1806, which first penetrated the Rockies and reached the Pacific coast. The background to this expedition is well known: in 1803 the American government bought from France the vast region then known as Louisiana, doubling at a stroke the size of the United States. Washington was well aware of the activities of Canadian-British fur traders in the Northwest, while California, Arizona, New Mexico and Nevada were still Spanish-Mexican territories. The Oregon coast therefore became the vital western maritime outlet of the newly enlarged United States, and it became imperative that the immense region from the Mississippi to Oregon be explored, mapped, described and appropriated; this was the purpose of the Lewis and Clark expedition. This was not simply an exploratory journey, it was a historical landmark, marking a turning point in the identity of the United States. It was the essential prelude to the huge migration to the West, to the process which would eventually make the United States synonymous with the North American continent from the Atlantic to the Pacific and from latitude 30° north to the Canadian border. Likewise the reports which came out of the journey are not merely travel narratives: they are the birth certificate of the modern United States.

Lewis and Clark's famous commission from President Jefferson, the charter of their expedition, opened by stating the aim of finding a waterway which would cross the entire continent 'for the purposes of commerce', an ambition that went back to Cartier and the sixteenth century. But Jefferson added important clauses requiring a scientific record to be compiled, describing exactly all that was seen and noted on the journey. Most important was the clause urging that good relations must be established with any native peoples whom they might encounter, assuring them of the Americans' wish for peaceful trade with them.

This last point suggests a considerable enigma at the heart of the Jefferson–Lewis–Clark enterprise: was this vast land empty or not? The United States had bought it from France, but what right did France have to sell it? The word 'frontier' normally meant the line between two nations or two entities, but as the concept of the frontier was to develop in America, it had to be altered to mean the line dividing civilisation from its opposite, from emptiness, wilderness and savagery. But how could these frontier lands be empty, when they were inhabited by several hundred thousand people? We are back with the problem of the Spanish and the Indians of Central America, for the only possible answer is that they were not seen as people; instead they were incidental features of the landscape – important in some ways, puzzling and problematic, but ultimately subservient to a grander scheme of history that was being imposed upon them.

As one would expect, the text of the Lewis and Clark expedition is a full and detailed account of the journey, a remarkable testimony to the courage and tenacity of the two leaders and their party of forty or so, mainly soldiers. They covered something approaching 8,000 miles, mostly through unknown territory, starting from St Louis, ascending the Missouri, crossing the Rockies in the Bitteroot Range, and descending the Columbia river to the coast, to return by almost exactly the same route. Journals were kept by Lewis and Clark in a collaborative effort, and were edited into an official two-volume memoir that appeared in 1814. This was the only form in which the records were known throughout the nineteenth century, but the much longer original journals are now available and run to a dozen volumes. Although this is a human story, it obviously had other and larger dimensions, and the text reflects them. They suffered only two fatalities, but there were innumerable near misses with grisly bears, difficulties with canoes, encounters with American Indians, friendly and unfriendly, discoveries of magnificent mountain passes and waterfalls. But the journals, always full of incident and inter-est, are neither personal records nor literary texts: this was an army expedition (the official title of the party was the Corps of Discovery) and military discipline was maintained throughout; it was an official expedition, to be reported in a way that satisfied the political motives behind it; and it was a scientific expedition, aimed at building a profile of this untravelled region, through maps and records of landscape, climate, flora and fauna. This official agenda does not overwhelm the narrative, but it is hard not to see the military and scientific mentality as a form of appropriation, as bringing these wild, unexplored regions within the realm of civilised knowledge and control, as now part of America. Nevertheless the journal-writers do occasionally respond to the landscape in aesthetic terms, to the beauty of the scenery and the abundance of wildlife, and part of the rhetoric of this response is the sense that this landscape is being seen for the first time because these are the first sightings by white, civilised men. The implication of this response is that this was virgin land, now for the first time offered by God or by nature to mankind.

On the purely human level, the best known aspect of the Lewis and Clark story is of course the presence in their party of the Shoshoni Indian woman Sacagawea, the wife of a French trapper guide, whose role as translator and intermediary between the Americans and the American Indians was to be enormously important. There has long been a tendency to romanticise her, but her presence was often crucial in negotiations for food, horses and geographical information, and thus she has become a human symbol of the fact that this new territory was not empty when the Lewis and Clark party explored it. On one typical occasion, the party came upon a group of American Indians who reacted with both fear and hostility, until 'the sight of this Indian woman ... assured these people of our friendly intentions ... no woman ever accompanied a war party in this quarter.' More recently Sacagawea has become an icon of feminism, of the unique power she wielded, albeit briefly, in a man's world. There is, however, a considerable irony in her role in assisting in the great historical event which was eventually to prove so destructive to her people and their entire way of life.

The Corps of Discovery returned to St Louis to a heroes' welcome, their journey having registered a historic shift in the geographical identity of the United States. However, they had clearly not succeeded in their primary aim of finding a waterway, or any easy route through the mountains to the Pacific; the complex geography of the Rockies would prove an enduring obstacle for many decades to come, and it was some time before the journey to the West would attract other parties or individuals in any numbers. Among the earliest significant literary responses was Washington Irving's *Tour on the Prairies* of 1835. This presented a colourful account of a two-month trip westwards from Oklahoma, in the buffalo-hunting grounds of the Pawnee. Irving established the familiar features of such narratives: the ambivalent nature of the American Indians, part noble and part savage; and the alternation between a romantic response to the virgin plains and forests – at times written in a style reminiscent of Chateaubriand – and the often brutal reality of the subsistence living among hunter–gatherers.

It was through the 1820s and 1830s that the famous trails westward became established, drawing many writers to explore and evoke the wild new territories that were now part of their country. One of these trails gave its name to perhaps the most significant literary text of these years, Francis Parkman's *The Oregon Trail*, of 1847 (published as a book in 1849). The young Parkman was an extraordinary character; a permanent semi-invalid with very poor eyesight, he nevertheless was already meditating the series of great studies of American history that would make him famous, and his journey through Wyoming and Colorado – but not all the way to the Oregon coast – was undertaken deliberately to gain an understanding of the pre-European character of America. Parkman travelled in a small group, but at one point they split up, and he lived for several weeks alone with the Sioux Indians, sharing their buffalo hunts and ceremonials. He tells of his adventures in a strong, clear, action-filled narrative style, but he has moments of inspiration as he contemplates the 'awful sublimity' of the prairie wilderness. There is not a great deal of intellectual analysis of what he sees and experiences, and his view of native American culture vis-à-vis that of the new America makes uncomfortable reading today. He foresees that the buffalo will be hunted to extinction by the white man, and that the Indian way of life will die with the herds. Parkman's lack of sentiment, lack of interpretation or myth-making perhaps explains his strength as a narrator: he is an honest eyewitness, showing us unemotionally the reality of this clash of cultures.

It is strangely ironic that the American Indians, whose fate was of no great concern to those travelling in the West, were nevertheless a chief feature of all their narratives; they were effectively icons of the West, along with the buffalo and the rifle, and to historians and critics they have now become a crucial factor in the story of the exploration and settlement of America. It was in 1841 that George Catlin published his monumental art volumes illustrating *The Manners, Customs and Condition of the North American Indians*, based on his eight years of travel and research in the West. Catlin's pictures and the troupes of American Indians he brought to the East aroused enormous interest and excitement, but were apparently unable to influence in the slightest degree the historic fate of the people he portrayed and celebrated. With the passage of time, this whole issue has inevitably become a crucial test not only of literary worth in these early travel accounts of the West, but of moral and social values.

Still less concerned with the American Indians was John Charles Fremont, whose western adventures throughout the 1840s were undertaken overtly for the purposes of American empire-building. Fremont's various reports of his assaults on the passes of the Rockies were aimed specifically at establishing routes for emigrants and for future railroads, and they caught the imagination of the public, with the image of Fremont raising a flag on a mountain peak entering the nation's iconography. Fremont's writing made a link between the political adventure of United States expansion and the physical adventure of taking possession of the prairies and the mountains, portraying the new, virgin territory in terms of an Edenic vision:

> Our route the next morning lay up the valley, which, bordered by hills with graceful slopes, looked uncommonly green and beautiful. The stream was about fifty feet wide, and three or four deep, fringed by cotton wood and willow, with frequent groves of oak tenanted by flocks of turkeys. Game here, too, makes its appearance in greater plenty. Elk were frequently seen on the hills, and now and then an antelope bounded across our path, or a deer broke from the groves.
>
> (*Narrative of the exploring expedition to the Rocky Mountains in the year 1842 and to Oregon and North California in the years 1843–44*, p. 115)

In Fremont's eyes, the sole blemish on this magical landscape were the Pawnees who 'infest' the area, of which he has evidently taken possession in his imagination for white America. Fremont was in the thick of the action when California seceded from Mexico to the United States; indeed he is remembered less as a travel writer than as a politician and expansionist soldier, becoming the first senator of the new state in 1849. That same year saw another transforming event in California's history, namely the Gold Rush, and among the many texts to come out of it was William Lewis Manly's dramatic *Death Valley '49*. Like many thousands of others, Manly and his party went off course seeking a more favourable southern route from Wyoming to the coast and the gold fields. Manly and one companion ended by trekking for almost a month on foot through the desert to seek help for the main party, and out of this harrowing experience he later penned what is probably the first description of Death Valley. He was awed by its inhuman grandeur, and immortalised its 'dreadful sands and shadows … its exhausting phantoms, its salty columns, bitter lakes, and wild, dreary sunken desolation'. It is a powerful but straightforward tale of despair, privation and selfless endurance. Manly kept a diary during his ordeal, and this formed the basis of a very long letter to his parents, which in turn became the book that was finally published in 1894.

The level of debate – if there was a debate – about Indian culture was significantly raised by the man who became the acknowledged founding father of anthropology in America, and indeed in the world, Lewis Henry Morgan. Morgan, a lawyer by profession, conceived a strong interest in Iroquois social customs, and made field trips to their reservations in upstate New York in the early 1840s. He was intrigued to learn that Iroquois people were subdivided into clans, and that within the clans the chieftanships, while always held by males, passed through the matrilineal line – that is, not from father to son but from mother's brother to sister's son; he had never found this described in any source before. His published results in this area marked the origin of kinship as one of the core problems within anthropology, and he naturally wished to extend his studies to other tribes. In the

1850s and 1860s he made field trips to Kansas and Nebraska and on through the Rockies into Canada, collecting data on kin classification among some eighty Indian nations. The ultimate question he wished to answer was whether all the many tribes of North America had been originally related, having one common point of origin, perhaps among the peoples who had migrated from Asia. He was never able to prove this, but he felt strongly that it was so. Morgan's greatest international fame came through his seminal work, *Ancient Society*, of 1877, in which, on the basis of his studies, Morgan proposed an overarching scheme of human development from savagery through barbarism to civilisation, corresponding to hunter–gathering, agriculture and urbanism. He gave lucid and accurate accounts of American Indian customs and beliefs, for example:

> the old practice was to bury the dead in a sitting position with face to the east ... for four nights after the burial it was customary to build a fire on the grave. With the body they buried food, and weapons and personal articles of the deceased in the belief that they would be useful to him on the journey.
>   They also believe that the souls of those who are killed in battle or that are killed in a village, do not go to heaven immediately, but are transmuted into thunderbirds. That it is the souls of these departed warriors who make the thunder and lightning, and they are represented as having the form of birds.   (p. 69)

The published journals of Morgan's field trips are naturally packed with details about Indian life, both traditional and in its newer, threatened context of the 1850s. The writing is serious, detached and unsentimental, but often quite memorable, and Morgan foresees quite clearly that the free, semi-nomadic, hunting phase of Indian history is now dying: the Indian must become a farmer in order to survive, and he commends the generous land settlements obtained by some tribes – up to 1,000 acres for a single family. He is severe in his judgement on some of the American Indians' addiction to whiskey, and he is absolutely honest in reporting the harsh attitude of the white settlers, by whom he is told repeatedly that 'you cannot domesticate the wolf', that no social policies conceived in Washington will tame the Indian, and that Indian culture is fated to die out, perhaps through intermarriage and racial dilution. He gives a long and searing account of the notorious Sun-Dance of the Sioux, its spiritual motivation and its self-imposed tortures. Morgan's anthropological studies did not automatically make him a campaigner for Indian rights, but he took their culture seriously, and championed their cause whenever he could. He showed that anthropology was impossible without travel, and that travel literature in turn could and should take note of the anthropologist's approach to his subject. Morgan's works were the scholarly, literary counterpart of Catlin's celebrated paintings.

Science, exploration and adventure were combined more sensationally in the career of John Wesley Powell, geologist, naturalist and ethnographer, who achieved national fame through his pioneer voyage down the Colorado river in 1869. His canoe journey through the wild canyons covered almost 1,000 miles in three months and his account of it in *Explorations of the Colorado River* (1875) is a classic blend of intellectual and physical excitement, scientific motivation and tenacious courage. Powell writes in a clear forceful style, casting his narrative in the present tense, giving a dramatic sense that the action is unfolding as we read:

> We have another short talk about the morrow, and he lies down again; but for me there is no sleep. All night long, I pace up and down a little path, on a few yards of sand beach, along by the river. Is it wise to go on? I go to the boats again, to look at our rations. I feel satisfied that we can get over the danger immediately before us; what there may be below I know not.
>
> (*Down the Colorado*, p. 137)

Powell is writing here about the tragic irony that partly marred this great exploit: three of his men left the party just before entering the deepest part of the Grand Canyon, arguing that it was too dangerous to continue; but only a few days after they had climbed up the walls to imagined safety, they encountered a group of hostile American Indians, and were killed. Powell returned for a second descent of the river in 1871, and one of the strangest aspects of his book is that, without informing the reader, it conflates the two trips, presenting incidents from both as if they were directly linked, and not even mentioning that there were two trips. Historians have been outraged by Powell's action, but he thought it perfectly legitimate, providing everything that he narrated was actually true.

At exactly the same time, Clarence King was exploring and writing of his climbing adventures in the Rockies, and his *Mountaineering in the Sierra Nevada* (1872) inspired a generation of American climbers to follow in his footsteps. King was a highly educated and cultured man, and his writing in his classic book works on two distinct levels. Parts of the book play for laughs, with highly coloured, if not invented, incidents and encounters. But elsewhere the author strives, not unsuccessfully, for a grandeur matching his subject. He sets the scene for his climbing narrative with a dramatic account of the geological origins of the Sierra:

> [The glaciers] gradually perished, leaving only a crest of snow. The ice melted, and upon the whole plateau, little by little, a thin layer of soil accumulated, and, replacing the snow, there sprang up a forest of pines, whose shadows fall pleasantly today over rocks which were once torrents of lava and across the burnished pathways of ice. Rivers, pure and sparkling, thread the bottom of these gigantic glacier valleys. The volcanoes are extinct, and the whole theatre of this impressive geological drama is now the most glorious and beautiful region of America.
>
> As the characters in the *Zauberflöte* passed safely through the trial of fire and the desperate ordeal of water, so, through the terror of volcanic fire and the chilling empire of ice, has the great Sierra come into the present age of tranquil grandeur. (pp. 4–5)

The blend of human comedy and poetic grandeur make King's book the first work of real mountaineering literature in America. Interestingly, King claimed the first ascent of Mount Whitney, the highest summit in North America outside Alaska; only later did it become clear that this was a complete mistake, and that even so expert a surveyor and scientist as King could identify and climb the wrong peak in these unexplored mountains.

Powell's and King's responses to the western territories emphasised the theme of grandeur, with the sense of excitement and adventure that came with exploring it. But both were high-ranking figures in the official bodies charged with mapping and administering the nation's natural resources; they believed strongly in public science, put to use for practical ends. A subtly different response came slightly later in the writings of John Muir, the Scottish-born immigrant to Wisconsin who made his later life in California, and spent many years wandering the Sierra and the entire mountain region. Muir was perhaps the first American writer to value and emphasise the wilderness experience for its own sake, as a transcendent experience which could and should reverberate through the life and mind of the wanderer. Although he did not speak in terms of conventional religious belief, Muir felt that contact with nature held a real, objective power for mankind, to enlighten him and heal him from the ills of civilisation. Muir was partly simply a poet, finding verbal equivalents for the delight he took in observing nature:

> Most people like to look at mountain rivers, and bear them in mind; but few care to look at the winds, though far more beautiful and sublime, and though they become at times about as visible as flowing water. When the north winds in winter are making upward sweeps over the curving summits of the High Sierra, the fact is sometimes published with flying snow-banners a mile long.
>
> (*The Wilderness World of John Muir*, p. 189)

But beneath the surface poetry lay a strongly mystical conviction that the life of nature and not the life of civilisation was reality. An epic traveller himself, Muir's mode of travel was always alone and on foot. 'Only by going alone and in silence,' he wrote, 'can one truly get into the heart of the wilderness. All other travel is mere dust and hotels and baggage and chatter ... In God's wilderness lies the hope of the world – the great fresh, unblighted, unredeemed wilderness. The galling harness of civilisation drops off, and the wounds heal ere we are aware.' Muir wrote and lobbied tirelessly in defence of the natural environment, and was the single most influential figure in founding the movement we now know as conservationism.

Muir postdated the most celebrated American nature writer of all, Henry David Thoreau, who shared the same perspective regarding nature and civilisation, but seen from the gentler countryside of the East rather than the spectacular mountain landscapes of the West. Muir knew Thoreau's work, and there are obviously strong parallels between Muir's ideas and those of the transcendental group, lead by Thoreau and Emerson; but Thoreau's voice is gentler, understated, almost minimalist. His great principle was the desire to simplify life, his own and others', and to achieve that a wild mountain environment is not essential. In some ways Thoreau was an anti-travel writer, who remarked humorously, 'I have travelled a good deal in Concord', making his fundamental point that the inner life was more important than the outer. Although firmly located in the woods around Walden Pond, it is not the precise character of the place which is important in his great book, but his vision of a possible human life lived in harmony with it; he did his 'adventuring at home', as he put it. In *Walden* he proved his point by writing an inverted travel book, one that was liberating in exactly the same way that travel literature is supposed to be – by opening our eyes to new possibilities of life outside the environment and the civilisation where we were born, and where our existence is rooted.

The role of travel writing in nineteenth-century America was immensely important, both politically and psychologically, creating an image of the new virgin lands that had been acquired through the Louisiana Purchase. The reports of travellers returning from the West created a renewed sense of nationhood, evoking the huge physical space, the physical beauty and the potential wealth of the region. This was a political and imaginative challenge which no European nation, for example, could have experienced. But it had about it an element of ruthlessness, a frontier mentality, that the land was there to be seized and exploited in a movement which equated freedom with rapaciousness. In *Roughing It* (1872), Mark Twain made comic or melodramatic capital out of the rough-and-ready life of the West, as he had experienced it in his travels there in the 1860s, much as Bret Harte did in fictional form with his tales of mountains and mining camps. In this environment the American Indians were the great historical losers, but there is a considerable paradox in the fact that the American Indians received so much attention from travel writers that they became essential icons in the story of the West. This initial phase was succeeded after the mid-century by a newer approach, which emphasised the rediscovery of the natural heritage of the American West, both its land and its people. Even without the understated spirituality of Thoreau, the works of Morgan, Powell, King and Muir encouraged a deepening insight into what had happened to the identity of America after 1803, when the nation's boundaries had suddenly extended far beyond the Mississippi.

The British in India

Intriguingly, the process of discovering and understanding a vast new territory was repeated by those British writers attempting to describe India. India of course was emphatically not virgin territory: it was home to millions of people of many races, with ancient roots and cultural traditions, yet in the nineteenth century this immense and mysterious region became – and not just metaphorically – part of Britain's social and political landscape, presenting a unique challenge to those who wrote about it. Britain's presence in India dated from 1600, but its interests in the country were, for approximately a century and half, purely commercial, channelled exclusively through the East India Company. It would be fair to say that of the thousands who sailed from England to serve the Company in Bombay, Madras or Calcutta, few in these early years had much care for India past, present or future except to sink their teeth into the decaying flesh of the Mughal Empire and draw some sustenance from it. An honourable exception must be made for the case of John Marshall, who spent nine years in Bengal from 1668 to 1677. A fairly low ranking employee, Marshall was intellectual and scholarly and made extensive notes on the beliefs and customs of India, on religion, astrology, medicine and folklore. He possessed immense curiosity and a striking turn of phrase, so that his journals are full of graphic images and stories, and he was undoubtedly the first Englishman to study seriously the ancient beliefs and customs of India. He never explains why his imagination was so captured, but he must have spent long hours with the Indian sages, for he devotes many pages attempting to tabulate the central tenets of Hinduism. He had considerable powers of description, writing of a great famine around Patna in 1671 that the Ganges was defiled with hundreds of corpses, that the sufferers were endeavouring to sell their children for half a rupee, and that at night he heard 'the sad noise of the poor starved people'.

The isolation, physical and mental, of the British in India began to change after 1750, when a series of conflicts, major and minor, with the regional rulers of India drew the Company, step by step, towards becoming the government of the country. But throughout the later eighteenth century, administration, justice and warfare still went hand in hand with trade, whose path was smoothed by gifts,

Aurungzeb's Mosque overlooking the Ganges at Benares, from Elliott's
Views in India, China, and on the Shores of the Red Sea, 1835.

perquisites and outright bribery on a massive scale. Calcutta was
then a city of elegant Palladian mansions, and the life of the Bengal
officer or merchant was magnificent, pampered and short. Edmund
Burke attacked these people as being 'animated with all the avarice of
age and all the impetuosity of youth', and this was the setting for the
impeachment of the Governor General, Warren Hastings, on charges
of corruption.

This was the world reflected in probably the most unbuttoned, outrageous text ever to come out of British India, the *Memoirs* of William
Hickey. Hickey was the reprobate son of a well-connected lawyer,
and having made London too hot to hold him, he was dispatched
by his family to Calcutta, where he made huge sums of money and
became the biggest party-giver in town. He caroused and womanised
and spent like a prince, maintaining fifty servants, including his own
personal hairdresser, and drove through the streets in a glittering
phaeton drawn by Arab stallions. If he had the slightest interest in the
Hindu and Muslim civilisations around him, he does not mention the

fact. After returning to England in 1809, he composed his memoirs as a series of candid and brilliantly lit tableaux, written in a racy, convivial style. Slightly zany, certainly bawdy, and probably unpublishable at the time, the manuscript languished, like Boswell's, until it saw the light of day in the 1920s, and brought back to life this extraordinary man and the unimaginable social world of Calcutta two centuries ago.

It was while Hickey was partying furiously that another man arrived in Calcutta who was his diametric opposite, and who inaugurated a new era in British attitudes to India. Sir William Jones was a member of England's intellectual elite, admired by Gibbon for his attainments as a linguist, which included Persian and Arabic as well as the more usual Latin and Greek. By profession he was a jurist, and he travelled to India to take up the post of Supreme Court Judge in Calcutta. In the moneyed and Philistine society of Calcutta he was a notably individual figure, for he immediately made it his life's work to uncover, understand and restore the ancient civilisation of India, whose mysterious and fragmentary remains surrounded him, and he identified a knowledge of the ancient languages as the key to this whole enterprise. He was not the first European to master Sanskrit, but he was the first to perceive its importance as the parent language of almost all the tongues of Europe. In 1786, after several years of diligent study at the feet of Indian scholars, he unveiled his great theory to the Asiatic Society, which he had founded, in words which have become justly famous in the history of linguistics:

> The *Sanscrit* language, whatever be its antiquity, is of a wonderful
> structure; more perfect than the *Greek*, more copious than the *Latin*,
> and more exquisitely refined than either, yet bearing to both of them
> a stronger affinity, both in the roots of verbs and in the forms of
> grammar, than could possibly have been produced by accident; ... there
> is a similar reason ... for supposing that the *Gothic* [i.e. Germanic] and
> *Celtick*, though blended with a different idiom, had the same origin with
> the *Sanscrit*; and the old *Persian* might be added to the same family.
>
> (*William Jones: Selected Poetical and Prose Works*, p. 361)

The implications of this were profound and revolutionary: if Sanskrit, the language of the Indians, were the root of the classical languages, then it must be ancient indeed, and moreover it was hard to understand how this language could have spread across Europe unless the people who spoke it had carried it with them, taking their gods too, to be worshipped under new names. So what were perceived as the rude, uncivilised, teeming, irrational, idolatrous people of India might have been the ancestors of the Greeks, of the Romans, and of the Sahibs themselves; it was an extraordinary thought. Jones's research was an Enlightenment project, an enquiry, like Gibbon's, into the origin and progress of civilisation. He conveyed his sense of excitement by comparing himself to a man who had stumbled into a world of fractured time zones, comparable to a world where the Greeks still worshipped Jupiter and Apollo, and where classical culture was unknown outside Greece. He had entered a mysterious culture, ancient but still living, which might prove to be the parent culture of Europe itself. Jones's discoveries made the field of Indian studies respectable in Britain, inspiring a generation of linguists and archaeologists to look with completely fresh eyes at Indian history and culture.

Following Jones's breakthrough came a series of landmarks in the appreciation of Indian art and memorials. The decipherment of the Asoka columns by James Prinsep in 1837 revealed the existence of the Mauryan kingdom and the centrality of Buddhism in the life of ancient India. Prinsep, a young official of the Bengal mint, drove himself to complete mental breakdown and an early death in the course of his studies. The nature and role of Buddhism, and the problem of its disappearance in the land of its birth, was gradually illuminated by a number of scholars, who began the work of excavating stupas, deciphering inscriptions and relating them to Buddhist texts. The central figure in this process was Alexander Cunningham, who progressed from being an outstanding army engineer to become the founding father of Indian archaeology. In 1851 in one stupa at

Sanchi, Cunningham found two ancient reliquaries containing human remains and bearing the names Sariputasa and Maha-Mogalanasa, two of the Buddha's leading disciples; translated into Christian terms, this was like finding the graves of St Peter and St Paul, undisturbed and inviolate for more than two thousand years.

Cunningham belonged to the generation after Jones, and it is surprising to find how many scholars and archaeologists were army officers, not the kind of men one would expect to become passionate about the ancient history and religious systems of India. None of these men was more colourful than Colonel James Tod, who between 1805 and 1825 reconstructed the history of Rajasthan, a region devastated by recent wars:

> All was desolate; even the traces of the footsteps of man were effaced. The babul and gigantic reed, which harboured the boar and the tiger, grew upon the highways; and every rising ground displayed a mass of ruin. Bhilwara, the commercial entrepôt of Rajputana, which ten years before contained 6,000 families, showed not a vestige of existence. All was silent in her streets – no living thing was seen except a solitary dog, that fled in dismay from his lurking-place in the temple, scared at the unaccustomed sight of man.
>
> (*Annals and Antiquities of Rajasthan*, vol. 1, p. 549)

Tod was captivated by the history of the Rajputs, a martial people with a strong chivalric code, whose legends seemed to awake echoes of Arthurian or medieval England. Like Jones, Tod learned at the feet of the pandits, in his case Jain pandits, and he conceived a deep interest in the strange and ascetic world of the Jains; later, when he was seriously ill, he had himself carried up Mount Abu, the 'Indian Olympus', to wander weakly but ecstatically through the Dilwara complex of temples:

> The pen is incompetent to describe the exuberant beauties of this proud monument of the Jains. ... When we reflect that all this magnificence is found on the summit of an isolated mountain on the

verge of the desert, now inhabited by a few simple and half-civilised people, the association cannot fail to enhance one's impression of wonder.   (p. 197)

Back in England, Tod wrote two important books, richly laden with factual material and personal feeling: first, *Annals and Antiquities of Rajasthan* (1829), and then *Travels in Western India* (1839). 'Heart and soul did I labour for the one,' he wrote, 'and with the same idolatrous affection for the subject have I given up every pursuit, every thought to this, in the hope of making the Rajputs known by their works.' Tod's passion for Rajasthan made him a legend in the region, and years later English visitors would still be asked if Tod-Sahib was still alive, and did they know him?

It was another young army officer, Captain Thomas Burt, who in 1838 had the distinction of unveiling to European eyes one of the most baffling of India's mysteries, the erotic temple sculptures of Khajuraho, whose first sight evoked this famous response:

> I found ... seven Hindoo temples, most beautifully and exquisitely carved as to workmanship, but the sculptor had at times allowed his subject to grow a little warmer than there was any absolute necessity for his doing; indeed some of the sculptures here were extremely indecent and offensive, which I was at first much surprised to find in temples that are professed to be erected for good purposes, and on account of religion.
>
> (*India Discovered*, p. 128)

Burt noted rather stiffly that his native porters took an unseemly delight in these novelties. It would take a great effort of study and understanding before the role of these sculptures in Hindu belief was appreciated; indeed many Europeans could never reconcile them with any religious system. Khajuraho was apparently a chance survival, preserved by the surrounding jungle from the iconoclasm of the invading Muslims. The rock temples of Elephanta and Ellora were likewise mysterious if less sensational, supposed by some early scholars to have been built by the Egyptians. The miraculously carved and painted caves of Ajanta were first described by a young lieutenant, James Alexander, in 1824, who found the cave floors littered with the remains of tribesmen's camps, and with clear evidence that they were also the haunt of jackals, bears, tigers and monkeys. Decades were to pass before it was understood that here was an entirely new and unknown realm in the history of world art, as revolutionary and important as if the Cathedral of Chartres or the Parthenon, hitherto unknown, had been discovered at the heart of a forest somewhere in Europe. The origin, their artistic quality and their value as evidence of Buddhist history, all were established slowly and painfully. Until the late nineteenth century, Indian art had meant only Moghul miniature paintings and the Taj Mahal. A prolonged intellectual effort was needed to arrive at a serious re-evaluation, yet that effort followed the amazing and fortuitous discoveries of a few curious army officers; the destruction wrought upon Indian art and architecture through centuries of neglect and vandalism can only be guessed at.

Some considerable time before all this, from the later eighteenth century onwards, India had been brought within the European range of vision through the work of the many fine artists who captured the image of its landscapes for the home market. Beginning in the 1780s, William Hodges, the Daniell brothers, James Fraser and Charles Gold all produced a flood of charming pictures, usually to accompany travel texts written by themselves or by others, which created an image of India clearly within the picturesque tradition. Forts and palaces, sometimes inhabited and sometimes in ruins, were placed against jungle, hillside or river, and given scale through picturesque native figures. This picturesque perception certainly became part of the travelogues of this period, in both its positive and its negative aspects. Writing in her *Letters on India* in 1814, Maria Graham (later Maria Callcott) spoke of 'the favoured country of Hindostan', enriched by nature's gifts, where 'under a pure sky and brilliant sun the soil produces the most exquisite fruits and the most abundant harvests; the rocks are rich in gems, the mountains teem with gold'. Here, she says, 'your eyes will often be enchanted with the most delicious landscapes ... where, if ever, you might realise the dreams of the poets.' But there are shadows in this paradise, the shadows left by historical conflicts and by cultural decay:

> But alas! it is not the natural riches of the country, not the exquisite beauty of its sylvan scenery, that will most attract your attention. Vast cities, now too large for their diminished inhabitants, towns embellished with temples and with tombs now falling to decay, and absolutely unpeopled, and stupendous monuments of art, which have not served to transmit even the names of their founders down to our times, will frequently arrest your steps; but while these are hastening to decay, the customs and habits of the natives seem immortal, and present us now with the same traits under which they are painted by the Greeks who visited them two thousand years ago.
>
> (*Letters on India*, pp. 6–7)

This image of India as a decayed paradise was common to writers and artists, and it is essentially the impression of an outsider, the first impression formed when the visitor is first dazzled by the teeming life of the country, then very soon afterwards saddened by thoughts of decay and the melancholy pleasure of ruins. India was never a colony in which the British settled permanently: the climate was inimical and often fatal, as it was to Jones; they were not permitted to buy land within the regions of Company control; and intermarriage was considered impossible. So the writers and artists, like all the other Europeans, came, saw, took what they could, and departed; the records of their experiences were rarely those of people with a deep intimate understanding of the country; in this situation, the picturesque image flourished. A tourist itinerary emerged of sites which had to be seen, in which the Taj Mahal was elevated to a unique status, while the more ancient Hindu and Buddhist memorials were less easily understood.

A considerable turning point in the British perception of India came in 1817 with the publication of James Mill's *The History of British India*, a highly influential book which presented a bitingly critical view of Indian culture as having been debased by centuries of political and religious tyranny, in which the British played the part of merely the latest villains. As a radical, a utilitarian, and more or less an atheist, Mill believed that reason and justice demanded that Britain reform its government of India along rational, efficient and humanitarian lines. The extraordinary thing about Mill's book and its widespread influence was that it came from the pen of a man who had never set foot in India. However, Mill's great political ally, Macaulay, had spent some time there, and he claimed that personal knowledge lay behind the deep contempt in which he held Indian culture:

> In no part of the world has a religion ever existed more unfavourable to the moral and intellectual health of our race. The Brahminical mythology is so absurd that it necessarily debases every mind which receives it as truth; and with this absurd mythology is bound up an absurd system of physics, an absurd geography, an absurd astronomy. ... All is hideous and grotesque and ignoble.
>
> ('The Gates of Somnauth', speech to the House of Commons, 1843)

This kind of vicious rhetoric also proved attractive to another very different group which began to interest itself in Indian affairs, namely the evangelical Christians, who shared with the radical utilitarians the conviction that Britain had an imperative duty to govern India responsibly, and to lead its people out of the darkness into light. In the atmosphere generated by the evangelicals and utilitarians, travel descriptions of India felt free to dwell on very unpicturesque aspects of Indian life, above all the curses of *suttee* and *thuggee* – the immolation of widows and the ritual murders – which were regarded with justifiable horror by Europeans. This approach had obviously no time for intellectual research on the Jones pattern, so that Cunningham's archaeological work was run on a shoestring. Why, it was asked, should Englishmen care for the bizarre works of art left by obscure and incomprehensible religious groups?

Yet the fascination with India continued to grow throughout the nineteenth century, as did the number of travelogues, so that scarcely a month passed without the appearance of yet another book of Indian description or memoirs. Thomas Twining, scion of the great tea-planting dynasty, had written a rare European eyewitness account of a suttee in 1792 which was quite heart-rending, in which he could barely restrain himself from intervening, and which left him shaken and sick. William Henry Sleeman, a senior officer charged with suppressing the thuggee movement, wrote sober, factual accounts of this religiously inspired campaign of murder, which had already been sensationally treated in *Confessions of a Thug* (1823) by Philip Meadows Taylor, a fictitious book with a strong basis in fact, assumed by many to be an authentic personal testimony. When Reginald Heber, the second Anglican Bishop of Calcutta, wrote his *Narrative of a Journey Through the Upper Provinces of India* (1828), he combined a traditional picturesque delight in the country with a deep religious sadness at the spiritual state of its people; in his eyes suttee and thuggee represented the depths of their darkness. Heber was the author of the celebrated hymn 'From Greenland's icy mountains / From India's coral strand', with its denunciation of 'The heathen in his blindness', who 'bows down to wood and stone'. He was stern in his verdict on the injustice and oppression formerly practised by the East India Company, and his guiding principle was 'That I might in some degree, however small, be enabled to conduce to the spiritual advantage of creatures so goodly, so gentle, and now so misled and blinded.' Heber wrote his text as a series of family letters to his wife and children, which gives them an appealing air of personal honesty, and following his premature death it was his wife who published them as a memorial to him.

At the opposite extremity were the rather odious journals and letters home of the upper-class memsahibs, such as Emily Eden's highly popular *Up the Country* of 1866. Eden was the sister of the Governor General, Lord Auckland, and had spent some years with him in India, before returning to the glittering society life of London. Her text is written in a continuous tone of tinkling laughter, in which everything Indian is made to sound deliciously absurd; even the story of her purchase of two young slave girls – with, it is true, the laudable aim of placing them in an orphanage – is told as if it were an episode of light-hearted self-amusement.

There were of course military memoirs by the score – *Nine Years on the North-West Frontier*, that kind of book; and when army officers were not writing about actual fighting or warfare, they were recalling their great days as *shikaris* – hunters, who made the deer and foxes of England seem like very small game. G.P. Sanderson, officer-in-charge of the government elephant-catching department, penned the splendidly entitled *Thirteen Years Among the Wild Beasts of India* (1870). There was Joseph Dalton Hooker's *Himalayan Journals* (1855), which show him to be almost the equal of Darwin in combining scientific observation – in his case botanical – with a humane and lucid record of the country and its people. There were numerous missionary memoirs, dwelling on the possibility of converting India to Christianity. There were historical works, political meditations, and accounts of folk customs and sketches of native life, all written within the framework of personal travel narratives, and all claiming to take the reader into 'the real India'. On a more intellectual level there began to emerge the stream of attempts to initiate western readers into the mysteries of the Indian religious systems. Of these, none was more remarkable than Sir Edwin Arnold's epic poem *The Light of Asia* (1879), a presentation of Buddhist history and belief in lush Tennysonian verse.

Some of this outpouring of books perpetuated the picturesque image of India, but a number of official or semi-official texts showed the shift away from the picturesque towards what we may call the

Village and fort of Dankan in Ladakh, from Moorcroft's
Travels in the Himalayan Provinces of Hindustan and the Panjab, 1841.

'survey mentality'. There were ethnographic surveys of India's people, archaeological surveys of historical remains, surveys of flora and fauna, and above all, perhaps, the Great Trigonometrical Survey, the body charged with mapping the country, whose roots lay back in the 1790s. All these activities suggest a surveillance mentality, an attempt to take control of the country through the accumulation of data, of centralised knowledge. This official approach was strengthened by the seismic event of the Mutiny in 1857, whose scale, violence and sudden, unforeseen eruption suggested there had been a failure to understand the country properly. Following the Mutiny there was an increase in anxiety levels in writings about India, meditations on the political future, and on 'the Problem of India'. How was India to be civilised – through sympathetic, humane understanding, or through still stricter control? Did the 'Problem of India' lie with the Indians or with the British? This anxiety also expressed itself in British approaches to the northern borderlands, Afghanistan, Kashmir, Nepal and Tibet, where it was feared that Russia and China had designs on the wealth and prestige that possession of India might bring to them. 'Frontiers', Lord Curzon wrote, 'are the razor's edge on which hang suspended the issue of war or peace and the life of nations.' Awareness of northern India as the place 'where three empires meet' inspired books of travel and of reflection on cultural and political conflict.

These Himalayan kingdoms were places of fable, and formidably difficult of access. Early information on these regions had been brought back by a succession of travellers: by Samuel Turner, who, as early as 1783, had been granted an audience at Tashilunpo with the infant designated as the new Dalai Lama; Turner left a memorable account of this formal diplomatic ceremony conducted under the grave, silent gaze of the eighteen-month-old child; by Thomas Manning, the querulous scholar and linguist, who in 1811 became the first Englishman to set foot in Lhasa, although he found the fabled city and its inhabitants to be filthy and poverty-stricken; by William Moorcroft, the East India Company's stud farmer, who, in his enthusiasm to improve the breed of his horses, made extraordinary trans-Himalayan journeys in the 1820s, first through the headwaters of the Ganges to Lake Manasarowar, and then through Kashmir, Ladakh and the Hindu Kush, returning via Afghanistan, where he met his death, possibly murdered. The surveying of the mountains fell to the Survey of India from 1850 onwards, and with it came the recognition that these were undoubtedly the highest mountains in the world; their remoteness and the physical challenges they presented meant that some time was to pass before European Alpinists could seriously contemplate climbing there. In 1892 a Royal Geographical Society expedition under Martin Conway succeeded in reaching and surveying the Baltoro Glacier in the heart of the Karakoram mountains, by then designated as a discrete range west of the Himalayas. By the mid-century the mountains and the border kingdoms, with the exception of Tibet, had become effectively part of the extended identity of India.

That identity was protean, elusive and ever-changing: it was political, aesthetic, commercial, scientific, cultural and racial, and in each of these areas India's identity could be seen as positive or negative. These were all valid identities, formed in the minds and the writings of the men and women who fell under the spell of India and sought to interpret her. Was there anything which united all these literary reconstructions of the country, the personal and the impersonal, the imaginative and the factual, anything that links the rampant party-going Hickey with the evangelical Bishop Heber, the imperious military commander and orchid hunter in the hills? If so, it can only be tentatively expressed as the experience of living in a parallel world. A state within a state, yes, but that expression is too formal, for to the British, India was really a theatre in which they were both actors and spectators; or, to put it even more frivolously, it was a playground, where they could play – politically, militarily, socially and intellectually. They could experiment with their own and other people's lives: from translating Sanskrit literature to shooting tigers; from mapping the Himalayas to running tea plantations; from excavating half-ruined temples to sentencing criminals in court – they could do all this without impact on Britain itself. They went there to experience this other world, and in most cases they returned home, but the minority who became addicted to it stayed all their lives. India was a realm of responsibility, but also of freedom – freedom from the rigidities of life in Britain; this explains why India was swarming with delicious British eccentrics, who had created alternative identities for themselves.

If there is any truth in this theory, it would explain the persistent myth that Britain did not seize India by force, that she stumbled into her empire in a fit of absent-mindedness, and that having done so, it transpired to be a gift of providence for the Indians themselves. Surely it was no accident that the great classical text taught in every school and every university in England for two centuries was Virgil's

Aeneid: the story of a man's noble and selfless response to an edict from the gods that he must voyage across the known world to found a new, divinely favoured empire. 'I do not see', said Lord Curzon, 'how Englishmen, contrasting India as it is with what it was or might have been, can fail to see that we came here in obedience to what I call a decree of Providence, for the lasting benefit of millions of the human race.' Duty and civilisation formed the dual creed which officially sustained British India, but beneath the surface perhaps it survived because it functioned as a form of theatre, a parallel world we find reflected in the myriad of memoirs and tributes to the country. We have only to compare the hold that India exercised over the British mind and imagination with that of Australia, for example, to perceive India's incomparably greater importance.

The Birth of Archaeology

By a long process stretching across centuries, travel ceased to be an optional activity and became a dimension of social and intellectual life. This can clearly be seen if we think of sciences and disciplines such as geology, natural history, archaeology or anthropology – studies of the earth and of mankind, whose development would have been impossible without travel, and which in turn provided a wholly new motive for travel writing. Sir Charles Lyell's revolutionary work, *Principles of Geology* (1830–33), the foundation text of modern geology, was based entirely on first-hand fieldwork in the Alps, the Pyrenees, France and Italy; what Lyell saw on those journeys and his interpretation of it form the substance of the book.

Perhaps the first large-scale public manifestation of archaeology had come from the work of the French scholars who accompanied Napoleon on his expedition to Egypt in 1798. The excavation, surveying and removal of thousands of antiquities were supervised by Baron Vivant Denon and recorded in the massive volumes *Description de l'Egypte* (1809 onwards), and in Denon's *Travels in Upper and Lower Egypt* (1803), texts which mark the dawn of modern Egyptology; they also mark the beginning of a rivalry between Britain and France that lasted for more than a century over the glory of great archaeological finds. The English public imagination was captured when Johann Burckhardt discovered the breathtaking ruins of Petra, cut into the living rock of the Jordanian desert, although he was also the first to describe the monumental statues of Abu Simbel. Burckhardt was a Swiss by birth, an Englishman by adoption, a linguistic genius able to pass as an Arab so well as to live for some months in Mecca, and after his death from fever in Cairo he was buried under his Muslim name; his *Travels in Syria and the Holy Land* appeared posthumously in 1822. Strangely, it was another Englishman by adoption, the colourful former pantomime strongman, Giovanni Belzoni, who enthralled the London public when he brought back Egyptian antiquities to the British Museum, including the great head of Rameses II. Belzoni recorded his excavations in his *Narrative of the operations and recent discoveries within the pyramids, temples and tombs in Egypt and Nubia* (1821–22).

Burckhardt never lived to enjoy his fame as a traveller, unlike another Englishman of Swiss origin, Austen Henry Layard, whose recovery of the lost culture of Assyria made him a national hero. Layard did not discover the great cities of Nineveh and Nimrud, but his excavations there from 1845 onwards unearthed sensational artefacts thrilling readers of his books with images of this ancient biblical civilisation, complete with its library of inscriptions in an unknown language. *Nineveh and its Remains* (1849) became a best-seller, the winged Assyrian bulls were carried in triumph to the British Museum rather than to the Louvre, Sir Henry Rawlinson deciphered cuneiform, and the vast buried library of the Assyrian kings was opened after two thousand years. This was the heroic age of archaeology, when diplomacy and large sums of money were manipulated by entrepreneurs like Layard to secure both treasures and national glory for England, France or Germany, as the case might be. There is no doubt that the excavation methods were crude, and that great damage was done on these sites, while the morality of this seizure of unique artefacts was at best questionable and at worst a form of naked imperialism. All these doubts apply just as strongly to Heinrich Schliemann, who found immortality as the discoverer of Troy and of the graves of the Mycenean kings, which yielded the famous 'Mask of Agamemnon'. The intrigue-and-adventure aspect of archaeology endured well into the twentieth century, and it is memorably recorded in Sir Wallis Budge's memoirs of his years collecting artefacts for the British Museum. Budge was a great scholar who interpreted the Egyptian 'Book of the Dead' for his generation; indeed he secured the celebrated Papyrus of Ani, but his book *By Nile and Tigris* (1920), with its tales of rivalry with Egyptian and French archaeologists, reads in parts like the plot of an adventure film. His 'collecting' activities brought matchless treasures to the museum, but involved ruthless bribery and duplicity.

These men were self-trained, obviously, and they blended the seriousness of the historian with the flair of the impresario. They would return home to write their memoirs – Schliemann's *Troja* was also an international best-seller – in which they strode across the stage of history, half-scholar, half-adventurer, ruling over large teams of indigenous workers who laboured in the deserts for them, paralleling in a strange way the hordes who had laboured thousands of years before to build these vanished cities. Their texts were the foundation stones of the discipline of archaeology, and they inspired the next generation of scholar-travellers, who longed above all for the moment when they might open a long-sealed tomb, or push aside the jungle screen to reveal the monuments of ancient civilisation, as John Lloyd Stephens and Frederick Catherwood did in Mexico in 1840. Catherwood's superb drawings of the Mayan and post-Mayan cities of Copan and Chichen Itza, published in Stephens's *Incidents of Travel in Central*

Layard's party removing the great winged Assyrian bulls from Nineveh for transport to London, from *Discoveries in the ruins of Nineveh and Babylon*, 1853. The nineteenth-century development of archaeology was both an offshoot of travel and an enormous spur to it.

America (1841) and *Incidents of Travel in Yucatan* (1843), provoked a surge of excitement in readers throughout Europe and America. It almost seemed that the firm ground of textbook history was dissolving under their feet: how many other unknown or lost civilisations might have flourished in the deserts and the world's jungles? How much did we really know about human origins?

Victorian Travel Classics

Questions about civilisation, our past, our beliefs, our identity vis-à-vis our own and other cultures may be detected behind many of the travel classics written in the Victorian era, a number of which show a fascination with the Middle East and the world of Islam. The best known was Alexander Kinglake's *Eothen*, published in 1844, a best-seller, a popular classic, still immensely readable, but full of ambiguities. Kinglake's journey, in a great arc from Belgrade to Cairo, took place in 1834, and he admitted in his Preface that he tried several times to write an account of it, but always failed because he found he was writing what he felt he ought to write, what people would expect from a travel book – full of discoveries, sound learning and cultural reflections. Finally he gave all that up, and found a way of writing 'the truth', what he really thought and felt on his journey, as if he were writing a letter to a friend. This apparently simple formula resulted in a text that is sometime poetic and solemn, but more often light-hearted and urbane. He appears sometimes as a philosopher, but sometimes as a schoolboy – he was 25 when he made his journey. He can shape an impressive rhetoric of strangeness:

> The Moslem quarter of a city is lonely and desolate; you go up and down, and on over shelving and hillocky paths through narrow lanes walled in by blank, windowless dwellings; you come out upon an open space strewed with the black ruins that some fire has left; you pass by a mountain of cast-away things, the rubbish of centuries, and on it you see a number of big, wolf-like dogs lying torpid under the sun, with limbs outstretched to the full, as if they were dead; storks, or cranes, sitting fearless upon the low roofs, look gravely down upon you; the still air that you breathe is loaded with the scent of citron, and pomegranate rinds scorched by the sun, or (as you approach the Bazaar) with the dry, dead perfume of strange spices. You long for some signs of life, and tread the ground more heavily, as though you would wake the sleepers with the heel of your boot; but the foot falls noiseless upon the crumbling soil of an eastern city, and Silence follows you still. Again and again you meet turbans, and faces of men, but they have nothing for you – no welcome – no wonder – no wrath – no scorn.
>
> (*Eothen*, pp. 7–8)

And yet a few moments later he can be recounting some comic, near-farcical encounter with a local dignitary. This is surely orientalism in its classic literary form: this is the mystery and colour of the east, the theatrical experience which could potentially end either way – in comedy or perhaps in tragedy, if the traveller is not equal to the challenge. Kinglake openly plays the English grandee, explaining how essential is the *dragoman*, the guide and interpreter who must smooth the traveller's path, and without whom he cannot possibly survive in the East – unless he is a linguist and actor of genius like Burckhardt, who can convincingly assume an eastern identity. As a classicist, Kinglake delights in wandering the plains of Troy, and in noticing that Homer *must* have passed there too, for he sees that the island of Samothrace is indeed visible as the poet says, though so far off, and when a modern map suggests that it must be completely hidden by the intervening island of Imbros. In the desert he takes no delight, but is grateful for the experience, for the austere solitude, the aching, self-immolating monotony of his toil across its emptiness. Kinglake sees eastern life as governed by ceremony and ritual, by imperatives of action and speech that may be noble and magnanimous, but are often ridiculous and deceitful. He views this life ironically, but evokes it superbly within the limits of his time and his mentality. This was the east which the British loved to imagine, and that love affair inspired many other books – those of Eliot Warburton, Robert Curzon, William Palgrave, Richard Burton, C.M. Doughty, Wilfred Blunt and T.E. Lawrence. These writers would increasingly shed Kinglake's ambiguous, ironic, consciously English control, and embrace the East and the desert as an escape from the decadence of western civilisation.

These orientalist texts had their visual counterpart in the highly artistic drawings made in the 1830s by David Roberts of Syria, the Holy Land and Egypt, with their superb renderings of architectural ruins and of the local peoples. Roberts was a wonderful topographical artist, and he seemed also to build a cunning subtext into his works: along with the beauty of his subjects, he seemed to evoke a quality of desolation, suggesting that the Muslim custodians were to blame for permitting this historic region to slide into decay, especially of course the Holy Land itself.

Roberts inspired a whole generation of artists, and now that the Near East was more friendly and more accessible than it had been for generations, it readily became a strong attraction for those seeking the picturesque, in landscape and in human terms. In his persona as a traveller, Edward Lear had no pretensions whatsoever: he was an eccentric, an oddity, and he knew it, representing no tradition of learning, no imperial or nationalist agenda, no viewpoint but his own. He was a sensitive and gifted artist who just missed the major importance that Roberts has, but as a writer he possessed a quirky genius that brought him immortality as an author of nonsense verse, and this same quirkiness colours all his travel writing. He formed the belief early on that the best evocation of place comes through a blend of text and pictures. He made his living for some forty years through incessant travel, producing journals on Italy, Greece, Albania, Egypt and India, illustrated with his own artworks. These writings are light-hearted and whimsical, with a sense of underlying strangeness and vulnerability:

> In the middle of the night, the roof of Seid Efféndi's house being slight, a restless stork put one of his legs through the crevice and could not extricate it; whereon ensued much kicking and screams, and at the summons came half the storks in Thessaly, and all night long the uproar was portentous. Four very wet jackdaws also came down the chimney and hopped over me and about the room till dawn.
>
> (*Edward Lear in Greece*, p. 220)

We wonder if this is fact or fiction, since it is easily recognisable as the same world Lear entered when composing his nonsense verse. He evidently had a fixation about birds, since they crop up repeatedly, as here, while he was sketching tomb ruins near Delhi:

> On the east, the broad stretch of river is imposing, the grimness of the dark gray and red fortress walls and the hopeless bareness of most of the scene very striking. We are going to breakfast on the step outside, though the wind and the dust are not agreeable; so we move on to the shade of a mimosa, which, small as it is, has this virtue and interest,

that it is full of birds, namely: one roller, six bee-eaters, 23 turtledoves and 11 Alexandrian parrots, for the foliage is so thin you may count all the party. Breakfast at 12.30 as usual on bread and cold mutton, eggs, sherry and soda water, little and good. Diversion afterwards from kites and crows intriguing about bones and scraps of bread.

(*Edward Lear's Indian Journal*, p. 99)

Lear clearly developed a technique of visual symbolism, expressing what he felt through what he saw, and there is surreal clarity about his writing. The artworks do not quite fit this mood, possessing always elegance, balance and clarity, with nothing threatening, not the hint of benign insanity that hovers in his writings. His blend of text and picture brought him fame and a certain measure of wealth, so their highly individual note must have struck a chord with Victorian England.

The traveller-eccentric became a familiar feature in the literary landscape, and none more so than George Borrow, who gave the nineteenth century another of its offbeat classics, *The Bible in Spain* (1843). Borrow was a lonely, secretive man who perhaps suffered from some form of manic depression, and whose mood swings appear in his books as 'the screaming horror'. His strange, aimless life took on a decisive new direction when he was recruited by the Bible Society to sell Bibles in Portugal and Spain, and this enterprise, which occupied four years, provided the background for his travels. Spain had never been on Europe's tourist trail, and what were perceived as its isolated, enigmatic, backward, violent, proud, passionate people provided the perfect spark to fire Borrow's imagination, especially since, at the time of his visit, the country was embroiled in civil war. His story is one of adventures and encounters, many of them taking place at night, with mysterious strangers, Gypsies, priests, Jews, partisans for one cause or another, beautiful women and threatening figures of authority. He defends Spain against the deep-rooted hatred felt by the English by arguing that the passionate nature of her people had somehow seduced her into playing 'the she-butcher ... of malignant Rome', but that the

Spanish themselves were not an irredeemably cruel or fanatical people. Through this dark pageant, Borrow moves as both a romantic and a man of action, in a form of travel writing in which it is impossible to disentangle fact from fiction, a picaresque adventure which we only half believe, if that. The book was an instant success, becoming an inextricable part of the English perception of Spain.

The towering figure among English travel writers was of course Sir Richard Burton. A restless, prolific, linguistic genius, able to penetrate and evoke the cultures of India, Africa and Arabia, Burton's protean nature makes him perhaps the most difficult of all travel writers to understand and summarise adequately: he wrote so much about so many places, and some of his work is frankly not deeply engaging – to the non-specialist it appears overlong and overdetailed. He achieved early fame through his feat of reaching Mecca – taking part in the hajj and maintaining for several months his disguise as an Indian Muslim – and for his role in exploring the lakes and rivers of East Africa, which led to his celebrated public conflict with Speke. But only rarely did he let the reader into his inner world, and explain the reason for his passionate love of travel, as he does here:

> Wonderful was the contrast between the steamer and that villa on the Mahmudiyah canal! Startling the sudden change from presto to adagio life! In thirteen days we had passed from the clammy grey fog, that atmosphere of industry which kept us at anchor off the Isle of Wight … and now we were sitting silent and still, listening to the monotonous melody of the East – the soft night-breeze wandering through starlit skies and tufted trees, with a voice of melancholy meaning.
>
> And this is the Arab's *kaif*. The savouring of animal existence; the passive enjoyment of mere sense; the pleasant languor, the dreamy tranquillity, the airy castle-building, which in Asia stand in lieu of the vigorous, intensive, passionate life of Europe. It is the result of a lively, impressible, excitable nature, and exquisite sensibility of nerve, – a facility for voluptuousness unknown to northern regions; … No wonder that *kaif* is a word untranslatable in our mother-tongue!
>
> (*Personal Narrative of a Pilgrimage to El-Medinah and Mecca*, pp. 12–13)

This sounds like the perfect charter for lingering forever among the sights and sounds of the East, and forgetting one's European identity. Yet this is what Burton would never do: he moved on restlessly from one destination to another, his travels always punctuated by periods in England where he played the social role of the upper-class army officer, scholar and diplomat. When he assumed his alien identities, was Burton a singular exception to the general pattern of appropriation, of Europeans taking possession of foreign cultures, or was he merely doing exactly that, but in his own unique way? In spite of all his brilliance, his courage, his imagination and his adaptability, was he also imprisoned in 'the imperial fantasy'? In his later life when travel became physically difficult, he set about bringing the East home to England through his translations of oriental classics like *The Arabian Nights* and the *Kama Sutra*, with their uninhibited avowal of a very un-English type of sexuality. The enigmas of Burton's personality and his true significance as a writer have generated an entire biographical industry, but no easy answers have emerged to either question.

In the range of his travels, Burton had a female counterpart in Isabella Bird, to whom conventional adjectives such as 'intrepid' and 'indefatigable' are commonly applied. Despite suffering from lifelong ill health, she travelled in Canada and the United States, Australia and the Pacific, Japan, China and Korea, India and Central Asia, and North Africa, writing extensive accounts of all these places. Most of her travelling was done after she was 50 years old, and her personality and her motives could hardly have been more different from Burton's, for she was a moral traveller. A devout, evangelical Christian, she was moved to undertake her extraordinary journeys largely by her sense of 'the desperate needs of the un-Christianised world'. Isabella Bird is not perhaps a brilliant travel writer, but she writes directly and sincerely about what she sees and feels, and occasionally she can be very powerful: her description of Chinese prison in *The Golden Chersonese* could scarcely be more horrifying. Her religious faith never comes to dominate her narratives, but in her letters home or in her lectures she could be both bitter and passionate, as here reflecting on her experience of Persia in the late 1880s:

> I have learned two things ... I think [Islam] the most blighting, withering, degrading influence of any of the false creeds. The second thing takes a very short time to learn, i.e. that if there is a more venal, devastating, and diabolical oppression on earth than that of the Turk it is that of the Shah. This is a ruined, played-out country. ...
>
> These false faiths ... degrade women with an infinite degradation. I have lived in zenanas and harems, and have seen the daily life of the secluded women, and I can speak from bitter experience of what their lives are – the intellect dwarfed ... while all the worst passions of human nature are stimulated and developed in a dreadful degree; jealousy, envy, murderous hate, intrigue ... It follows necessarily that there is also an infinite degradation of men.
>
> (*This Grand Beyond: The Travels of Isabella Bird Bishop*, p. 24)

One is left with a feeling of genuine wonder at the character of this woman, as she travels calmly for thousands of miles by horseback among the most remote peoples, through mountains, deserts and jungles, none of them apparently ever inspiring her with fear or self-doubt. Perhaps our judgement is coloured by our knowledge that the great inspiration of her life was evangelical religion, but wherever she goes she seems anxious to find the good in the people she encounters, to see mankind as essentially one family, in spite of what she calls the 'moral shadows of the darkest kind' which may hang over their lives; to dispel those shadows was evidently her deepest wish, and her journeys and her books were her chosen means of doing so.

Alongside intrepid figures like Burton and Isabella Bird, lighter classics of travel writing came from the pens of Robert Louis Stevenson and Mark Twain. The subtle comedy of Stevenson's *Travels with a Donkey in the Cevennes* (1879) is mild and engaging, with a touch so light that it could be thought of as demonstrating to perfection the old-fashioned essayist's art of writing about nothing; but its child-like good humour made it into a classic of camping. Twain's *The Innocents Abroad* (1869) is a deliberately provocative American view of other cultures in Europe and the Near East, so scornful in places that we are reminded of Smollett's tirade against eighteenth-century France. But there is more, because Twain's book is surely the first anti-travel, or rather anti-tourist, polemic: whatever you go to see is spoiled because you must see it with hundreds – or thousands – of other people, and because it is degraded by the hideous apparatus of tourism – the hoteliers, the mendacious guides and the hordes of hangers-on demanding baksheesh. Twain's obstinate refusal to be impressed by anything he saw produced a masterpiece of abrasive American humour.

Travellers to the Near East like Burton were reporting on a rich, puzzling, alien civilisation, but public interest was still more concerned with a vast region that was beyond civilisation entirely, a region repeatedly characterised by images of darkness – Africa. Here even Burton paled into insignificance compared with the two lords of African travel, Livingstone and Stanley. Although they both wrote important and best-selling books, it is impossible to treat these two men merely as travel writers: they were a joint phenomenon, they were heroes, they represented history being made before the eyes of the public. On the face of it there was a world of difference between them: Livingstone was the missionary who proclaimed again and again that the purpose of his journeying was to bring Christianity and civilisation to Africa, and that this could be achieved only through commerce, through driving out the iniquitous slave trade and replacing it with farming and manufacturing on the European model. To this end, the mapping of the rivers was essential, for only they could offer routes into the African heartland. He dreamed of a British colony in the fertile highlands on either side of the Zambezi, in modern-day Zambia and Zimbabwe. 'Those two pioneers of civilisation,' he declared, 'Christianity and commerce, should ever be inseparable; and Englishmen should be warned by the fruits of neglecting that principle as exemplified in the result of the management of Indian affairs.' This was written in 1858, the year following the Indian Mutiny, and it was music to the ears of the British public. Livingstone's outstanding courage, dedication and modesty were all reflected in his *Missionary Travels and Researches in South Africa* of 1857; his later expeditions were far less productive, but his legendary status was assured.

Stanley was a very different character, a self-made journalist, showman and adventurer, who constructed a new and heroic identity for himself, almost certainly to heal the wounds of his tragic childhood. He bathed in Livingstone's glory when he was sent by the *New York Herald* to find Livingstone, who in 1872 was presumed lost in the jungle. A year later, Livingstone was dead and Stanley assumed his mantle as the explorer of Africa, and, in so far as he possessed any intellectual agenda for what he was doing, he too promoted himself as the bringer of light, civilisation and commerce to the continent; Christianity was now given a lesser role. Stanley's first descent of the Congo was a triumph of resourcefulness and determination, but on this and still more on his second Congo journey in search of Emin Pasha, Stanley and his team behaved more like conquistadors than Victorian explorers, not hesitating to use weapons and intimidation against the indigenous peoples, or to ally themselves with notorious Islamic slave-traders. His accounts of these expeditions in *Through the Dark Continent* (1878) and *In Darkest Africa* (1890) became best-sellers, but they also drew strong criticism from some in England, uneasy at the price the arrival of civilisation exacted in central Africa. Nevertheless the adulation continued, as it had for Livingstone himself: the medals and receptions at the Royal Geographical Society, the audiences with Queen Victoria, the lecture tours, the honorary degrees, and for Stanley a knighthood, a seat in Parliament and a wedding in Westminster Abbey.

Even Livingstone's later reputation has not been able to escape being tainted by the subsequent history of central Africa – the way that the British South Africa Company took possession and exploited

Livingstone's boat capsized by a hippopotamus, from his
Missionary Travels and Researches in South Africa, 1857.

both land and people. For Stanley, however, it was even worse, for in the final years of his life the horror of the Belgian exploitation of the Congo was publicly exposed. Stanley had played a key role as the personal agent of King Leopold II in opening up the Congo, and although he was not directly involved in the brutality that followed, his reputation was all but ruined. For him there was no funeral in Westminster Abbey as there had been for Livingstone. In the case of these two men, travel and travel writing became bound up with the highest ideals and the deepest evils of their society in a way that had not been seen perhaps since the navigators and conquistadors of Spain took possession of the new world in the sixteenth century.

What Livingstone and Stanley wrote about Africa was deeply implicated in Britain's collective understanding of her place in the world, and in the strategy of empire, and likewise what Kinglake or Burton wrote about the Near East, and what everyone from Maria Graham to Lord Curzon wrote about India. But there were still areas of travel far removed from all that, areas where the individual could explore, be alone, and match his strength and wits against the elemental forces of nature. Mountaineering was largely the invention of a few cultured and imaginative Englishmen – gentlemen, officers, diplomats and scholars – who were nevertheless in partial rebellion against the restrictions of their society. Mountains have always been there, but their beauty was not seen and their freedom not valued until the ugliness and monotony of the Victorian industrial city made them visible and appreciated. By 1850 a small group among the many thousands swarming to the Alps had transformed themselves from tourists into climbers, seeking a different kind of experience of the mountains. The first classic of Alpine literature was Edward Whymper's *Scrambles Amongst the Alps* (1871), a book made all the more memorable through its first-hand account of the notorious accident which marred Whymper's first ascent of the Matterhorn in 1865, when four members of his party fell to their deaths. Whymper was an accomplished artist, and this and all his subsequent books were illustrated with his fine woodcuts. Whymper wrote about climbing in a robust rather than a poetic style, and he had a dry, ironic sense of humour, which he certainly needed when he set out to attempt the peaks of the Andes in 1880. His *Travels Amongst the Great Andes of the Equator* (1892) is a magisterial work of adventure travel, the climbing itself told in a rather clipped, stiff-upper-lip style, but enlivened by his campfire stories and his observations on South American life. Whymper was a great but cold and solitary man. Only once perhaps did he write of the spiritual dimension of climbing, and that was while describing what happened a few hours after the Matterhorn tragedy, when the three survivors beheld a mysterious pattern in the sky, formed out of the mountain mist:

> Pale, colourless, and noiseless, but perfectly sharp and defined, except
> where it was lost in the clouds, this unearthly apparition seemed
> like a vision from another world; and, almost appalled, we watched
> with amazement the development of two vast crosses, one on either
> side ... our movements had no effect upon it. The spectral forms

A vignette of climbers on the summit of the Matterhorn,
from Whymper, *Scrambles Amongst the Alps*, 1871.

remained motionless. It was a fearful and wonderful sight; unique in
my experience, and impressive beyond description, coming at such a
moment.

(*The Ascent of the Matterhorn*, pp. 288–9)

The man who stood outside the narrower climbing fraternity but
who made it intellectually respectable was the great literary scholar
Sir Leslie Stephen. His essays contributed to *The Alpine Journal* and

elsewhere were collected in *The Playground of Europe* (1871), a book which conveyed to a wide audience the power of mountaineering to enrich one's life. Writing in an elegant and imaginative style, he made climbing appear to be as much a part of civilised, gentlemanly life as a knowledge of Plato, a seat in Parliament or running a country estate. He confesses the absurdities and discomforts of climbing, but convinces us that its rewards are still greater; in one essay he describes a bad day's climbing over rock and ice which had begun at 2 a.m. but then, on the sudden realisation that the summit was within reach, he remarks, 'For the first time that day it occurred to me that life was not altogether a mistake.' After the Matterhorn accident there were many voices – Queen Victoria's among them – suggesting that mountaineering should be banned, but the writings of men like Whymper and Stephen in this early golden age helped to establish climbing as an occupation for gentlemen. Climbing in the Himalayas emerged at the end of the century as a natural extension to military surveying and mapping activities in India.

Given the ever-growing importance of travel in so many aspects of life and thought, it seems surprising that the Victorian novelists did not make greater use of it in their settings or their plots. The literary novel in England remained determinedly a portrayal of society and character in England. Sea travel and exotic settings were regarded as part of the apparatus of adventure stories for younger and more popular audiences, as in the work of Frederick Marryat, R.M. Ballantyne and, later, Rider Haggard. In America, it was Melville who seized on the adventure and sea story as a basis upon which to build his characteristic vision of the human struggle. Beginning with *Typee* and *Omoo*, and culminating in *Moby-Dick*, Melville took the serious novel out of society, away from conventional plots about love, marriage and money, and into the elemental environment of the ocean and the people who live on the ocean. In his early novels, Melville strongly endorsed the view of the Pacific as an Eden corrupted by western commerce and western missionaries. Henry James took the novel back again into Byzantine complexities of social and psychological analysis, but James used travel as a dimension in which his themes might unfold. James, of course, left America and settled in England, citing his deep personal need to be surrounded by the rich accumulation of cultural history to be found in Europe, and where he sensed not only culture but subtle, refined forms of evil. Out of this grew his favourite theme of the conflict of values between the New World and the Old, America and Europe, played out in the lives and minds of the characters who moved from one sphere to the other.

It was in France that the nineteenth-century idea of travel really achieved expression in fictional form, first in Jules Verne's works, then in Pierre Loti's. In Verne's fantasies, *A Journey to the Centre of the Earth*, *The First Men in the Moon* and *Twenty Thousand Leagues Under the Sea*, travel is both a dream of human power and a revelation of nature's magnificence. The destiny of modern scientific man to explore and master the earth, and perhaps the entire universe, could receive no greater expression. In *Around the World in Eighty Days*, surely the most perfect travel fiction ever written, this theme is given realistic social setting. In the process it poses in a delightful, subtle and satiric form the question why we travel, why we employ steamers, railways, carriages, yachts, sledges and elephants to rush around the world; in the final lines Verne produces a novelist's tongue-in-cheek answer – to find true love – which we are not intended to believe for a moment. The real reason is that we *can* do it: the steamers and the railways exist, the world is at our disposal.

A more subjective and romantic use of travel as a fictional device is to be found in the many novels of Pierre Loti. Loti was a naval officer, and almost all his works are sentimental adventures in idealised settings, evoking the familiar travel experience of loving and sailing away, part of the mythology of the sailor. His first novel, *Aziyadé* (1879), was inspired by his own love affair with a Turkish woman, and tells of his audacious plan to free her from a harem, a plan which failed and left them estranged, apparently forever; in a tearful sequel, *Fantôme d'Orient* (1892), Loti returns to Istanbul to find that she has died, perhaps killed by her vengeful husband. In his life, Loti acted like one of the heroes of his romances, building an escapist, dream image of himself as a man of multiple, exotic identities. There was no English novelist who corresponded to Loti, using locations like Constantinople, Senegal, Tahiti and Japan, evoking them in a romantic spirit and an impressionistic style.

The unofficial laureate of the British Empire was of course Rudyard Kipling. He was born and brought up in India, so technically perhaps his fictional realisations of India may not come under the heading of travel literature, but his evocations of the country became definitive, even though their viewpoint can be as puzzling as their prose style: if Kipling was simply an apostle of empire, how could he write with such warmth and understanding about the indigenous peoples? His masterpiece, *Kim*, is a dazzling portrayal of a nation which is a tangled web of contrasting cultures and sub-cultures, a novel that, with its surface colour and elusive structure, is very like India herself. But some of Kipling's other tales are disturbing and definitely non-humorous, suggesting a much darker sense of India. Is 'The Man Who Would be King' a horrifying parable of the British role in India, in which the two Englishmen who have ruled and deceived their native subjects must suffer terrible retribution? Is 'The Mark of the Beast' a Conradian tale of savagery released when the veneer of civilisation breaks down? Kipling's work is very far removed from any picturesque or sentimental view of India.

At the very end of the century, it was the expatriate Pole Joseph Conrad who introduced travel as a symbol or metaphor of shifting identity into the English novel. He did this by transforming the sea story into a study of psychological tension and self-discovery, whether in a Pacific storm, in the jungles of Africa, or in a South American revolutionary war. Conrad's characters are men placed *in extremis*, in situations beyond those of European social life, where they are faced with what is alien, with their own loneliness, weakness or irrationality. Conrad's interest in foreign cultures in their own right is minimal, for his attention is fixed on his European protagonists and their inner conflicts. Even his much-discussed novella *Heart of Darkness* has been criticised for leaving the Africans without reality and without voices; they are merely figures inhabiting the darkness, symbols of savagery, and the tragedy the story contains is not theirs but that of the European, Kurtz, corrupted by what he has seen and done outside the confines of civilisation. There is an elaborate strangeness about Conrad's style and thought which often makes his message elusive, but the fear, alienation, crisis and self-doubt that threaten his characters are his unmistakable trademark, and it is this which places him among the founders of modernism. Travel is not associated here with power, with pleasure, with commerce, with the furtherance of science or civilisation at any level, but with the unknown and the alien, with solitude and the void. Conrad's work is a fitting bridge between the nineteenth and twentieth centuries, for the first had opened with the romantic, posturing restlessness of Byron, the second with Conrad's nervous dissection of the threatened self. The horizons of travel writing in the nineteenth century had shifted and fragmented with the intellectual horizons of the century itself.

SIX

The Twentieth Century:
No Foreign Land

To travel in Europe is to assume a foreseen inheritance; in Islam, to inspect that of a close and familiar cousin. But to travel in farther Asia is to discover a novelty previously unsuspected and unimaginable. It is not a question of probing this novelty, of analysing its sociological, artistic, or religious origins, but of learning, simply, that it exists. Suddenly, as it were in the opening of an eye, the potential world – the field of man and his environment – is doubly extended. The stimulus is inconceivable to those who have not experienced it.

Robert Byron (*First Russia then Tibet*, p. 155)

The snow, sprinkled over every rock and gleaming in the sun, was of a radiant beauty that touched me to the heart. I had never seen such complete transparency; I was living in a world of crystal. Sounds were indistinct, the atmosphere like cotton wool.

An astonishing happiness welled up in me, but I could not define it. Everything was so new, so utterly unprecedented. It was not in the least like anything I had known in the Alps ... This was a different universe – withered, desert, lifeless; a fantastic universe where the presence of man was not foreseen, perhaps not desired. We were braving an interdict, overstepping a boundary, and yet we had no fear as we continued upwards.

Maurice Herzog (*Annapurna*, p. 158)

The dead men looked wonderfully beautiful. The night was shining
gently down, softening them into new ivory. Turks were white on the
clothed parts of their bodies, much whiter than the Arabs among whom
I was living; and these soldiers had been very young. Close round them
lapped the dark wormwood, now heavy with dew, in which the ends
of the moonbeams sparkled like sea-spray. Dead men seemed flung so
pitifully on the ground, huddled anyhow in low heaps that one wished to
straighten them to lie comfortably at last. So I put them all in order, one
by one, very wearied in mind and body, and longing to be of these quiet
ones, not of the restless noisy aching mob up the valley, quarrelling over
the plunder, boasting of their speed and strength, to endure God knew
how many toils and pains of this sort, till death, whether we succeeded
or failed, wrote the last chapter in our history.

T.E. Lawrence (The Seven Pillars of Wisdom, p. 331)

EACH OF THESE three passages offers a powerful clue to the paradigm
shift in travel writing in the past hundred years – the desire to evoke
what it truly *feels* like to be in a foreign environment, an alien culture
or landscape. After its long history of experimentation, approaching
and circling around but never quite grasping certain central truths,
travel writing in the twentieth century finally came to focus on two
crucial insights: that foreign travel has something vital to teach us, and
that the writers must undergo some form of personal transformation as
they travel, otherwise their experience and their writing will be merely
formulaic. In other words, travel writing acquired depth and honesty,
humility and vision, as it proved the truth of Robert Louis Stevenson's
dictum that 'There is no foreign land; it is the traveller only who is
foreign.' Discovery had to become once again central to travel writing
– but discovery that was subjective, disturbing, existential, even spiritual: it was self-discovery because it modified, perhaps transformed,
the accepted picture of the world we inhabit, and the sense of our
own selfhood. The formal reasons for travel – exploration, science,
religion, trade, political reconnaissance, colonialism, anthropology
and knowledge-gathering of all kinds – these now become separate

fields of their own, separate areas of action and discourse, leaving a purer form of travel literature, free to wander in the realms of personal discovery. This discovery began on the physical plane, which itself was – rather surprisingly – something novel, for as long as the traveller had assumed the stance of dominance, superiority and control, he had been reluctant to evoke the sheer physicality of his surroundings and impressions. Now, however, it became perhaps the principal aim of the travel writer to convey the strangeness, exhilaration, fear or loneliness that may wait in alien landscapes. Yet physicality was seen as the gateway to something else, for in this sense travel means the opening of other worlds of being, worlds which the travel writer attempts to articulate, something that goes beyond the curiosity, the description, the knowledge-gathering and the humour of travel writing in earlier centuries.

This process of discovery had still to compete with all the established modes of travel writing, with all the long-cherished assumptions of cultural superiority which lay behind so many narratives from the Age of Discovery to the nineteenth century. It had to compete with the democratisation of travel, and the revolution which re-created travel as tourism, as an aspect of consumerism. Having functioned for so long as an index of western psychology, the travel narrative found a new *raison d'être* as a critique of it, and of western culture. To put it crudely, after centuries in which the European traveller swaggered around the world laughing at foreigners – when he wasn't killing them – he finally realised that his own culture wasn't perfect, and that he might perhaps learn from others. We can see this theme prefigured long ago in many guises: in the eighteenth-century quest for the noble savage; in the romanticism of Byron and Ruskin; in the wilderness experience of John Muir; in the passion for India felt by scholars like William Jones, James Tod, Alexander Cunningham, and many more; in the orientalism of Richard Burton and Charles Doughty; and in the fiction of Conrad. The traveller writer had at last to shed his civilised skin and understand what foreign lands were offering him. In the 1930s, Robert Byron expressed this clearly, although in rather pompous language, when he wrote, 'As a member of a community and heir to a culture whose joint worth is now in dispute, I would discover what ideas, if those of the West be inadequate, can with greater advantage be found to guide the world.' He might have added that his generation was fired by the urgent desire to escape, escape at all costs from what they felt was the grey, haunted, dishonest, war-crippled world of northern Europe; a longer perspective suggests that the escape motive goes back further, at least to the romantic era.

Polar Regions and Mountain Ranges

The twentieth century opened, however, with a piece of unfinished business from the nineteenth century: polar exploration. The Arctic and Antarctic continents were the last regions on earth to defy Europe's explorers, scientists and adventurers, and as late as the 1850s the old dream of the Northwest Passage remained still a lure to commercial and imperial ambitions. The disappearance of the expedition led by Sir John Franklin in the Canadian Arctic in 1846 became a cause célèbre in Britain, and initiated a dozen rescue expeditions in as many years before the truth was discovered. That truth was disturbing: that every Englishman had died, some on the ice-bound ships, but most while trekking overland to seek aid, succumbing helplessly to an environment where the Innuit people were able to dwell permanently and to flourish. Franklin's widow proclaimed that the 130 men of the expedition had 'laid down their lives in the service of their country as truly as if they had perished by the rifle, the canon-ball or the bayonet'. Yet the commercial and naval importance claimed for the Northwest Passage had been a myth, and the real motive was national pride, the European drive to appropriate – psychologically if not politically – even such remote regions.

The same was still more true of the Poles themselves, two unique but featureless geographical points on the planet, whose inaccessibility acted like a goad to generations of explorers. There was no reason to go there, except to test the limits of human endurance, to proclaim that mankind was master of the planet, and to establish which of the nations of mankind was really the best at this kind of thing. The North Pole was reached first in 1909 by the American naval officer Robert Peary, but a decade earlier the Norwegian, Fridtjof Nansen, had survived probably the most extraordinary of polar journeys, locked in his ship in the ice for three years as it drifted almost two thousand miles, thus demonstrating that the Arctic was not a land-mass but a moving ice cap. Nansen's narrative of this wilderness experience in *Farthest North* is remarkably sane, good-tempered and humorous, as he sees himself transformed into filthy savage living on bear meat and walrus blubber.

The South Pole generally produced literature of a bleaker but more exalted kind, where the traveller is brought face to face with intense physical suffering, and with the existential question, Why am I here? Scott's own diary of his last fatal expedition of 1912 was found with his body, and the entries are mostly clipped and factual as he attempts to rationalise the fate he now knows he cannot escape: 'We are showing that Englishmen can still die with a bold spirit.' But there is a sharper poignancy about those entries when his officer-trained mask slips away and he confronts the fact that he has been brought here solely by his own choice, perhaps by his own vanity: 'All the day-dreams must go ... Great God, this is an awful place.' His fate was made all the more unbearable to him by his sense of failure, knowing he had been beaten by Amundsen in the race to be first to the Pole, and he must have been additionally tormented by the question whether ordinary people, including their own families, would sympathise, and understand what had driven them on: 'Surely a great rich country like ours will see that those who are dependent upon us are provided for.' And the final entry seems to ache with a sense of personal guilt

Scott at the Pole (*left*), his faced marked with physical suffering and with
the desolate sense of failure.

for his family: 'For God's sake look after our people.' Scott need not
have feared, for failure and death made him a hero perhaps even more
securely than success could have, or rather his story forced people
to re-examine what success and failure mean, for he had pursued his
vision to the ultimate end, and given his life for an idea. This form
of idealism was seen as essential to the process of nation-building,
and still more of empire-building. The sacrifice of the individual self
in a noble cause: this was what Scott came to symbolise, and surely
there could be no higher destiny that that. Scott became part of the
mythology of Britishness, and the ideal of sacrifice was one which
millions were called upon to consider, to embrace or to reject, in the
Great War.

Scott would undoubtedly have produced his own major book
about the polar quest, but instead his fragmentary notes provide unforgettable insights into the world of Antarctic exploration. The definitive work on this expedition is probably Apsley Cherry-Garrard's

The Worst Journey in the World (1922). The author was a member of the expedition, but was not chosen for the final assault on the Pole, which is not the central episode in the book; instead he focuses on the earlier, subsidiary trek which he and two others had made in the most agonising conditions of the Antarctic winter, from which they returned only after coming close to death. 'This journey', he wrote, 'had beggared our language: no words could express its horror', and 'We were beginning to think of death as a friend.' Cherry-Garrard was one of those who waited in vain at the base camp for Scott's party to return, and who found their bodies eight months after their deaths. His book dwells on the feelings of guilt which assailed him for years afterwards, and the question whether the whole enterprise had been futile. By any standard of rationality or practicality, no doubt it was so, but for him it was a defining experience which carried him into realms of being which would otherwise have remained unknown. This experience and the character of his comrades, especially Edward Wilson, gave him hope for the future of humanity. 'In such a world, violent, angry and tired, Wilson sets a standard of faith and work. In a world which destroys itself and beauty, desperately and impotently desiring peace, he helps.' Looking back on the agonising mystery of the expedition, he reflected that 'Exploration is the physical expression of the Intellectual Passion'.

The Australian scientist Douglas Mawson had turned down the chance to go with Scott, and instead led his own expedition in 1912–13, which turned into an epic of survival in nightmare conditions, recorded in his memorable book *The Home of the Blizzard* (1915). But the most long-drawn-out of all the Antarctic journeys was the expedition led by Shackleton in 1914–16, which turned into a two-year battle for life over ice and sea, in which every man was saved, thanks largely to Shackelton's tenacious leadership. Ironically the expedition never set foot on Antarctica, because their ship was crushed and destroyed by ice in the Weddell Sea. The tangible results of this expedition were non-existent, but as a narrative of adventure and courage *in extremis* the book *South* (1919) is unforgettable. One of the most poignant moments comes when Shackleton reaches civilisation after the ordeal, and asks about the war – his party had left England in August 1914 just days after the outbreak of the Great War – and was told that it was still raging and that millions had been killed, that 'the world had gone mad'; locked in their private battle for survival, he and his men had known nothing of the slaughter taking place in Europe. Scott and Shackleton became national figures, almost as celebrated as Livingstone and Stanley had been, and the narratives of their journeys were raised above the level of mere travel literature to become part of the nation's history.

The narrative of discovery and endurance amid savage landscapes became the *raison d'être* of the enormous volume of mountaineering literature – and seafaring literature too – which the twentieth century produced. Both these forms of writing have a large technical component, absorbing to fellow climbers and sailors; but to non-specialists there is always the feeling that these technical descriptions are a diversion, giving the appearance that the problems faced on a mountainside or on the high seas are merely technical problems, whereas the heart of the matter is psychological: why is the writer there, risking his life in that alien environment? The extent to which the writer confronts this question – even if he does not answer it – determines the success, the spiritual depth and the beauty that a text achieves. Although it serves no practical purpose, the mountaineering experience or the seafaring experience brings about inner changes within the life and the mind, bringing mankind face to face with those elemental forces which have been banished from normal life. Consider this account by Georges Sonnier of a solitary climber lost in a crevasse on Mont Blanc:

> He was alive. Alive, but alone, abandoned, lost at the bottom of an ice hole, above which he saw but a narrow stretch of blue sky and, at night, a few faint twinkling stars.

He was there for eight days and seven nights, eating only a little chocolate which he melted over the flame of a candle and diluted with the glacier water that dripped over him.

Eight days and seven nights! No search party had found anything. Everybody thought he was dead, even his friends.... For living people, this living man was but a name and a shadow.

And yet, obstinately, he persisted in living. His ice-axe had become stuck in the broken snow-bridge. With a frightful exertion he managed to climb up to within one metre of it; a single metre from light, freedom, warmth and life. But that one last metre was beyond him. His strength gave way and he fell back.

He tried again seven times and always in vain. Clutching at the ice with his bleeding hands, which were now without sensation, he crept up the terrible, steel-coloured wall, and finally dropped back into the night of his ice prison. He was exhausted and had to abandon his attempts. Then, on the evening of the fourth day, the ice-axe fell beside him. It was useless now, for he no longer had the strength to use it.

Sometimes he heard parties passing above him. He heard words, songs, laughter, and he shouted in vain. The edges of the crevasse were formed in such a way that they magnified the sounds that came from outside, while shutting in those which might come from below. So the prisoner's voice was captive too....

I can picture to myself the wounded man, fighting against so much cruelty, against the exquisite torture of the mountain; abandoned by everything, left at the gate of the next world and yet fighting, still fighting in the shadows.... There is no word to describe such courage.

And yet he was saved at last by a miracle – a lesser miracle than that of his dogged, protracted fight. Passing near the crevasse, a guide noticed the broken bridge, drew near and saw the prisoner. That very night he was brought down to the valley, half his body frozen and his burnt eyes full of shadow.

(*Mont Blanc*, pp. 168–9)

This surely is the heart of the mountain experience in its most extreme form: to travel into the realm of death, and to return alive. This is the ultimate journey, bringing echoes of ancient mythological descents into the underworld: a brief, terrifying experience which has the power to transform forever our perspectives on life.

A New Primitivism

Physical harshness, alien landscapes, dissolved identities – these things add up to what we might think of as a new primitivism in travel writing, paralleling the psychological void that lurks below the surface in Conrad's fiction, and that was made explicit at exactly this time in the paintings of Picasso and the music of Stravinsky – the sense of flight from the conventional canons of western art and thought. Some of the most characteristic travel writers of the period set out to shed their narrow English identities and penetrate into a different level of being. Perhaps the most overt act of self-transformation was that of T.E. Lawrence, whose experience of desert life and the Arab struggle formed the basis for the last great romantic war book. *The Seven Pillars of Wisdom* (1926) uses a highly wrought prose style to cast a mantle of poetry, even spirituality, over conflict, suffering, pain and death. It is not the events of the war which are central, but the desert and the people who inhabit it: this is why, although not a travel book in the usual sense, it has become indelibly linked with our image of the desert. It is also the ultimate escape book, the personal testament of an upper-class soldier and scholar turning his back on conventional English life and writing his will across the pages of history, not in cavalry charges, not in the uniform of a British officer, but in the robes of a desert nomad and surrounded by wild guerrilla forces. It was, he said, like travelling in imprisoning valleys, and then coming out upon a hilltop to behold a vision of freedom, 'a window in the wall of life'. The story moves endlessly across the desert in a narrative filled with heat, thirst, sickness, pain, loneliness, degradation and violence. The effect of his years in the desert was to rid him of his English self forever; they made him, he said, 'look at the West and its conventions with new eyes: they destroyed it all for me'. Lawrence was that highly unusual creature, an intellectual who had wallowed in bloodshed, and this strange dichotomy gives his writing its exceptional power.

Lawrence's exact contemporary and namesake D.H. Lawrence was another man pursuing a personal quest away from Englishness towards something that had been lost, something more elemental and physical. Of course this urge to escape was not restricted to exceptional visionary beings like Lawrence; in fact the 1920s and 1930s saw something like a literary exodus from England: think of Norman Douglas in Italy, Robert Graves in Majorca, Somerset Maugham in the Pacific and the South of France, Gerald Brennan in Spain, Auden in China and Iceland, Isherwood in Berlin, Lawrence Durrell in the Greek islands, Aldous Huxley in California; and at the same time, Pound, HD, Stein, Eliot, Cummings, Hemingway, Macleish and Henry Miller left the United States for Europe. Perhaps some of this was mere fashion, but D.H. Lawrence was deliberately seeking a level of being untainted by civilisation, a primitive energy which he felt was the key to the regeneration of western man, now paralysed, corrupted and alienated from his true being. Lawrence travelled restlessly in search of an environment and culture that was uncorrupted, where he could settle or find inspiration. The places he chose were always in the south, always filled with sun and almost always associated with an ancient civilisation: Italy, Sri Lanka, Tahiti, Australia, Mexico. He never found his ideal, and was aware at some level that he never would. 'Travel seems to me a splendid lesson in disillusion', he admitted in a letter to Mary Cannan. He wrote four books of explicit travel memoirs, on Italy, Sardinia, Mexico and Etruria, and all four display Lawrence's overwhelmingly subjective approach to travel writing. For the facts of geography and history, for information or conventional description of any kind he cares nothing. All that interests him is unseen, the processes taking place in the soul – his own and those of the indigenous people as he projects them in his imagination.

Twilight in Italy (1916) subverts the expected images of Italian beauty and sensuousness by discovering everywhere the transition from traditional agrarian life to industrialisation, and the inexorable dwindling of population as the young emigrate, mainly to America. This is one meaning of the 'twilight' in the title, but there is a second more subtle meaning: that Lawrence had expected from Italy a blend of sun and darkness, wisdom and emotion, but had not found it. 'Where is the transcendent knowledge in our hearts, uniting sun and darkness, day and night, spirit and senses?', he asks. 'Why do we not know that the two in consummation are one?' It is the 'great mechanised society' which has reached out even to Italy, and destroyed this ideal which Lawrence was always seeking. Thus *Twilight in Italy* is an early example of something that would become central to primitivist travel writing – the sense that the author is witnessing a turning point, a vanishing world, which the readers of the future will never see.

Disillusioned with Italy, Lawrence turned his attention to Mexico and New Mexico in his search for a place that might truly have the power to transfigure his life. *Mornings in Mexico* (1927) reiterates again and again that the American Indian consciousness is quite different from that of the white man, that his world is animated by powerful non-intellectual forces. But the book itself is rather thin in comparison with Lawrence's fictional treatment of his response to Mexico in *The Plumed Serpent*, which chronicles a revival of the ancient blood religion as a path of human rebirth. The same theme informs one of Lawrence's strangest and most disturbing short stories, 'The Woman Who Rode Away', in which a white woman offers herself as a sacrificial victim so that the reign of the 'dark powers' may continue. That Lawrence truly believed in these things is unlikely; in both fiction and travel writing he was exploring a realm of symbols to express what he wished to say about the necessity for human regeneration. Likewise his last travel book, *Etruscan Places*, published in 1932 after his death, is unmistakably part of his emotional preparation for his own death, for it dwells on imagery of the Etruscan tombs, which Lawrence was convinced showed a confidence in a continuing existence after death. The tomb sculptures were natural, spontaneous, smiling and full of life, and the entire culture of the Etruscans contrasted strongly with the grim authoritarianism of the Romans who supplanted them. Lawrence represents in the most extreme form the travel writer who reimagines the places he has seen in his own image, and more even than that, for the whole world becomes a mirror of his mind:

> And death, to the Etruscan, was a pleasant continuance of life, with jewels and wine and flutes playing for the dance. It was neither an ecstasy of bliss, a heaven, nor a purgatory of torment. It was just a natural continuance of the fullness of life. ...
>
> To the Etruscan all was alive; the whole universe lived; and the business of man was himself to live amid it all. He had to draw life into himself, out of the wandering huge vitalities of the world. The cosmos was alive, like a vast creature.
>
> (*Etruscan Places*, pp. 28, 89)

This escape, this return to primitivism, vitality, freedom, paganism, ancient wisdom – call it what you will – appears again and again in the travel literature of the first half of the century, very often with an explicitly anti-English colouring.

Throughout his work E.M. Forster used foreign settings to attack conventional English barriers of class, race and gender. To him, genuine travel meant knowing the people of a place; he was less interested in landscape or picturesque impressions. From his earliest fantasy stories set in Italy and Greece, through to his mature novels, Forster plays off the figures of passionless, grey English men and women against the southern peoples, who live by instinct, retaining a sense of the mystery and beauty of the irrational. Italy is the scene of comic misunderstanding, where glimpses of love and freedom challenge characters' former lives. India offers a still more profound psychological shock, exposing people to spiritual forces incomprehensible in the west, transforming their lives through cultural conflict. Forster's non-fictional travel works, *Alexandria* and *The Hill of Devi*, represent strictly censored accounts of his experiences in Egypt and India, and are less remarkable.

Forster's early stories involve magical events and forms of life, suggesting the survival of pagan nature cults. Literary paganism had deep roots in nineteenth-century romanticism and aestheticism, and these stories have a tongue-in-cheek quality. The travel books of Norman Douglas, however, seem to offer a more serious and consistent creed of hedonistic paganism. Like Forster, Douglas felt himself to be a sexual outsider in England, but unlike Forster he was not afraid to admit it. In his books on Southern Italy, fiction and non-fiction, he advances an ideal of what life and travel writing should be: they should both be animated by physicality, subjectivity and aestheticism, a rule of life completely impossible in England. Douglas came from an elite, aristocratic family, and as a man and as a writer he clearly felt himself to be a law unto himself, one who could live exclusively for leisure and pleasure, both suitably intellectualised. *Siren Land*, his account of the Sorrentine Peninsula, appeared as early as 1911, and *South Wind*, his novel of the scandalous life of Capri, in 1917. The latter was a sensational success, creating the modern legend of Capri as a hedonistic paradise, and being widely condemned as indecent by those who were avidly prosecuting the Great War; it could be seen as Douglas's defence of the passionate vitality of southern Europe against the insane death wish of the north. The figure of the Siren was the perfect double-edged symbol for the dangerous, seductive creed preached by Douglas: the Sirens were vampire-like demons, hiding beneath a mask of irresistible sweetness and beauty. Yet Douglas makes it clear that, for him, a life lived within reach of the Sirens' song was worth whatever punishments they might inflict. Douglas's works appear to have no formal structure; they are discursive and fluid, moving between narrative, descriptive, didactic and meditative passages. They all contain harsh, even brutal comments, reflecting Douglas's elitist psychology, and make uncomfortable reading today. *Fountains in the Sand* (1912) is a book on Tunisia, showing little sympathy for Arab culture. 'They die like flies', he writes of the country's poor. 'Naturally enough, for it is not too much to say of the poorer classes that they eat dirt, and that only once a day.' For him the life of Southern Italy was both harsh and sensuous, taking one back, cleansing one of the grey, diseased breath of civilisation. In *Old Calabria* (1915) he writes:

> Meanwhile it is good to rest here, immovable but alert, in the breathless hush of noon. Showers of benevolent heat stream down upon this desolation; not the faintest wisp of vapour floats upon the horizon; not a sail, not a ripple, disquiets the waters. The silence can be felt. Slumber is brooding over the things of the earth.
>
> (*Old Calabria*, p. 321)

Anti-Christian, anti-imperialist and anti-authoritarian, Douglas hovers somewhere between the Wildean nineties and Bloomsbury. As a writer and philosopher he is superbly dated in his elitist faith that the world exists as a sensuous playground for those courageous enough to seize upon it. Related to Douglas but safer and less satyresque were the works of his friend Sir Osbert Sitwell, who offered himself as the well-bred guide to life's finer pleasures in countries like Italy and Greece. Sitwell was the traveller as connoisseur, publishing his memoirs in a series of what he called 'discursions' on travel, art and life, for a public willing to be patronised by such an aristocratic guide.

Literary Travel in the Interwar Years

The end of the war in 1918, and of the restrictions it had placed on travel, had released a new wave of travel literature, and of course there were many writers of the ensuing two decades who did not fit at all into the pattern of new primitivism or new paganism, which was a literary, avant-garde creed. Some of the most popular travel writers took a very different approach, and among them none was more successful than Peter Fleming. Fleming's literary career began in 1932 when he joined a press-sponsored expedition to South America to search for the missing explorer Percy Fawcett, out of which came his first book, *Brazilian Adventure* (1933). The expedition was disorganised and comic, and Fleming seized the opportunity to debunk the romantic view of travel and travel literature, portraying his party as rather bad actors in a rather awful play, and he made no secret of the fact that their jungle journey was, in part at least, a media stunt, which he nevertheless enjoyed in a public-school-games spirit. The dangers and heroism of off-the-map travel he dismisses breezily with remarks like, 'It requires less courage to be an explorer than to be a chartered accountant.' The book was enthusiastically received, and was welcomed as exploding the psychological or cultural pretensions of 'serious' travel writing. Fleming followed this up with accounts of new journeys into Russia, China and Central Asia, which developed still further the frivolous, episodic approach. Accomplished and readable as they are, even Fleming himself recognised that they were really just a higher form of journalism, in which he created a carefree, adventurous role for himself, then played it for all it was worth. After three books, Fleming drifted away from travel writing, describing this kind of commissioned work frankly as 'a rut' and 'a racket', saying he hoped to travel again but never with a publisher's contract in his pocket. He later wrote a short story titled 'A Tent in Tibet', about a dying explorer who knows that he has never really told the truth about his travel experiences, but has dressed them up for publication. On this, his last expedition, he keeps a diary in which he does reveal the truth about his motives and what has really happened to him, imagining it will be found by a search party, and that it will immortalise his name. But finally, to gain a little life-giving warmth in his final hours, he is driven to burn it, and this at last is a final deed of truth, of authenticity, springing from the reality of his life, not from some pathetic desire for publicity. The story obviously reveals Fleming's deep scepticism about the values that lay behind the modern business of travel writing.

The question of the writer's role, persona and voice loomed ever larger, and it was one of the ways in which travel writing approached nearer to fiction in the interwar years. Originality of mind and style became more and more important, making the travel book an image of the world refracted by each writer's distinct personality. In this respect, Robert Byron has been the most acclaimed, and hailed as virtually the inventor of the modern travel book, but so has Norman Douglas, and the two certainly have much in common. Both were elitist, sustained by an invincible belief that they were a law unto themselves; both were aesthetes proclaiming their personal view of what constituted the life of the mind and of the senses; and both chose omniscience as their foible. The latter gave them the full confidence to build their texts out of unrelated fragments – art, history, landscapes, encounters, incidents, conversations – which are made to cohere purely through the force of the writer's imagination. Byron produced a handful of books, of which *The Road to Oxiana* (1937) is considered his masterpiece, a journey through Persia in search of little-known monuments of ancient architecture. It is written mostly in a style of offhand but calculated wit, in which people, places and impressions are impaled with pin-sharp, offensive phrases, like specimens of lower life-forms, which today make for uncomfortable reading:

> We went to the Lido this morning, and the Doge's Palace looked
> more beautiful from a speed-boat than it ever did from a gondola. The
> bathing, on a calm day, must be the worst in Europe: water like hot
> saliva, cigar ends floating into one's mouth, and shoals of jelly-fish.

> Physically, Jews can look the best or the worst bred people in the world.
> These were the worst. They stank, stared, shoved, and shrieked.

> Mesopotamia has remained a land of mud deprived of mud's only
> possible advantage, vegetable fertility. It is a mud plain. ... From this
> plain rise villages of mud and cities of mud. The rivers flow with liquid
> mud. The air is composed of mud refined into a gas. The people are
> mud-coloured; they wear mud-coloured clothes, and their national hat
> is nothing more than a formalised mud-pie.   (pp. 3, 14–15, 37)

... and so on. The book is not long, but it was three years in the writing, for everything that happened to Byron on this journey was refined and intensified in his imagination. *Oxiana* used to be extravagantly praised, claimed to be as important to travel writing as *The Waste Land* to poetry or *Ulysses* to the novel, and identified as *the* classic interwar travel text. But to many later readers it has dated unpleasantly; it now appears posturing, embodying some of the most irritating features of travel literature – above all its social elitism. Byron seemed to regard it as his perfect right to cut his way through any country, any journey, manipulating high commissioners, local rulers, religious leaders, old Etonian friends and servants at will. Unwittingly perhaps, his carefully crafted, biting prose reveals a refined heartlessness, a power complex that must surely be a hangover from the age of imperialism. Sometimes silky and exquisite, sometimes caustic and brutal, it is a prose of domination, in which the writer's ego is everywhere supreme, in which any and every experience reveals the author's superior mind and personality. Open the book where you will, and you are reminded of Holden Caulfield's tired cynicism: 'Witty bastard; all I ever meet is witty bastards.' Each reader must make up his or her own mind about the high claims made for *The Road to Oxiana*, but no book of this period could show more clearly the travel writer's proud descent from the conquistadors and the imperial agents of the past.

Did all the travel writers of the 1920s and 1930s have to be, like Fleming and Byron, products of Eton and Oxford? Sometimes it seemed that way, especially when those of them who were building careers as novelists deliberately chose travel writing in order to boost their public profile. Evelyn Waugh's half-dozen travel works were all produced to commission, to put his name around. The first of them, *Labels: A Mediterranean Journal* (1930), is relatively good-humoured, written frankly as a tourist rather than as a traveller, an account of a luxury cruise through the seaports of the Mediterranean. The point of the title was to examine the stereotyped images, the 'labels', attached to the places he visited, and see whether they were valid. Waugh uses devices borrowed from fiction, including wholly invented characters, to frame his own reflections, and in most cases the result is to explode the stereotypes.

But Waugh's absurdist humour and the bitterness of his mind very soon grew deeper and uglier, so that his travel books became an all too accurate mirror of his personality, the stylish frivolity corresponding to a blank despair beneath the surface. In his African books, and more especially in *Ninety-Two Days*, his disgust with himself is only faintly masked by a disgust for the world. By deliberately seeking what is abnormal, especially the squalor, disease and desolation of Guiana, he explores what is abnormal in himself, almost like an act of religious penance. Out of this South American journey came the bleakest of all his novels, *A Handful of Dust*, and out of the absurd experience of acting as a war correspondent in Abyssinia came *Scoop*. In Waugh the link between travel writing and fiction is exceptionally clear: the disorder and bleakness of life are reflected, but not redeemed, in the refined cruelty of his art. Waugh made absolutely no claim to sympathy or sensitivity about any country or its people. He wrote as only a querulous, chauvinistic Englishman of his class and time could write; this was his integrity as a literary artist.

In this respect Waugh is close to Graham Greene, whose *Journey Without Maps* (1936) resembles in places a psychological thriller. The book describes a trek through the jungles and squalid villages of Sierra Leone and Liberia, thoughout which there was apparently no culture to see or describe; it was an ordeal, undertaken to plumb the depths of existential boredom, a deliberate journey into a personal heart of darkness. Researching the awful conditions in those countries while planning the trip, Greene commented, 'It really seemed as though you couldn't go deeper than that.' What he found there was fear, emptiness, disease and boredom, a void, an experience which might become a rock-bottom point from which his life might somehow be redeemed or at least raised. Greene's narrative drive is more exciting than Waugh's, and the writing is grittier, tense, nervous and more willing to take risks. Greene's plunge into the horrors of West Africa was repeated in his experience of Mexico in *The Lawless Roads* (1939), a commissioned work of reportage on the hostility of the then Mexican government to the Catholic Church. Greene wrote no other explicit travel books, but he consistently used foreign locations in the same way that Conrad did, to place his characters *in extremis*. Strange as it sounds, with these two upper-class Oxford-educated Catholic converts we are back in a realm of strangeness with the neo-primitivists, desperately seeking for something that might make them feel that they exist. Greene is the only writer to have a country, albeit an imaginary one, named after him; 'Greeneland', with its grim sense of squalor, violence, guilt and possible redemption, is a psychological reality, if not a geographical one.

From 1936 onwards, reports from war fronts added a new dimension to travel literature. There was Waugh in Abyssinia and Orwell in Spain with *Homage to Catalonia* (1938), while W.H. Auden and Christopher Isherwood were commissioned to go to China to observe the Sino-Japanese war. Auden turned his impressions into poetry, and took many photographs, while Isherwood provided a diary of their travels, and the result was *Journey to a War* (1938). Neither of them spoke a word of Chinese, so their exchanges with ordinary people were strictly limited. Isherwood, however, was a skilled and perceptive observer, very open to personal impressions, and this was a new form of socially committed travel writing. With his subversive stories of 1930s' Berlin, Isherwood had already identified himself as a writer determined to escape the stifling dullness of England. Orwell described his experiences in Spain with his characteristic voice of passionate decency, very different from Waugh's celebration of Italian imperialism in Africa, and very different from a persona like that of Byron, Fleming or Douglas.

There was, however, one celebrated travel writer of the 1930s whose works outsold those of all the aesthetes and adventurers combined. H.V. Morton was a journalist whose series of books *In Search of...* dominated the middlebrow market for some three decades. Morton had no pretensions at all to being an explorer or the possessor of any special knowledge; he was merely a decent, thoughtful Everyman-figure, touring in comfort, observing and recording what he saw with charm and humour. The resulting books were guidebooks with a personal touch, imbued with the agreeable personality of their author. He began with his own country – *In Search of England*, then Wales, Scotland and Ireland – before venturing further afield, to southern Europe, the Middle East and South Africa. His masterpieces were *In the Steps of the Master* (1934), about the Holy Land, and *In the Steps of St Paul* (1936), about the Eastern Mediterranean, both of which sold in their hundreds of thousands. Morton may have been unpretentious, but he did have his own homespun philosophy: a strong faith in the ideal of rural life, an antipathy to industrialism and urbanisation, and his books dwelt largely on the history and traditions of the places he described. When the war came, he almost seemed to welcome it as a possible way out of the slide into social decay which he sensed all around him. He was also a sincere Christian, and wrote his religious travel books to recall his countrymen to their historic faith, while *In the Steps of the Master* is plainly intended as a pilgrimage narrative. His books are extremely well written in an old-fashioned sense:

> As the sun goes down, a stillness falls over Egypt. Water channels that cross the fields turn to the colour of blood, then to bright yellow that fades into silver. The palm trees might be cut from black paper and pasted against the incandescence of the sky. The brown hawks that hang all day above the sugar-cane and the growing wheat are seen no more and, one by one, the stars burn over the sandhills and lie caught in the stiff fronds of the date palms.
>
> It is this moment which remains for ever as a memory of Egypt, a moment when day is over and night has not yet unfolded her wings,

a strange between-time in whose tremendous hush the earth seems listening for a message from the sky. The fierce day dies and the sand loses its heat and all things are for a brief space without shadow.

During this hush I stepped into a little boat on the Suez Canal. The water that fell from the oars was red, but before we had crossed the narrow canal to El Kantara it was silver, and the moon was shining.

(p. 1)

It might be the opening page of a novel. As an ageing reactionary, Morton finally emigrated to South Africa, which he believed resembled England as it had been in the 1920s. He was a publishing phenomenon, whose prolific works from the 1930s and 1940s are still to be found abundantly in the second-hand book shops.

In 1939, in a bittersweet footnote to the rage for travel writing between the wars, Anthony Powell published his novel *What's Become of Waring?* in which it emerges that the admired travel writer T.T. Waring has never travelled to any of the places he has written about, but has half-invented and half-plagiarised the entire contents of his best-selling books, until he becomes sick of the whole thing and fakes his own death. But if Powell – one of the few novelists of this era to resist the lure of travel – thought that his satire might help to kill off an over-hyped literary fashion, he was much mistaken, for nothing it seemed could now stop its progress. The great mountaineer H.W. Tilman would soon write sarcastically in the preface to *China to Chitral*: 'Comparatively few travellers have visited Chinese Turkestan; which is perhaps just as well because of those fortunate few, not many have refrained from writing a book.'

Post-war English Travel Writing

So far as travel literature was concerned, World War II did not function as any kind of watershed or set any radical changes in motion. Several writers enjoyed careers which spanned the war. Freya Stark, for example, had written accounts of her courageous ventures into little-known and hostile parts of the Middle East in the 1930s, which were engaging but heavily influenced by the 'romance of the desert' tradition. In later years Stark became elevated into an establishment figure, an official doyenne among travel writers, able to do no wrong in the eyes of critics. Her prestige became enormous; she knew everybody, she was consulted by governments, and she socialised with the diplomatic and military elite of Europe. Yet her books, published into the 1980s, became less and less attractive, full of expert knowledge and rather heavy-handed wisdom. She had a weakness for fine writing, a prose that was almost Ruskinian, as if she were fulfilling the traditional expectation of what a travel book should be. The sharp edge of real personal experience seemed to slip away from her, and her writing became rather stagy.

The tradition of southern paganism found a new post-war advocate in Lawrence Durrell, although he often pointed out that his three famous evocations of Greek islands were not strictly travel books but place books. *Prospero's Cell* (1945), *Reflections on a Marine Venus* (1953) and *Bitter Lemons* (1957) describe the author's life on Corfu, Rhodes and Cyprus respectively. Durrell was the archetypal escape-writer, devoting his life to a deliberate search for an elemental environment where he might find passion, release and creativity. He was convinced that neither personality nor culture is the product of human will, but of place, hence he lived the life of an exile, although not, in his own terms, that of a traveller, but that of a settler, one who had found a new life. In *Bitter Lemons* he remarked that journeys 'flower spontaneously out of the demands of our natures – and the best of them lead us not only outwards in space, but inwards as well.' His sense of Greece was not that of a scholar of the past, but of a lover of the present:

> The whole Mediterranean – the sculptures, the palms, the gold beads, the bearded heroes, the wine, the ideas, the ships, the moonlight, the winged gorgons, the bronze men, the philosophers – all of it seems to

rise in the sour, pungent taste of these black olives between the teeth. A taste older than meat, older than wine. A taste as old as cold water.

(*Prospero's Cell*, p. 96)

Durrell's status as an outsider in this idealised world only became a problem in Cyprus, because of Britain's involvement in the political conflict there. The book ends with a tragedy, when Durrell's close friend is shot dead for the crime of fraternising with him, an event signalling the end of his Greek dream. His great fictional work, *The Alexandria Quartet*, is likewise dominated by the spirit of place, for the city of Alexandria is the sole organising principle in a story in which personal reality is refracted and dissolved. Durrell's politics became increasingly right-wing, rejecting mass democracy and industrialism, in favour of a pagan ideal. His rejection of Englishness was total, and his entire adult life was lived abroad.

Durrell was an important force in forming the modern image of Greece as an idealised land of sun, sea and a rich traditional culture. His influence was carried even further by Patrick Leigh Fermor, perhaps the most highly regarded of all the travel writers of the mid-century. The achievement of his long lifetime has been just half a dozen books, all written with a controlled passion, composing a portrait of his own personality as much as the places he describes. Fermor is one of the very few travel writers whose works have been so deeply admired that they have spurred people to leave England and settle in the places he evoked so feelingly.

Fermor was a rebel in his youth, a heroic soldier during the war, a scholar and a master of prose; all his books seem offered as hymns of praise to an ideal of nobility, freedom, generosity and imagination, which he found above all in Greece, but also in other parts of Europe before the war. Not surprisingly these virtues are everywhere under threat, and consequently his work has a persistently elegiac quality. He is bitter in his denunciations of tourism, bitter that his beloved Greece should be doomed to destruction in what he describes as 'the Coca-Cola age'. Guidebooks should be publicly burned, he rages, for they have opened Greece to the most dangerous invasion since Xerxes. Tourism destroys the object of its love, turning dignified islands and serene coasts into polluted hells. What tourism has destroyed is not tabulated in statements or arguments, but emerges slowly, from the images and remembered experiences in his carefully wrought prose. This is his description of the house of the painter Ghika, on the island of Hydra:

> It lies above and beyond the town at the end of a precipitous ascent
> by mule or on foot, for the island, thanks to its steepness, is as empty
> of wheels as pre-Columbian America. A saddle of rock to the east,
> covered with white houses which flow down and fill a ravine that
> sinks to the shore, conceals the main town. This valley divides the
> seaman's from the shepherd's realm, for the roughly-ledged hillsides
> to the west, bare except for occasional almond and olive trees, are
> sprinkled with black goats. Beyond, in either direction, ascends
> a wilderness of grey and wrinkled mountains. The sea, showing
> through the rugged hills, stretches away to the Argive coast. Islands
> follow each other along leagues of water ... White-walled and
> massive, built as a defence against the attacks of pirates, the house
> climbs the flank of the central watershed in four dazzling tiers. ...
> A tilted, fortress-like wall encloses its nine strata of tree-shaded
> terraces. ... This ziggurat is honeycombed with rooms and elaborate
> cedarwood ceilings enclose the larger ones like the lids of caskets.
>
> (*Ghika: Paintings, Drawings, Sculpture*, p. 26)

This is evidently more than a description of a house: it suggests that the structure has grown, or been shaped by some natural force, out of the landscape and out of the history of the island. Almost every feature and incident of Fermor's books is re-created with this kind of care. True, it results in a prose that may be criticised as fussy and elaborate, but it explains why Fermor holds his position as the culmination of modern literary travel writing. In the 1930s, when he was still under 20 years of age, Fermor had walked alone across Europe, from Amsterdam to Istanbul. He chose to let forty years pass before embodying this journey into two books, *A Time of Gifts* (1977) and *Between the Woods and the Water* (1986). This extraordinary lapse of time inevitably turns the books into an encounter between an old man and his younger self, and an encounter between two worlds. On this journey he was received everywhere with hospitality and generosity, and he recollects a sense of freedom and civility in the life of Europe which would now be impossible.

Probably the only travel writer of this period to approach the veneration in which Fermor is held was Wilfred Thesiger, whose oeuvre is even more slender, consisting really of just two classic books, *Arabian Sands* (1959) and *The Marsh Arabs* (1964). Although he came from a socially elite English family – Eton and Oxford, and an uncle who was Viceroy of India – Thesiger carried the primitivist spirit to new heights. He seems a twentieth-century throwback to the explorer-adventurers of a century before like Burton, eager to test their physical endurance and perhaps dissolve their identities, in the encounter with desert and mountain and savage people. Of one of his first expeditions in Ethiopia as a very young man, Thesiger recalled:

> As I looked round the clearing at the ranks of squatting warriors and the small isolated group of my own men, I knew that this moonlight meeting in unknown Africa with a savage potentate who hated Europeans was the realization of my boyhood dreams. I had come here in search of adventure: the mapping, the collecting of animals and birds were all incidental. The knowledge that somewhere in this neighbourhood three previous expeditions had been exterminated, that we were far beyond any hope of assistance, that even our whereabouts were unknown, I found wholly satisfying.
>
> (*The Life of My Choice*, p. 146)

These are the thoughts of a boy who had grown up with the novels of Rider Haggard, but Thesiger would build his experiences of

wildernesses and the people who lived there into a thoroughgoing critique of civilisation, a hatred of life in the modern West. To Thesiger,
the strength, simplicity and nobility of the desert nomad or the African
plain-dweller were bitter reproaches to the so-called achievements of
civilisation – the technology, the greed, the blindness to nature, the
corruption of the spirit. The style of his books is lean and economical,
sometimes fierce, sometimes gently lyrical, a style perfectly adapted
to his message. But so extreme did his anti-civilisation stance become
that some readers have been repelled by what seemed to be a fascist
worship of the will and of physical toughness, and his apparent rejection of any of the gifts of higher culture. In Thesiger, the ideal of the
noble savage is revived, and contrasted passionately with the evils
of the industrial age. He completely reverses the nineteenth-century
ambition of carrying civilisation to primitive peoples; he is the fugitive
from civilisation, escaping back into elemental simplicity.

Spirituality played no part in Thesiger's world-view; his desert
experiences seemed to him revelations only of the endless capacities of
the will and of the body. Laurens van der Post has at first sight some
strong points of contact with Thesiger, for he too saw the 'primitive' traditions of Africa as representing instinct, emotion, openness,
freedom and warmth. But for Van der Post, this nexus of positive
life values was held together only because they revealed an organic
and psychic unity between man and his environment, indeed with
the cosmos as a whole. Van der Post's books, *Venture to the Interior*
(1952), *The Lost World of the Kalahari* (1958), and so on, were praised
as outstanding books of their time, transcending the travel genre, as
books of vision or philosophy, that could reach out to anyone, and
so it proved when they sold in their hundreds of thousands. They
were adventure stories overlaid with a quasi-religious wisdom which
today would be termed partly ecological, partly mystical. Van der
Post's Kalahari Bushmen, like Thesiger's Bedu, represented a nobler,
more authentic sense of life and of the universe, a sense of nature now

utterly lost and destroyed in the West. He cast his narrative within a framework of Jungian concepts, archetypal images of harmony or destruction, paradise or alienation, which may be projected outwards from the human spirit and become part of the world he creates. Reason, control, commerce, claims of racial superiority – these are the forces which had decimated indigenous cultures in Southern Africa. But the African interior and the traditions of its peoples still remained as

> [an] example to us of what we should recover in our own spirit. And they are also a warning to us, that if we do not recover this sense nature will turn on us one day, and we will be eliminated as the Bushmen were eliminated – because you cannot eliminate something precious in life without killing something in your own soul.
>
> (*A Walk with a White Bushman*, p. 31)

Easily ridiculed – as he has been by many critics – for wrapping up his reports from Africa in a veil of pseudo-philosophy and vague mysticism, Van der Post set out to make the travel experience a vehicle for teaching what he saw as an urgent message. It is also clear that he was prepared to shape and reshape the incidents and the overall pattern of his narrative to make them serve this message.

If there is an opposite experience to that mediated by Thesiger and Van der Post, it is that of the traveller whose subject is really the faces of human civilisation, above all the civilisation embodied in the world's cities. Jan Morris has made a speciality of books which explore the history of British India, of Venetian civilisation, of Oxford, or of quintessentially modern American cities from New York to Los Angeles. Highly regarded among cultural travellers, Morris nevertheless has her critics. To some, her prose is simply too smooth, too clever, too omniscient, too grand; nothing ruffles or defeats her. Her style is both impressionistic and digressive, proceeding through lists, through accumulation, the piling up of disparate facts, details, images and impressions. In Los Angeles she suggests that the freeways are the city's most exciting feature:

> Snaky, sinuous, undulating, high on stilts or sunk in cuttings, they are like so many concrete tentacles, winding themselves around each block, each district, burrowing, evading, clambering, clasping every corner of the metropolis as if they are squeezing it all together to make the parts stick.
>
> (Destinations, p. 86)

Some of her many commissioned journalistic pieces are collected into books including *Destinations*, *Among the Cities*, *Locations* and *Journeys*, their contents brief essays in local colour. With her intelligent eye and prolific knowledge, she is undoubtedly the virtuoso of recent travel writers. Yet some critics might say that the overall feel is that of travel writing that has become too slick, too polished.

New Horizons

The comic tradition of travel writing is a long one: the ironic self-mockery of the naive, exploited, insulted tourist got going in the eighteenth century, and became a fixture. Eric Newby revived the genre with his self-portraits as the parody-explorer, the bumbling amateur wandering innocently through chaotic or hostile environments. *A Short Walk in the Hindu Kush* (1958) and *Slowly Down the Ganges* (1966) reverse the older image of the masterful, omnicompetent Englishman in India, bringing the country to life in a very personal way, quite without literary fireworks. Wry and charming, Newby constructs no intellectual framework or argument, but convinces us immediately of his honesty – no mean feat in a travel writer. He is nevertheless capable of penetrating judgement, as when, in *A Short Walk in the Hindu Kush*, he thankfully left Afghanistan with the thought that he 'had the sensation of emerging from a country that would continue to exist more or less unchanged, whatever disasters overtook the rest of mankind'. Newby's hilarious portrait of Thesiger at the end of this book has become justly famous, more famous probably than any single passage from Thesiger himself. Newby offers a more serious personal memoir in *Love and War in the Apennines,* where he recalls his experiences as an escaped prisoner of war in Italy, when he was helped and protected by the hill farmers, and where he met his future wife, who later accompanied him on his travels, her distinct point of view enriching the narrative, and adding to the air of rough DIY adventure and offbeat humour.

Newby gave a foretaste of a new approach to the travel genre. Many of the leading travel writers of the century have striven for literary artistry in the traditional sense. Douglas, Byron, Waugh, Durrell, Fermor, Thesiger, Morris, all in their various ways were exploring the forms civilisation takes, and it was part of their message to use a prose that was precise, highly crafted, commensurate with their subject. By the 1970s a new approach had emerged, an approach that was much less rooted in the past, that was faster, more colourful, colloquial and improvisatory, that set out to act as a truer mirror to the world we live in. While not going to the extremes of gonzo journalism, it was recognisably American: brash, hip, demotic and attention-seeking. This was a watershed, a fundamental change, and if we look for some explanation why this style emerged when it did, we find that it coincided with the revolution in exotic foreign travel for the masses. With thousands of cheap flights to every corner of the world, anyone could now travel not merely to traditional destinations in Europe, but throughout Asia, Africa, the Pacific and the Americas, to places formerly the preserve of the serious, wealthy, leisured traveller, or even the explorer. This new wave of travellers constituted a huge new market for travel writing, and they wanted not elitist cultural critiques, but the experience – the feel of the heat, the sea, the cities, the faces they would see and the voices they would hear. But the revolution in mass travel cut two ways, for it also forced the travel writer to seek new destinations inaccessible to the tourist, and to write about them in novel ways, ways that distinguished them absolutely from the stagy, upper-class cultural travel writing of the past.

The leading figure in this major new style of travel writing was undoubtedly the American Paul Theroux. Many writers have sought to escape the label of travel author by going on to write novels, but with Theroux it worked in reverse: he had already written several novels, set in the exotic locations where he had lived, in Africa and the Far East, novels peopled with bizarre, visionary, driven characters, their lives captured in sharp, aggressive prose. The same approach brought his *The Great Railway Bazaar* (1975) and *The Old Patagonian Express* (1979) enormous popular success, as his train journeys across Asia and America cut a swathe through the scores of random lives with whom he collided. It is impossible to imagine these hilarious and mercilessly readable books being written by a non-novelist, for they are really a sequence of whimsical tableaux, linked in a narrative chain. History and cultural analysis are out: this is in-your-face reportage; what we get is what Theroux sees and feels — a crazy world flung down on the page in language to match. The result is a satirical debunking of the conventional travel experience: romance and beauty are in short supply, and when Theroux is tired, frightened, bored or utterly sick of some dreadful place and its dreadful people, he says so. In classical travel-narrative terms, almost nothing happens: no discoveries, no drama, no enlightenment. All that happens happens in Theroux's brilliant, satirical imagination and in the deadly fire of his prose, as he mows down virtually every cliché of the traditional travel book. We recognise his books as panoramic pictures of our contemporary world, just as we recognise the eighteenth century in the novels of Fielding or the nineteenth in those of Dickens, while the mad world of *Gulliver's Travels* is not far away. Theroux was demythologising travel writing, knocking it off its refined, upper-class pedestal, speeding it up and bringing it into the modern world.

Theroux's English counterpart was Jonathan Raban, who made no secret of the American influences on his innovative work – the risk-taking, confessional writers such as Roth in the novel and Lowell in poetry – who possessed a verve and daring which Raban wished to apply to travel writing. His first book, *Arabia Through the Looking Glass* (1979), was a very incomplete survey of its subject, but was nevertheless important in its time in signalling a new awareness of the fast-changing Middle East and the impact of oil politics and oil money on the region itself and on the West. Raban admitted that his interest in the Middle East was first aroused by the increased number of Arabs in West London, and his curiosity to know what this meant, but he really got into his stride with *Old Glory* (1981), the story of a river-boat journey down the Mississippi, written in a hip, streetwise style that is not so much impressionist as expressionist. Especially curious to see the city of St Louis, where T.S. Eliot spent his early years, he found a desolation he could easily identify with, finding ready-made literary echoes:

> Pushing one's face against the glass, one could see all that any human being could reasonably bear of St Louis: mile after mile of biscuit-coloured housing projects, torn-up streets, blackened Victorian factories and the purplish, urban scar tissue of vacant lots and pits in the ground. It was the Waste Land.
>
> (*Old Glory*, p. 329)

But overwhelmed by New Orleans he accepts defeat:

> I wasn't a traveller at all, I was just another rubberneck in a city which made its living out of credulous rubbernecks. Go buy a guidebook! Take a buggy ride! Eat *beignets*! Listen to the sounds of Old Dixie! ... then *go home*, schmuck! (p. 503)

Raban later developed a passion for sailing, and moved away from these modish collage effects to find a voice that was starker and more personal in *Passage to Juneau* (1999), describing a voyage from Seattle into the Gulf of Alaska. Having undertaken a professional assignment to explore rich historical and literary associations, the author finds his life unexpectedly and dramatically changed in the course of it by his father's death and his wife's desertion; life as a journey can take on new and unexpected meanings even for the professional traveller writer.

As well as expressionist energy imported from America, a second new force appeared in travel writing in the 1970s, namely feminism. Women have always written travel texts of course, going back to the age of pilgrimage, and more prolifically in the nineteenth century, but this did not mean that their works embodied any feminist agenda. What is new in the last three or four decades is a desire to change, to open up, possibly to subvert the genre itself by exposing the mentality of male power underlying much travel writing. A landmark text in this respect was Robyn Davidson's *Tracks* (1980), the story of a camel journey across the Australian desert. In the tradition of such narratives, the physical hardship and loneliness are central themes, but Davidson breaks new ground when she uses the story to criticise stereotyped Australian attitudes to race and femininity. She also gives an unusual exposé of the commercial framework of her journey, her difficulties with her sponsors, for example – matters usually kept hidden. The result was a discussion of identity such as one would expect from such an experience, but also a move towards freeing the idea of exploration and endurance from some of its historical burdens. She demonstrated that women could endure and suffer, but also bring additional understanding to the process of travel, hitherto the province only of masculine ambitions. Another Australian writer, Sara Wheeler, echoes many of Davidson's themes in her account of her epic crossing of Antarctica, *Terra Incognita* (1999), in which the mechanics of the journey and its psychological aspects are highlighted, although not at the expense of some fine writing about the questions of selfhood that are so difficult to evade in this environment of extreme harshness and solitude.

The late 1970s saw the publication of possibly the most admired and discussed single travel book of the age, the first book by the young Bruce Chatwin, *In Patagonia* (1977). The effect of this slim volume was so instantaneous and deeply felt that its status in modern travel literature almost resembles that of Wittgenstein's *Tractatus* in modern philosophy – the more so since it consists of a series of brief, enigmatic passages, not easily related to one another or to any central theme, and spoken in a cool, laconic, self-possessed voice, a voice that declines to identify itself or to establish any conventional context. Less funny than Theroux, but hinting at greater psychological depths, this is travel writing as postmodern collage, very close to fiction, playing games with the reader, dissolving reality into a series of encounters and impressions. Yet there is also a strong link to the upper-class British traveller of the past: nothing can faze him, frighten him or defeat him, because at heart he is a nomad, a free spirit; he is another of those civilised, literate rebels in flight from the commonplace, in search of the alien, the primitive or the exotic – anything that can prove to him that the world is unpredictably alive. His favourite literary models are both revealing: Robert Byron, the rebel aesthete, naturally enough; but more surprisingly Ernest Hemingway, the tough guy, the adventurer with the lean, macho prose style that left unspoken as much as it revealed. Chatwin's life, his revolutionary approach to travel writing, and his early death, have generated many legends and a considerable biographical industry. His work was another powerful force in breaking down the conventions of the travel book.

Yet in the midst of all this modish experimentation – postmodernism, satire, hyped-up prose, dissolving genres – there is still room for serious, informative, compassionate objectivity in the travel narrative. Colin Thubron is the acknowledged master of this form of civilised analysis: expert in the languages and history of his chosen places, he nevertheless has the imagination of the novelist to present what he sees and hears as unfolding dramas, springing from the cultures and landscapes he is attempting to understand. His style is supple, lucid but unfussy, as befits a man who claims descent from Dryden. He began his career writing about the Middle East and the Greek world, before going on to the larger, riskier subjects of Russia and China. *Among the Russians* (1983) was a cold-war journey, undertaken in considerable fear of this ruthless enemy power, and dogged by officials guides and minders, while *In Siberia* (1999) explores regions of the country Thubron was not permitted to see before. Both books add up to a bleak and disturbing picture of a vast land and a huge population enslaved by a pseudo-religion that claimed infallibility for itself. It was not merely communism that haunted Russia, but some deeper obstinacy or irrationality that reigned throughout her history; mistrust, conspiracy and drunkenness are the national pastimes. Yet Thubron's trademark is the reported conversation, through which he permits his Russian hosts to speak for themselves. He acknowledges that he disguised the identities of some of these people in order to protect them from possible trouble. Thubron is a man seeking understanding, travelling in these remote and difficult places almost as our representative, so that we do not have to. But he is also seeking to understand what the people themselves do not, because you do not understand what you are in the middle of, while the outsider can see more clearly. These are high claims for travel writing, the reverse of the romantic traveller seeking his own personal escape. If anyone can meet these high demands it is Thubron, with his modest, civilised voice, and his own personality kept largely in the background. He has claimed that for him there is no serious relationship between travel writing and fiction, for the hallmark of the former is that curiosity is projected outwards into the world, and of the latter that it is projected inwards into the self. Consequently what shines out of his travel writing is a respect for that elusive and old-fashioned quality, the truth.

The American Perspective

In America, the development of modern travel literature shared some features of the genre in Britain, but with some very distinctive shifts of emphasis. There was one travel book of the mid-century that attained mythic status: Jack Kerouac's *On the Road* (1957) was utterly unlike any British work, and it became the classic text of the Beat movement. Writing in a spontaneous, stream-of-consciousness prose, Kerouac criss-crosses America by car, exploring its cities and its landscapes, drinking, womanising, philosophising and building his intense, intimate friendship with the shaman-like figure of Dean Moriarty. Moriarty is a portrait of the real-life Neal Cassady, and the whole novel is deeply autobiographical. While functioning on one level as a celebration of America, beneath its surface *On the Road* is full of sadness and loneliness, a search for escape as urgent as that of Lawrence or Thesiger: escape from the political, industrial, militaristic wasteland of the United States. But instead of escaping abroad, Kerouac escapes into restless movement within his own country, roaming backwards and forwards, from east to west, seeking out the interstices of this diseased society, where he can find his own being. Skirting the edge of the Buddhism which becomes explicit in some of his other books, Kerouac is seeking escape on more than a social level. The book was reviled as an anarchist tract when it appeared, the critics failing to see how conservative and religious Kerouac's stance was, in the tradition of Emerson and Thoreau, seeking individual freedom, something that would transcend life's pain and striving. More clearly than any other twentieth-century writer, Kerouac underpinned this radically modern novel with the ancient idea of travel as a quest.

Another real-life figure who appears in Kerouac's work is Gary Snyder, who taught Kerouac Buddhism and mountaineering in the Sierra Nevada, and who is portrayed as Japhy Ryder in *The Dharma Bums* (1958). Snyder's poetry and his philosophical prose works from the late 1950s onwards embody the story of an inner journey, away from modern America and back to an order of being based on nature, on Eastern mysticism and on the belief systems of the American Indians. He is among the first of those who may be described as 'environmental writers', whose travels – not necessarily abroad – result in rediscovery of man's lost identity, and in a severe critique of modern western society. 'What we are witnessing in the world today', he wrote, 'is an unparalleled waterfall of destruction of a diversity of human cultures.'

Loosely associated with Kerouac and the Beat writers was Paul Bowles, who did escape abroad, via Paris to Tangier, where he found inspiration for poetry, fiction and non-fiction. Bowles's novels and short stories portray characters who have moved away physically from civilisation, usually into the North African desert, and who fight for survival and for some new identity; his novel *The Sheltering Sky* (1949) has been described as a kind of North African *Heart of Darkness*. Bowles was fascinated by African life and culture as being closer to the earth and the soul than those of the west. Americans, he said contemptuously, live 'like larvae in their cocoons', and were caught in their 'voluntary crystal shells'. Some of his short stories culminate in experiences of terror and suffering, through which the author dramatises the collision between civilisation and it opposite. He wrote many perceptive travel essays, collected in *Their Heads are Green* (1963). Describing 'the baptism of solitude' that is the desert experience, he writes:

> There are probably few accessible places on the face of the globe where you can get less comfort for your money than the Sahara. In the past few years the prices in dollars or sterling have more than quadrupled, and the accommodations are as miserable as ever. You can still get something flat to lie down on, stewed turnips and sand, noodles and jam, and a few tendons of something euphemistically called chicken to eat, and the stub of a candle to undress by at night, but you will pay heavily for these luxuries. Inasmuch as you must carry your own food and stove with you in any case, it sometimes

seems scarcely worthwhile to bother with the 'meals' provided by the hotels. ... Everything disappears eventually anyway – your coffee, tea, sugar, cigarettes – and you settle down to a life devoid of these superfluities, using a pile of soiled clothing as a pillow for your head at night and your burnous for a blanket.

Perhaps the logical question to ask at this point is: Why go? The answer is that once you have been there and undergone the baptism of solitude you cannot help yourself. Once you have been under the spell of the vast, luminous, silent country, no other place is quite strong enough, no other surroundings can provide the supremely satisfying sensations of existing in the midst of something that is absolute.

(*Their Heads are Green*, p. 143)

The link between Bowles and other exiles like Lawrence, Thesiger and Durrell is obviously a strong one.

In the west, in the Beat era of the 1950s, when Snyder began looking at nature through the eyes of a Zen Buddhist or an Indian Shaman, what we call ecology simply did not figure in the public mind. Twenty-five years later this situation had changed dramatically, and a new generation of writers had marked out a territory that brought together travel, nature-awareness, anti-industrialism and landscape poetry, forging what amounted to a new genre of environmental literature. Sometimes this took the form of visionary or overtly religious experiences, although still focused on geographical locations, as in the much praised *Pilgrim at Tinker Creek* by Annie Dillard (1974). It could also be built more recognisably on science, as in the works of Barry Lopez, who has used travel both within America and beyond, to open his reader's eyes to issues of ecology, politics and human ethical values. *Of Wolves and Men* (1978) blended fieldwork and scholarship to probe the mythology of the wolf, to ask why men have been so afraid of the wolf that they have sought to exterminate it, when its practical threat was really quite small. He suggests that it represents mankind's fear of the wild, and his need to master and tame the environment. For *Arctic Dreams* (1986) Lopez traversed North America between the

Bering Strait and Davis Strait in the company of Eskimos, recording the way in which their way of life had been virtually destroyed by the impact of the white man and his industries. In *The Rediscovery of North America* (1990), one of the many books prompted by the quincentenary of Columbus, Lopez surveys the history of the continent over five centuries, remarking bitterly how this whole story from the very beginning had been marked by the perception of America as a place to be seized, plundered, exploited and savaged, as a place whose one social ideal had been to grow rich, no matter what damage was done to the indigenous people, to the landscape and to the inner lives of Americans themselves. For Lopez, the purpose of his travel and environmental writing is an attempt to move forward into a new perception of what human social and political life might be.

This represents a considerable extension of the role of travel literature, and still another extension can be found in works of regional autobiography and social commentary, a kind of travelling at home, where the writer's role is that of a stranger, almost a visitor in an alien world. Joan Didion has offered bleakly powerful pictures of her native California in *Slouching Towards Bethlehem* (1968) and *The White Album* (1979), showing contemporary life as an increasingly sinister social void. She has also placed novels of violent despair in Central America, and there is disturbingly little difference in the ethos of *A Book of Common Prayer* (1977) and her Californian essays. Unlike Snyder or Lopez, she refrains from offering any intellectual or spiritual construct which might function as a way out of these maimed worlds.

The culmination of moral, environmental travel writing probably came in the work of Peter Matthiessen. His travels have taken him throughout North America and South America, to Africa, Siberia and to sea on many of the world's oceans. Like Snyder and Lopez, he combines ecological science with a profound concern for non-western cultures, saying of one group in New Guinea that they 'offered a unique chance, perhaps the last, to describe a lost culture in the terrible beauty of its pure estate', before they become 'no more than another backward people crouched in the long shadow of the white man' (*Under the Mountain Wall*, 1963). A Zen Buddhist, Matthiessen was struck by the similarity between Eastern spirituality and the traditions of the American Indians. The central lesson he drew from the natural world is that nature offers unobscured signs of being. 'The secret of the mountains is that the mountains simply exist ... they have no meaning, they *are* meaning.' Unlike man, the other creatures of the natural world 'have no need to find the secret of true being'. This is clearly indebted to the 'deep ecology' of the existential philosophers such as Heidegger. Matthiessen's work is filled with a sense of wonder of natural things as they are, not, as in the western system, for their potential value, for how they may be used and exploited. His most celebrated book is *The Snow Leopard* (1978), the story of a trek in Western Nepal, where he finds in the traditional Buddhist culture 'the last citadel of all that present-day humanity is longing for, either because it has been lost or not yet realised.' A subsidiary ambition is to observe the elusive snow leopard, one of the rarest animals on earth, which ends by carrying the central message of the book, for it is never seen. He knows it is there, nearby, but it remains just out of reach, just as the secret of being remains out of reach of western thought and western achievement. The snow leopard becomes therefore the symbol of a new, or rather an old and lost, attitude of the spirit, in which western power, language and intellect meet and finally accept their limitations. Matthiessen's book is interesting above all in showing that travel is a genre in which matters of ultimate spiritual importance can be discussed; by contrast, in public discourse here, in the west, they are out of place, they are banished because they represent what we have lost and forgotten.

It is appropriate that a survey of the history of travel literature should end with a writer like Matthiessen, for he shows how the genre has come full circle from the era when it was the servant of conquest and domination, political or cultural. Matthiessen and the other environmental writers are the fulfilment of the specifically American intellectual tradition of Emerson, Thoreau and Muir: here the traveller represents potentially a new beginning for mankind, starting again from scratch in the attempt to understand the world and himself.

Postscript: Re-imagining the World

This book has identified some of the many different paradigms of travel and travel writing that have been dominant through succeeding periods of history. These paradigms sprang from the psychology of their time, and they reveal why people travelled and how they viewed the world beyond their own cultural boundaries. The obvious question therefore is whether a new paradigm exists in the modern age, capable of illuminating the aims and motives of today's traveller, and more especially the travel writer.

The new paradigm – if there is one – seems to be the search for identity, or perhaps the redefinition of identity. The twentieth century was an age of dislocation, the shattering of European cultural claims, undermined by its own destructive wars, the dissolution of certainties in science, in the arts and in our understanding of our own nature. The time was ripe for western travellers to explore the world in a new spirit of openness, ready to learn from other cultures or alien environments, and in the process to learn about themselves. 'I have spent most of my life,' wrote the anthropologist, Margaret Mead, 'studying the lives of other peoples, faraway peoples, so that Americans might better understand themselves.'

We in the West have created a complex, pressurised, dehumanised society in which the need to escape has become endemic: escape and understanding have therefore become the twin poles around which the travel literature of the last hundred years has revolved. The prevalence of the theme of escape is striking, the desire to return to something elemental, noble, primitive or pagan, suggesting a flight from civilisation and its discontents. There is a distinct sense that western society has taken a wrong turning, and that by looking at other cultures we may regain what we have lost. We see this is in the 'quest' motif so common in travel books – the quest for a lost tribe, a lost valley, a lost species, a lost island, a lost ruin of an ancient civilisation, or an ancient route through desert or mountains – and also in the reconstruction of former journeys and voyages – the voyage of Sinbad or Jason, the journey in the footsteps of Captain Scott or Marco Polo. No doubt these projects are commercial – they are often linked to films – and the 'footsteps' motif is a marketing ploy; but their appeal has a strong psychological basis – that the act of retracing these journeys in space might reconnect us in time with a freer, nobler, more adventurous age, as perhaps it may, while the journey lasts.

Freedom is after all among the greatest ideals of the human mind, and the travel writer is manifestly free, while we, the readers, are not. In this sense there is perhaps still a link between travel and social privilege, a link to the past when it was the aristocratic elite alone who could roam the world at will. And today, even when stuck in a flea-bitten train in India, when freezing and sick on a Baltic ferry, or trekking in some searing desert, the traveller is still free from the deathliness of everyday reality, and even these experiences can be later transformed in the imagination. We are constantly told that true travel is now dead, killed by the age of mass tourism; but isn't this pure elitism? If the essence of travel is the inner journey, then the experience of foreign places can still be a transforming one. Avoiding the tourist crowds is now simply another part of the art of travel. Even the hellish airport and the numbing in-flight experience can be seen as modern purgatories, through which the traveller must pass to reach his desired paradise. Isn't even the common tourist seeking to move, for a brief space of time, into some freer realm of existence, out of the fetters of his everyday anonymity, out of non-being into being?

But this only serves to confirm the closeness of travel writing to other forms of imaginative literature, and as in a drama or a novel, a range of characters is essential: the great hallmark of the modern travel text is the personal encounters in which the traveller allows unfamiliar voices from anywhere in the world to be heard. Without these voices, the books of writers like Theroux, Chatwin, Thubron and all the others would lose much of their charm and their authenticity. But are we to believe that these conversations occurred as they are reported, word for word? Surely they must have been edited and sharpened? Norman Douglas admitted that some of his 'encounters' were complete inventions. 'One suppresses much,' he said candidly, 'why not add a little?' Consider this passage, as Colin Thubron parts from two friends he has made in Russia, and whom he is sure he will never meet again:

> We hugged Russian-fashion, and from far down the street I saw them still waving, silhouetted in a lake of lamplight. For a few days their valedictory shapes had incarnated Leningrad for me – its Western beauty and native generosity, its grace and sadness.
>
> (*Among the Russians*, p. 104)

Is this bare, factual reporting, or something else? Likewise this little exchange between Thubron and a Uighur nomad in Kazakhstan:

> Their lives were hard, he said. In summer they wandered; in winter they just survived, hibernating with their herds as best they could.
> 'But would you prefer city life?'
> He said: 'We know nothing about working in the city. We've lived like this since childhood. So I prefer the nomad way.'
> 'And what of your children?'
> ... 'I want them to go to the city and find jobs there ... Otherwise they will gain nothing here – and become the same as me.'
> Was this, I wondered, the start of their end? Perhaps this was how the Uighur had felt eight centuries ago, drifting into the oases towns.

I said: 'Do most of your people feel the same as you?'
He looked at me with an odd, wan emptiness, and said: 'The same.'

(*Great Journeys*, pp. 20–21)

The words of the Uighur may be accurately reported, but the entire cultural divide that Thubron is presenting between his way of life and ours is concentrated into the phrase 'with an odd, wan emptiness'. This tells us the author's sense of the forces of change, and the decline of a traditional culture; it functions like a stage direction, bringing out the feeling of the scene; it comes from the author's emotional intelligence; it is not objective. So this brief report, perhaps composed some months, or even years, after the events it describes, is a small act of re-imagining the world. So too are some of the much larger themes of modern travel writing: the mysticism of Van der Post, the formal beauty embodied in Fermor's prose, Theroux's expressionist daring, Durrell's pagan praise of Mediterranean places – they are all strategies for re-imagining the world, which is perhaps what travel writers have always done, always mingling the objective with the subjective, the world they saw and what they felt within themselves.

As modern tourist travel has been derided as existentially empty, so travel writing has often been dismissed as an elitist survival from the past, having no real role in a modern, democratic, information-rich society. All the world is accessible in a few hours by plane; and at home, reports, images and experiences are flashed from every corner of the world in minutes. We no longer need travellers like Sir Robert Sherley in the seventeenth century, Bougainville in the eighteenth or Livingstone in the nineteenth to tell us what the countries of Asia or the Pacific or Africa are like. Once, on a Japanese train, Theroux tried to persuade a sceptical fellow-American that travel writing was worthwhile. 'Why?' asks his friend. 'Everyone travels, so who wants to read about it?' To which Theroux responds: 'Everyone gets laid too, but that doesn't eliminate screwing as a subject – I mean people still write about it.' With travel, then, as with love, or with anything else, we read to check that we are really alive and at least half-sane, to see how our experience corresponds with the rest of humanity. So the flood of information about the outside world does not signal the end of travel writing – on the contrary, it makes the need for it more urgent. Travel writing must respond by becoming sharper, more perceptive, more analytical, more imaginative, cutting through the stereotypes, and understanding the reality behind the images and superficial reports that fill a few moments of media time and are then forgotten. Unfortunately perhaps, there is no escaping the world, and no escaping the effort to understand it. In this task the travel writer, at his or her best, can act as our representative.

Principal Works Discussed

CHAPTER I

ARCULF, *The Pilgrimage of Arculfus in the Holy Land*, trans. J.R. Macpherson, London, 1895.

ARRIAN, *The Life of Alexander the Great*, trans. Aubrey de Selincourt, London, 1970.

BATTUTA, *Travels in Asia and Africa, 1325–1354*, ed. H.A.R. Gibb, London, 1929.

BENJAMIN OF TUDELA, *The World of Benjamin of Tudela: A Medieval Mediterranean Travelogue*, trans. Sarah Benjamin, London, 1995.

BREYDENBACH, *Die Reise ins heilige Land 1483*, facsimile, ed. E. Geck, Wiesbaden, 1961.

CAESAR, *The Gallic War*, trans. H.J. Edwards, London, 1994.

CATULLUS, *The Poems of Gaius Valerious Catullus*, trans. F.W. Cornish, Cambridge, 1904.

EGERIA, *Diary of a Pilgrimage*, trans. George E. Gingras, New York, 1970.

ERICSSON, *The Norse Discoveries of America: The Wineland Sagas*, trans. G. Gathorne-Hardy, Oxford, 1970.

FRAZER, *Pausanias and Other Greek Sketches*, London, 1900.

FULCHER OF CHARTRES and ODO OF DEUIL, *The Crusades: A Documentary Survey*, James A. Brundage, Milwaukee, 1962.

GILGAMESH, *The Epic of Gilgamesh*, trans. N.L. Sandars, London, 1960.

HERODOTUS, *The Histories*, trans. Henry Cary, London, 1992.

MANDEVILLE, *Mandeville's Travels*, trans. Malcolm Letts, London, 1953.

PAUSANIAS, *Guide to Greece*, trans. Peter Levi, London, 1971.

PETRARCH, *The Ascent of Mount Ventoux*, trans. J.H. Robinson, New York, 1989.

PLINY THE ELDER, *Natural History*, selections trans. J.F. Healy, London, 1991.

POLO, *The Travels of Marco Polo*, trans. Aldo Ricci, London, 1931.

POLYBIUS, *The Rise of the Roman Empire*, trans. Ian Scott-Kilvert, London, 1979.

THE SEAFARER, *Old and Middle English, c. 1090–1400*, ed. Elaine Treharne, Oxford, 2004.

WEY, *The Itineraries of William Wey*, ed. R. Badinel, London, 1857.

WILLEM OF RUBRUCK and GIOVANNI CARPINI, *The Contemporaries of Marco Polo*, ed. M. Komroff, London, 1928.

XENOPHON, *The Persian Expedition*, trans. Rex Warner, London, 1972.

CHAPTER 2

BARENTSZ, *The Three Voyages of Willem Barentsz to the Arctic Regions*, ed. C.T. Beke, London, 1876.

CABEZA DE VACA, *Cabeza de Vaca's Adventures in the Unknown Interior of America*, trans. C. Covey, New York, 1972.

CAMÕES, *The Lusiads*, prose trans. W.C. Atkinson, London 1973; verse trans. Richard Burton, London, 1880.

CARTIER, *The Voyages of Jacques Cartier*, trans. H.P. Biggar, Toronto, 1993.

CAVENDISH, *The Last Voyage of Thomas Cavendish 1591–1592*, ed. D.B. Quinn, Chicago, 1975.

CIEZA DE LEÓN, *The Incas*, trans. H. de Onis, Oklahoma, 1959.

COLUMBUS, *The Four Voyages of Columbus*, ed. Cecil Jane, New York, 1988.

CORTÉS, *Hernando Cortés: Five Letters 1519–1526*, trans. J. Bayard Morris, New York, 1991.

DE BRY, *America 1590–1634*, facsimile, ed. G. Sievernich, Berlin, 1990.

DRAKE, *The World Encompassed by Sir Francis Drake*, ed. W.S.W. Vaux, London, 1854.

DIAZ DEL CASTILLO, *The Conquest of New Spain*, trans. J.M. Cohen, London, 1974.

FOXE and JAMES, *The Voyages of Captain Luke Foxe of Hull and Captain Thomas James of Bristol in search of a North-West Passage*, 2 vols, ed. M. Christy, London, 1894.

FROBISHER, *The Three Voyages of Martin Frobisher in search of a passage to Cathia and India by the North-West*, ed. R. Collinson, London, 1867.

HAKLUYT, *The Principal Navigations Voyages Traffiques & Discoveries of the English Nation made by sea or over-land to the remote and farthest distant quarters of the earth at any time within the compasse of these 1600 yeeres* (1589), 12 vols, Glasgow, 1903–05.

HARIOT, *A Brief and True Report of the New Found Land of Virginia*, facsimile, New York, 1992.

MAGELLAN, *Magellan's Voyage: a narrative of the first circumnavigation*, by Antonio Pigafetta, trans. R.A. Skelton, New York, 1994.

MONTAIGNE, 'Of Carriages', in *Essays of Michel, Seigneur de Montaigne*, trans. Charles Cotton, London, 1889.

MORE, *Utopia*, trans. G.M. Logan and R.M. Adams, Cambridge, 1989.

MÜNSTER, *Cosmographia Universalis*, Basle, 1544.

ORELLANA, *The Discovery of the Amazon according to the account of Friar Gaspar de Carvajal*, trans. B.T. Lee, New York, 1970.

PURCHAS, *Hakluytus Posthumus or Purchas his Pilgrimes* (1625), 20 vols, Glasgow, 1905–07.

RALEGH, *The Discoverie of the large and bewtiful Empire of Guiana*, ed. V.T. Harlow, London, 1928.

VESPUCCI, *Letters from a New World*, trans. L. Formisiano, New York, 1992.

WILLOUGHBY and CHANCELLOR, *England and Russia: The Voyages of Sir Hugh Willoughby and Richard Chancellor to the White Sea*, London, 1854.

CHAPTER 3

ADAMS, *Memorials of the Empire of Japan in the XVIth and XVIIth Centuries*, ed. T. Rundall, London, 1850.

ANTHONY and ROBERT SHERLEY, *The Sherleian Odyssey*, ed. Boies Penrose, London, 1938.

BATTELL, *The Strange Adventures of Andrew Battell of Leigh in Angola and the adjoining regions* (1625), ed. E.G. Ravenstein, London, 1901.

BLOUNT, *A Voyage into the Levant*, London, 1636.

CARDER and KNIVET, in Purchas, *Hakluytus Posthumus, or Purchas his Pilgrimes* (1625), 20 vols, Glasgow, 1905–07.

CORYATE, *Coryat's Crudities hastily gobbled up in five Monthes travells...*(1611), 2 vols, Glasgow, 1905.

DAMPIER, *A New Voyage Around the World*, 1697; *A Voyage to New Holland*, 1703, ed. John Masefield, 2 vols, London, 1906.

ESQUEMELIN, *The Buccaneers of America* (*c.* 1678), trans. A. Brown, London, 1969.

FITCH, *Ralph Fitch: England's Pioneer to India and Burma*, ed. J.H. Ryley, London, 1899.

GOES and ANDRADE, *Early Jesuit Travellers in Central Asia*, ed. C. Wessels, The Hague, 1924.

HALL, *Mundus Alter et Idem*, London, 1605, translated as *Another World and Yet the Same*, 1609.

HASLETON, *The strange and wonderful things which happened to Richard Hasleton...*, London, 1595.

HERBERSTEIN, *Notes upon Russia*, trans. R.H. Major, 2 vols, London, 1851–52.

HERBERT, *A Relation of Some Yeares Travaile into Afrique, Asia, Indies*, London, 1634; facsimile, Amsterdam, 1971.

HORTOP, *The Travails of an English Man...*, London, 1591.

JENKINSON, *Early voyages and travels to Russia and Persia*, ed. E. Morgan and C.H. Coote, 2 vols, London, 1886.

LITHGOW, *The Rare Adventures and Painful Peregrinations of William Lithgow* (1614), ed. G. Phelps, London, 1974.

MORYSON, *An Itinerary containing his ten years travell* (1617), 4 vols, Glasgow, 1907–08.

MUNDY, *The Travels of Peter Mundy in Europe and Asia, 1608–1667*, ed. Sir Richard Temple, 5 vols, London, 1907–36.

NASHE, *The Unfortunate Traveller*, London, 1594.

PINTO, *The Travels of Mendes Pinto*, trans. R.D. Catz, Chicago, 1989.

RICCI, *China in the 16th Century: The Journals of Matthew Ricci*, trans. L.J. Gallagher, New York, 1953.

ROE, *The Embassy of Sir Thomas Roe to the Court of the Great Mogul, 1615–1619*, ed. W. Foster, 2 vols, London, 1899.

SANDYS, *A Relation of a Journey Begun An: Dom: 1610. Foure Bookes containing a description of the Turkish Empire...*, 5th edn, London, 1652.

VARTHEMA, *The Travels of Ludovico di Varthema*, trans. J.W. Jones, ed. G.P. Badger, London, 1863.

WEBBE, *The rare and most wonderful things which Edward Webbe hath seen...*, London, 1590.

XAVIER, *The Life and Letters of St Francis Xavier*, ed. H.J. Coleridge, 2 vols, London, 1872.

CHAPTER 4

ADDISON, *Remarks on Several Parts of Italy*, London, 1705; *A Letter from Italy*, London, 1709.

ANSON, *Voyage Around the World*, London, 1748.

BANKS, *Journal of the Rt. Hon. Sir Joseph Banks during Captain Cook's first voyage in H.M.S. Endeavour in 1768–71...*, ed. Sir J.D. Hooker, London, 1896.

BECKFORD, *Travel Diaries of William Beckford of Fonthill*, ed. G. Chapman, 2 vols, Cambridge, 1928; *Dreams, Waking Thoughts and Incidents; in a series of letters from various parts of Europe*, London, 1783.

BOSWELL, *Boswell on the Grand Tour*, ed. F.A. Pottle, London, 1953.

BOUGAINVILLE, *A Voyage Round the World*, trans. R. Forster, London, 1772.

Principal Works

BRUCE, *Travels to Discover the Source of the Nile*, London, 1790; selections ed. C.F. Beckingham, London, 1964.

BURKE, *Memoir of the life and character of the Right Hon. Edmund Burke*, ed. J. Prior, London, 1824.

BURNEY, *Dr Charles Burney's Continental Travels*, ed. C.H. Glover, London and Glasgow, 1927.

BYRON, *The Wreck of the Wager: the narratives of John Bulkeley and the Hon. John Byron*, ed. C. Hibbert, London, 1983.

BYRON, WALLIS, COOK, CARTERET, BANKS, *An Account of all the Voyages undertaken by the order of His Present Majesty...* ed. John Hawkesworth, 3 vols, London, 1773.

COMMERSON, *The Quest and Occupation of Tahiti during the Years 1772–1776*, vol. 2, ed. Bolton Corney, London, 1915; *French Explorers in the Pacific*, by John Dunmore, Oxford, 1965.

COOK, *Captain Cook's Journal during his First voyage round the world made in H.M. Bark 'Endeavour' 1768–71*, ed. W.J.L. Wharton, London, 1893; *The Journals of Captain Cook*, 3 vols, ed. J.C. Beaglehole, Cambridge, 1969.

DIDEROT, *Supplément au Voyage de Bougainville*, Paris, 1796.

EVELYN, *The Diary of John Evelyn*, ed. Austin Dobson, 3 vols, London, 1906.

GIBBON, *Memoirs of my Life*, ed. B. Radice, London, 1991.

GOETHE, *Italian Journey*, trans. R.Heitner, New York, 1989.

GRAY, *The Letters of Thomas Gray*, ed. J.Beresford, Oxford, 1925.

HAWKESWORTH, *An Account of the Voyages undertaken by the order of His Present Majesty for Making Discoveries in the southern Hemisphere*, London, 1773.

JOHNSON, *Boswell's Life of Johnson*, ed. J.W. Croker, London, 1848.

LA PEROUSE, *A Voyage Round the World in the Years 1785–88*, 3 vols, London, 1798; *Pacific Explorer: The Life of Jean-François de la Perouse*, ed. J. Dunmore, Palmerston North, 1985.

MACARTNEY, *An Embassy to China*, ed. J.L. Cranmer-Byng, London, 1962.

MORRISON, *The Journal of James Morrison, Boatswain's Mate of the 'Bounty'*, ed. O. Rutter, London, 1935.

NUGENT, *The Grand Tour*, 4 vols, London, 1749.

ROGGEVEEN, *The Journal of Jacob Roggeveen*, ed. A. Sharp, Oxford, 1970.

SMOLLETT, *The Works of Tobias Smollett*, vol. VIII, ed. J.P. Brown, London, 1872.

STERLING, *Essays and Tales*, ed. J.C. Hare, vol. I, London, 1848.

STERNE, *A Sentimental Journey through France and Italy*, London, 1768.

VASON, *An authentic narrative of four years' residence of Tongataboo*, London, 1810.

VOLTAIRE, *Letters Concerning the English Nation*, London, 1733; *Lettres Philosophiques*, Paris, 1734.

WALLIS, *An Account of the Discovery of Tahiti from the Journal of George Robertson*, ed. O. Warner, London, 1955.

Travel

WALPOLE, *The Letters of Horace Walpole*, ed. P. Toynbee, Oxford, 1903–18.

WILSON, *A Missionary Voyage to the South Pacific Ocean*, London, 1799.

WOOD and DAWKINS, *The Ruins of Palmyra*, 1753; facsimile, Farnborough, 1971.

WORTLEY MONTAGU, *Embassy to Constantinople: The Travels of Lady Mary Wortley Montagu*, ed. C. Pick, London, 1988.

CHAPTER 5

BELZONI, *Narrative of the operations and recent discoveries within the pyramids...*, London, 1821–22.

BIRD, *This Grand Beyond: The Travels of Isabella Bird Bishop*, ed. C.P. Havely, London, 1984.

BORROW, *The Bible in Spain*, London, 1843.

BURCKHARDT, *Travels in Syria and the Holy Land*, London, 1822; *Travels in Arabia*, London, 1829.

BURT on Khajuraho and ALEXANDER on Ajanta, reports in the *Journal of the Asiatic Society of Bengal*, and *Transactions of the Royal Asiatic Society*; quoted in John Keay, *India Discovered*, Leicester, 1981.

BURTON, *Of No Country: An Anthology of the Works of Sir Richard Burton*, ed. F. McLynn, London, 1990; *Personal Narrative of a Pilgrimage to El-Medinah and Meccah*, London, 1855–6.

BYRON, *Childe Harold's Pilgrimage*, Cantos I–IV, London, 1812–18; *Don Juan*, London, 1819–24; *Letters and Journals of Lord Byron*, ed. Thomas Moore, Paris, 1830.

CATLIN, *The Manners, Customs and Conditions of the North American Indians*, 2 vols, London, 1841.

CHATEAUBRIAND, *Voyage en Amérique*, Paris, 1867; *Chateaubriand's America*, ed. Richard Switzer, Wisconsin, 1968.

CURZON, *Frontiers*, The Romanes Lecture Series, Oxford, 1907.

DISRAELI, *Vivian Grey*, London, 1926.

DARWIN, *Journal of Researches into the Natural History and Geology of the Countries Visited during the Voyage of H.M.S. Beagle Round the World*, 2 vols, New York, 1846; *The Correspondence of Charles Darwin*, vol. 1, Cambridge, 1985.

DENON, *Travels in Upper and Lower Egypt*, trans. A. Aiken, London, 1803.

EDEN, *Up the Country*, London, 1866.

FREMONT, *Narrative of the exploring expedition to the Rocky Mountains in the year 1842 and to Oregon and North California in the years 1843–44*, Washington, 1845.

GRAHAM, *Journal of a Residence in India*, Edinburgh, 1812; *Letters on India*, Edinburgh, 1814; *Travellers' India*, ed. H.K. Kaul, Delhi, 1979.

HEBER, *Narrative of a Journey through the Upper Provinces of India...*, 2nd edn, London, 1828.

Principal Works

HICKEY, *Memoirs of a Georgian Rake*, ed. R. Hudson, London, 1995.

IRVING, *A Tour on the Prairies*, Paris, 1835.

JONES, *Sir William Jones: Poetical and Prose Selected Works*, ed. M. Franklin, Cardiff, 1995.

KING, *Mountaineering in the Sierra Nevada*, ed. F.P. Farquar, London, 1947.

KINGLAKE, *Eothen*, London, 1844.

LAYARD, *Nineveh and its Remains*, London, 1849; *The Discovery of the Ruins of Nineveh and Babylon*, London, 1853.

LEAR, *Edward Lear in Greece: Journals of a Landscape Painter in Greece and Albania*, London, 1965; *Edward Lear's Indian Journal*, ed. R. Murphy, London, 1953.

LEWIS and CLARK, *History of the Expedition under the Command of Lewis and Clark*, ed. Elliott Coues, 4 vols, New York, 1893.

LIVINGSTONE, *Missionary Travels and Researches in South Africa*, London, 1857.

LOTI, *Pierre Loti: Portrait of an Escapist*, ed. L. Blanche, London, 1983.

MACAULAY, *Speeches of Lord Macaulay*, London, 1860.

MANLY, *Death Valley '49*, San José, 1894.

MARSHALL, *John Marshall in India*, ed. S.A. Khan, London, 1927.

MOORCROFT, *Travels in the Himalayan Provinces of Hindustan*, London, 1841.

MORGAN, *The Indian Journals, 1859–62*, ed. L.A. White, Ann Arbor, 1959.

MUIR, *The Eight Wilderness Discovery Books of John Muir*, London, 1992; *The Wilderness World of John Muir*, ed. E.W. Teale, New York, 2001.

PARKMAN, *The California and Oregon Trail*, London, 1849.

POWELL, *Down the Colorado*, ed. D.D. Fowler, London, 1969.

RADCLIFFE, *The Mysteries of Udolpho*, London, 1794; *Journey Made in the Summer of 1794... down the Rhine*, London, 1795.

ROBERTS, *Egypt and Nubia from drawings made on the spot*, London, 1846–49; *The Holy Land, Syria etc, from drawings made on the spot*, London, 1842–43.

ROGERS, *Italy: a poem*, London, 1822.

RUSKIN, *Praeterita*, intro. Kenneth Clarke, London, 1949; *The Diaries of John Ruskin*, ed. J. Everns and J.H. Whitehouse, Oxford, 1956; *John Ruskin: The Early Years*, by Tim Hilton, New Haven, 1985,

SHELLEY, *Prometheus Unbound and other Poems*, London, 1910.

STANLEY, *Through the Dark Continent*, London, 1878; *In Darkest Africa*, London, 1890.

STEPHEN, *The Playground of Europe*, London, 1871.

STEPHENS, *Incidents of Travel in Central America, Chiapas and Yucatan*, 2 vols, London, 1841.

STEVENSON, R.L., *Travels with a Donkey in the Cévennes*, London, 1879; *The Silverado Squatters*, London, 1883.

THACKERAY, *The Irish Sketch book*, London, 1886.

THOREAU, *Walden*, Boston, 1854; *The Maine Woods*, Boston, 1864.

TOD, *Travels in Western India, embracing a visit to the sacred mounts of the Jains,*

London, 1839; *Annals and Antiquities of Rajasthan*, London, 1829; John Keay, *India Discovered*, Leicester, 1981.

TURNER, *An Account of an Embassy to the Court of Teshoo Lama in Tibet*, London, 1800.

TWAIN, *Innocents Abroad, or The New Pilgrim's Progress*, London, 1869; *Roughing It*, London, 1872.

VERNE, *Around the World in Eighty Days*, trans. George Makepeace Towle, London, 1874.

VON HUMBOLDT, *Personal narrative of travels to the equinoctial regions of America, during the years 1799–1804; Letters of Alexander von Humboldt*, trans. Thomasina Ross, London, 1852.

WHYMPER, *Scrambles Amongst the Alps*, London, 1871; *The Ascent of the Matterhorn*, London, 1880; *Travels amongst the Great Andes of the Equator*, London, 1892.

CHAPTER 6

AUDEN and ISHERWOOD, *Journey to a War*, London, 1938.

BOWLES, *The Sheltering Sky*, London, 1949; *Their Heads are Green*, London, 1963.

BYRON, *The Road to Oxiana*, London, 1937; *First Russia, then Tibet: Travels through a Changing World*, London, 1933.

CHATWIN, *In Patagonia*, London, 1977.

CHERRY-GARRARD, *The Worst Journey in the World*, London, 1922.

DAVIDSON, *Tracks*, London, 1980.

DIDION, *Slouching Towards Bethlehem*, 1968; *The White Album*, 1979; *A Book of Common Prayer*, London, 1977.

DILLARD, *Pilgrim at Tinker Creek*, New York, 1974.

DOUGLAS, *Siren Land*, London, 1911; *Fountains in the Sand*, London, 1912; *Old Calabria*, London, 1915; *South Wind*, London, 1917; *Alone*, London, 1921.

DURRELL, *Prospero's Cell*, London, 1945; *Reflections on a Marine Venus*, London, 1953; *Bitter Lemons*, London, 1957.

FERMOR, *Mani: Travels in the Southern Pelopennese*, London, 1958; with Stephen Spender, *Ghika: Paintings, Drawings, Sculpture*, London, 1964; *Roumeli: Travels in Northern Greece*, London, 1966; *A Time of Gifts*, London, 1977; *Between the Woods and the Water*, London, 1986.

FLEMING, *Brazilian Adventure*, London, 1933; *News from Tartary*, London, 1936.

FORSTER, *Alexandria*, 1922; *The Hill of Devi*, London, 1953.

FRANKLIN, *As affecting the fate of my absent husband: Selected Letters of Lady Franklin*, ed. Erika Behrisch Elce, Montreal, 2009.

GREENE, *Journey Without Maps*, London, 1936; *The Lawless Roads*, London, 1939.

HERZOG, *Annapurna*, trans. M. Morin and J.A. Smith, London, 1986.

Principal Works

KEROUAC, *On the Road*, London, 1957; *The Dharma Bums*, London, 1958.

D.H. LAWRENCE, *Twilight in Italy*, London, 1916; *Mornings in Mexico*, London, 1927; *Etruscan Places*, London, 1932; *The Letters of D.H. Lawrence*, vol. v, ed. James T. Boulton and Lindeth Vasey, Cambridge, 1989.

T.E. LAWRENCE, *The Complete 1922 Seven Pillars of Wisdom*, ed. J. and N. Wilson, Fordingbridge, 2004.

LOPEZ, *Of Wolves and Men*, London, 1978; *Arctic Dreams*, London, 1986; *The Rediscovery of North America*, Lexington, 1990.

MATTHIESSEN, *Under the Mountain Wall: A Chronicle of the Seasons in Stone Age New Guinea*, London, 1963; *The Snow Leopard*, London, 1978.

MEAD, *Blackberry Winter*, New York, 1972.

MORRIS, *Venice*, London, 1960; *Oxford*, London, 1965; *Cities*, London, 1963; *Destinations*, Oxford, 1980.

MORTON, *In the Steps of the Master*, London, 1934; *In the Steps of St Paul*, London, 1936.

NANSEN, *Farthest North*, London, 1898.

NEWBY, *A Short Walk in the Hindu Kush*, London, 1958; *Slowly Down the Ganges*, London, 1966; *Love & War in the Apennines*, London, 1971.

ORWELL, *Homage to Catalonia*, London, 1938.

POWELL, *What's Become of Waring?*, London, 1939.

RABAN, *Arabia Through the Looking Glass*, London, 1979; *Old Glory*, London, 1981; *Passage to Juneau*, London, 1999.

SCOTT, *Scott's Last Expedition*, ed. L. Huxley, London, 1913.

SHACKLETON, *South*, London, 1919.

SNYDER, 'The Politics of Ethnopoetics', in *Ethno Poetics: A First International Symposium*, Boston, 1976.

SONNIER, *Où règne la lumière*, trans. in *Mont Blanc: An Anthology*, compiled by C.E. Engel, London, 1965.

THEROUX, *The Great Railway Bazaar*, London, 1975; *The Old Patagonian Express*, London, 1979.

THESIGER, *Arabian Sands*, London, 1959; *The Marsh Arabs*, London, 1964; *The Life of My Choice*, London, 1987.

THUBRON, *Among the Russians*, London, 1983; *The Lost Heart of Asia*, London, 1994; 'The Silk Road', *Great Journeys*, London, 1989; *In Siberia*, London, 1999.

TILMAN, *China to Chitral*, London, 1951.

VAN DER POST, *Venture into the Interior*, London, 1952; *The Lost World of the Kalahari*, London, 1958; *A Walk with a White Bushman*, London, 1986.

WAUGH, *Labels: A Mediterranean Journal*, London, 1930; *Ninety-Two Days*, London, 1934; *Waugh in Abyssinia*, London, 1936.

WHEELER, *Terra Incognita: Travels in Antarctica*, London, 1996.

Acknowledgements

Acknowledgements

p. 209 Elliott, *Views in India, China, and on the Shores of the Red Sea*, 1835, Vol. 1. Oxford, Sackler Library, 914.84 H.Ell, opposite p. 5.

p. 219 Moorcroft, *Travels in the Himalayan Provinces of Hindustan and the Panjab*, 1841. Oxford, Bodleian Library, 41.1204, Vol. 2 (frontispiece).

p. 225 Layard, *Discoveries in the ruins of Nineveh and Babylon*, London, 1853. Oxford, Bodleian Library, 230.1 N.83.

p. 235 David Livingstone, *Missionary Travels and Researches in South Africa*, 1857. Oxford, Bodleian Library, 580. S. 1, opposite p. 498.

p. 237 Whymper, *Scrambles Amongst the Alps in the years 1860–69*, 1871. Oxford, Bodleian Library, 203 e. 205, p. 390.

p. 247 'At the South Pole', Photograph by Lieutenant H.R. Bowers, from *Scott's Last Expedition*, 1931, Vol. I. Arranged by Leonard Huxley. Image courtesy of the Union Library, Oxford.

PLATE SECTION

p. 1 Bernhard von Breydenbach, Map of the Holy Land, *Peregrinatio in terram sanctam*, 1486. Oxford, Bodleian Library, Arch. B c.25.

p. 2 Map of the Holy Land. Oxford, Bodleian Library, MS. Douce 389.

p. 3 Oxford, Bodleian Library, MS. Bodl. 264, fol. 220r.

p. 3 Oxford, Bodleian Library, MS. Marsh 458, fol. 45r.

p. 4 Desceliers World Map, 1898 edn, Oxford, Bodleian Library, B1 a.14, sheet 1.

p. 4 BN Cartes et Plans, Res.Ge B 1148, © Bibliothèque nationale de France.

p. 5 Sir Thomas More, *Utopia*, 1895 edition, courtesy of the Union Library.

p. 6 Portrait of Sir Robert Sherley, painted in Rome in 1622, in the Red Room at Petworth House, West Sussex © NTPL/Derrick E. Witty.

p. 7 Oxford, Bodleian Library, MS. Douce Or. b. 3, fol. 21r.

p. 8 La Perouse in 1784, by Nicolas André Monsiau (1754–1837). © RMN (Château de Versailles)/Gérard Blot.

p. 9 The Piazzetta, Venice by Carlevarijs, *c.* 1720. WA1949.6 © Ashmolean Museum, University of Oxford.

p. 10 Goethe in the Roman countryside by Tischbein, 1787. © U. Edelmann–Städel Museum/ARTOTHEK.

p. 11 Print of Wood and Dawkins discovering the ruins of Palmyra in 1751, from an oil painting by Gavin Hamilton, 1758. Photograph © Victoria and Albert Museum, London.

p. 11 Lord Macartney's embassy to China, 1792, by James Gillray. © Trustees of the British Museum.

p. 12 Portrait of Lord Byron in Albanian costume, replica by Thomas Phillips. Oil on canvas, *c.* 1835 (1813). © National Portrait Gallery, London.

p. 13 'Company Officer and Nobles on a terrace', Jameel Centre object LI 118.27. © Ashmolean Museum, University of Oxford.

p. 13 Colonel James Tod. Photograph © V&A Images/Victoria and Albert Museum, London.

p. 14 Samuel Rogers, *Italy*, 1842. Oxford, Bodleian Library, Dunston B 1538, pp. 165, 191, 197, 224.

p. 15 'Morning in spring with north-east wind, Vevey', watercolour by John Ruskin, *c.* 1849. WA.RS.ED.298b. © Ashmolean Museum, University of Oxford.

p. 16 El Khasnè, a lithograph by Louis Haghe after a watercolour by David Roberts, *The Holy Land, Idumea, Arabia, Egypt and Nubia* (1842–49). © Trustees of the British Museum.

TEXT

p. 18 Extract from 'The Seafarer', translated by Elaine Treharne in *Old and Middle English c. 890–c. 1400*, ed. Elaine Treharne, published by Blackwell Publishing.

p. 242 Extract from *First Russia, then Tibet* (1933) by Robert Byron reprinted by permission of Peters Fraser & Dunlop on behalf of the estate of Robert Byron.

p. 242 Extract from *Annapurna* by Maurice Herzog (1952), translated by Janet Adam Smith and Nea Morin, published by Vintage Books. Courtesy of Professor A.D. Roberts.

p. 250 Extract from *Où règne la lumière* by Georges Sonnier, translated in *Mont Blanc: An Anthology*, edited by C.E. Engel (1965), published by Allen & Unwin Ltd.

p. 256 Extract from *Old Calabria* by Norman Douglas (1915), published by Orion Books.

p. 258 Extract from *The Road to Oxiana* (1937) by Robert Byron reprinted by permission of Peters Fraser & Dunlop on behalf of the estate of Robert Byron.

p. 262 Extract from *In the Steps of the Master* by H.V. Morton (1934), published by Methuen. © Marion Wasdell and Brian de Villiers.

p. 264 Extract from *Prospero's Cell* by Lawrence Durrell (1945), published by Faber & Faber.

p. 266 Extract from *Ghika: Paintings, Drawings, Sculpture* by Patrick Leigh Fermor (1964), published by Lund Humphries. Reprinted by permission of John Murray.

p. 267 Extract from *The Life of My Choice* by Wilfred Thesiger (1987). Reprinted by permission of HarperCollins Publishers Ltd. © 1987 Wilfred Thesiger.

p. 269 Extract from *A Walk With a White Bushman* by Laurens van der Post (1986), published by Vintage Books (UK) and HarperCollins Publisher (USA). Reprinted by permission of The Random House Group Ltd and HarperCollins Publishers.

p. 270 Extract from *Destinations* by Jan Morris (1980), published by Oxford University Press. By permission of Oxford University Press, Inc.

p. 273 Extract from *Old Glory* by Jonathan Raban (1981) published by Macmillan Publishers.

p 278 Extract from *Their Heads are Green* by Paul Bowles (1963). © 1957, 1963, The Estate of Paul Bowles.

p. 284 Extract from *Among the Russians* by Colin Thubron (1983), published by Vintage Books. Reprinted by permission of The Random House Group Ltd.

p. 284 Extract from *Great Journeys* (1989) published by BBC Books. © Colin Thubron.

Index

Index

Index

Thorne, Robert, 65
Thubron, Colin, 275–7, 285
thuggee, 217
Tibet, first European account of, 101
Tilman, H.W. 263
Tod, Captain James, 212–13
tourism, impact on travel literature, ix, 233, 286
Troy, excavation of, 224
Turner, Samuel, 220
Twain, Mark, 207, 232–3
Twining, Thomas, 217

Van der Post, Laurens, 268–9
Varthema, Ludovico, 80
Vason, George, 152–3
Verne, Jules, 239–40
Vespucci, Amerigo, 47–48
Vinland 19
Virgil, *Aeneid*, 10

Voltaire (François-Marie Arouet), vii, 160, *Candide*, 178

Waldseemüller, Martin, 49
Wallis, Captain Samuel, 133–4
Walpole, Horace, 160–61, 166, 174
Waugh, Evelyn, 259–60
Webbe, Edward, 110
Wey, William, 34–5
Wheeler, Sara, 274
Whymper, Edward, 236–7
Willoughby, Sir Hugh, and Richard Chancellor, 65
Wilson, William, missionary, 152
Wonders of the East, 12, 31
Wood and Dawkins discover Palmyra and Balbec, 173–4

Xavier, St Francis, 83, 97–9
Xenophon, *Anabasis*, 6–7

SEPTENTRIO

Illandia

Ibernia

Anglia

Mosco
uia

Ta
na

is

Dacia
Germania   Sarmatia

Sarmatia
Asiatica

Paludes

Nœotides

EVRO   PA

Euxinus

Arme
nia

Gallia

Ita
lia

Græcia

Tunchia

Hispa
nia

Assy
ria

Lisbona

Mare
mediterra
neum

Syria

Arabia
deserta

anctus
der
Canarie

Barbaria

Atlas mons

Aegyp
tus

Terra alba

Getulia

Dargin
Alba
Gazera
boni asus
ns magnus
Sagres
ru   Deus

Caput album

NIGRITAE

Arabia

Hodeni
Caput uiride
Gambra regnu

Aethiopia

Sanga flu.

Me
roe

Mare
rubrum

Besigne
Ginega

APHRICA

AETHIOPIA
interior

Tro
glodite

30   10   20   30   40   50   60   70   8

Regnum
Melli &
Nebeorum

Regnum
Melin
cæ